EVALUATION AND REGULATION
OF BODY BUILD
AND COMPOSITION

INTERNATIONAL
RESEARCH MONOGRAPH SERIES
IN PHYSICAL EDUCATION

Archimedes is said to have requested his friends and relatives to place upon his tomb a representation of a cylinder circumscribing a sphere within it, together with an inscription giving the ratio which the cylinder bears to the sphere; from which we may infer that he himself regarded the discovery of this ratio as his greatest achievement.

> *Any cylinder having its base equal to the diameter of the sphere, is itself (i.e., in content) half as large again as the sphere, and its surface also (including its bases) is half as large again as the surface of the sphere.*

From Professor T. L. Heath, *The Works of Archimedes* (New York: Dover Publications, 1953).

Evaluation and Regulation
of Body Build
and Composition

ALBERT R. BEHNKE
JACK H. WILMORE

Prentice-Hall, Inc.

Englewood Cliffs, New Jersey

Library of Congress Cataloging in Publication Data

BEHNKE, ALBERT RICHARD
 Evaluation and regulation of body build and composition.

 (International research monograph series in physical education)
 Bibliography: p.
 1. Somatotypes. 2. Body composition.
3. Exercise—Physiological effect. I. Wilmore, Jack H., joint author. II. Title.
[DNLM: 1. Body composition. 2. Somatotypes. QU100 B419e 1974]
QP34.5.B42 573'.6 73–9890
ISBN 0-13-292284-3

QP
34.5
.B42

Printed in the United States of America

10 9 8 7 6 5 4 3 2 1

Fig. 2.4 from University of California Lawrence Berkeley Laboratory.

PRENTICE-HALL INTERNATIONAL, INC., *London*
PRENTICE-HALL OF AUSTRALIA, PTY. LTD., *Sydney*
PRENTICE-HALL OF CANADA, LTD., *Toronto*
PRENTICE-HALL OF INDIA PRIVATE LIMITED, *New Delhi*
PRENTICE-HALL OF JAPAN, INC., *Tokyo*

Contents

9/ Alterations in Body Composition with
Physical Activity

Preface

During the past 30 years interest in the gross composition, size, and shape of the human body has accelerated as a result of development and validation of densitometric, radiogrammetric, and radioisotopic techniques. The scientific community, in no small measure due to the scholarly leadership of Josef Brožek and Francis Moore, has become aware of quantitative procedures in health and disease which divide the body into chemical entities and anatomic components such as total body fat, water, blood volume, red cell mass, cellular (potassium space) water, extracellular (sodium and chloride space) water, and define lean body or "fat-free" mass and active metabolic structure of the body. Currently, sophisticated tracer and other techniques are directed to quantitation of elusive bone mineral and protein as well as lipid per fat cell (with DNA analysis) and vital cell moieties such as mitochondria.

Because these analyses require the application of high technical skill to elaborate equipment, relatively few individuals can engage in them. We turn then to deceptively facile techniques which require carefully defined measurements of external form in order to classify all individuals in various population samples, not primarily by statistical indices but according to biologically meaningful interrelationships. With due recognition to the presumptive value of somatotyping from photographs according to Sheldon's technique, directed to classical description of body form in terms of rotundity, muscularity, and linearity, it has long been an objective to implement anthropometry for large-scale quantitative assessment of body build. In the late '30s,

Albert Behnke with Dr. Walter Welham (now Rear Admiral, USN, Ret.) sought the help of the eminent physical anthropologist, Dr. Aleš Hrdlička, which led to incorporation of girth measurements of chest and abdomen in conjunction with underwater weighing in the examination of Navy personnel and professional football players.

A reservoir of reference measurements in large part came fortuitously as a by-product of the successful application of anthropometry to the design of military equipment. This noteworthy advance, made possible by Professor Hooten of Harvard and the foresight of Captain Otis Benson (now Major General, retired), was implemented by highly qualified professional anthropologists as Albert Damon, Francis Randall, Russell Newman, Robert White, and the biometrician Edmund Churchill. From Army Quartermaster surveys of some 100,000 men, we have derived much of our basic data for a reference man. Especially valuable have been the techniques and their reliable application in the Air Forces by Hertzberg, Daniels, and Churchill. Anthropometry of Air Force women (WAF) provided essential proportions of the reference woman.

With reference to the civilian population, special credit is due Ruth O'Brien, Meyer Girshick, Eleanor Hunt, and William Shelton of the United States Department of Agriculture for their unexcelled national surveys in the late '30s of children, adolescents, and adult females. Thus, there is available (although not directed to classification of man), a large body of reliable anthropometric data essential as standards of reference.

Little use heretofore has been made of these measurements for quantitative evaluation of body build. The conversions of the voluminous data for individual assessment of body size, shape, and variation have been lacking. Apart from formulations by Matiegka and by Willoughby, there was, on the one hand, no systematization of relationships which rendered anthropometric data meaningful other than as statistical derivations in the interest of human engineering requirements, and, on the other hand, no intercorrelated standards of reference to which a given individual's measurements could be compared, apart from stature and weight.

The chief anthropometric contribution of this monograph is the conversion of anthropometric dimensions to ponderal equivalents by elementary formulations which apply both to the 10 kg infant and the 150 kg longshoreman. The authors measured some 3500 individuals to test the principles outlined in the text, and brief mention follows of those who participated in these endeavors.

Beginning in 1955, Drs. Otto Guttentag and Carroll Brodsky, physicians who were also anthropologists, conducted a comprehensive survey of girths and breadths of 31 males at the Radiological Defense Laboratory. The subjects, selected for diversity of body build, were also assessed by Dr. William Siri for volume (helium dilution chamber technique) and total body water at the Donner Laboratory of Medical Physics at the University of California, Berkeley. Subsequently, over a period of 15 years Dr. Siri has made the services of his laboratory available for examination of Navy personnel, Berkeley adolescents, and for studies on one of the authors.

In 1961, Dr. Nemat Borhani and Robert Buechley of the California State Department of Public Health conducted an anthropometric examination of 2300 longshoremen. This exercise proved to be a severe test of the techniques employed; as many as 100 men were measured daily during the course of a primitive type of screening examination.

In the Berkeley Nutritional-Anthropometric Survey* (N-A S) initiated also in 1961 under the direction of Dr. Ruth Huenemann, Nutrition Division, School of Public Health, University of California (Berkeley), two basic approaches were followed in the attempt to compare anthropometric growth parameters during adolescence with densitometric and total body potassium (^{40}K) determinations conducted by Dr. Robert Martin at the Naval Radiological Defense Laboratory. Data were recorded on an entire class of Berkeley adolescents (450 boys and 500 girls) in their progress from ninth to twelfth grade, at mean ages equal or close to 14.5, 15.2, 16.2, and 17.2 years. It was a privilege for Albert Behnke, as research physician, to be a member of the "grass-roots" team with Mary Hampton and Leona Shapiro. In this survey, Dr. Frank Katch from University of California (Santa Barbara) played an important ancillary role in programming and analysis of computerized data.

In the late '60s, steps were taken to provide an independent validation of anthropometric-densitometric data with the cooperation of Dr. Joseph Royce of the Department of Physical Education, University of California (Berkeley). When he left on special assignment, Dr. Jack Wilmore willingly undertook the task of conducting the independent evaluations on 133 Berkeley males and 128 females.

Dr. J. Edmund Welch made a major contribution in 1967 in his biography of Edward Hitchcock, M.D. (professor and "Founder of Physical Education in the College Curriculum," 1861 to 1911). From Hitchcock's measurements (9 of 11 girths as measured currently) it can be stated that the Amherst man of 1882 (age 19), although 7 cm shorter and 8.5 kg less in weight adjusted for stature than the Amherst man (age 18) of 1957, nevertheless had girth proportions very similar to those we have derived for the reference man from military data.

The authors are deeply indebted to the outstanding persons previously mentioned. We would like to pay special deference to Robert Buechley and

*The Berkeley N-A Survey was supported by a grant from the National Institute of of Child Health and Human Development, N.I.H., Public Health Service, U.S. Dept. of Health, Education, and Welfare. Additional assistance was supplied by a General Research Support Grant from the School of Public Health (U. C. Berkeley) for statistical and editorial services.

Mr. H. Hechter for their statistical treatment of data pertaining to long-shoremen and Navy groups.

For the overall investigative endeavor we acknowledge the essential and pioneer contributions of the following investigators:

In the early Navy studies, Nello Pace and Edith Rathbun for their fundamental *in vivo* and *in vitro* studies, and further to Dr. Pace for the introduction of tritiated water (HTO) for estimation of total body water,

Manuel Morales and Robert E. Smith for their mathematical and biological groundwork which has been the foundation of all subsequent studies,

Grover Pitts for the only continuous quantification of adipose tissue during the course of 25 years,

J. Murray Steele, Bernard Brodie, and their co-workers for the antipyrine technique in determination of total body water.

At the Radiological Defense Laboratory, we recognize the importance of analyses of human adipose tissue by Dr. Cecil Entenman and William Goldwater. The tritiated water and meticulously executed radioisotopic analysis by Dr. Eldon Boling were essential to our synthesis of individual compositional components. These were furthered by collaborative studies in the 4 pi 'human' counter at Los Alamos under the direction of Ernie Anderson and Wright Langham. At all times, Dr. Ulrich Luft of the Lovelace Foundation and Dr. Thomas Allen and Harry Krzywicki have made available to us their classical contributions which constitute the solid core of body compositional analysis.

We gratefully acknowledge the pioneer determinations of lean body weight of young women by Dr. Charlotte Young of Cornell University, and the innovative 'head out of water' technique for body volume determination.

Our radiologic and anthropometric studies have been enhanced by the unstinting cooperation of Dr. Marion Maresh of the Child Research Council of the University of Colorado. There are no other data comparable to the multi-disciplinary longitudinal studies of the renowned Colorado investigators.

Through the years, two distinguished investigators from abroad, Dr. Jana Pařízková of Prague and Dr. Wilhelm von Döbeln of Stockholm have been our esteemed colleagues *in absentia*.

It is with the greatest satisfaction and pride that we have always had technical assistance exemplary in competence and dedication. Finally, we are indebted to Dr. H. Harrison Clarke for the invitation to prepare this monograph.

Albert R. Behnke
Jack H. Wilmore

EVALUATION AND REGULATION
OF BODY BUILD
AND COMPOSITION

Chapter 1 / **Introduction and Orientation**

Objectives and Scope

The purpose of this monograph is to describe, validate, and demonstrate the routine application of the following techniques for assessment of body build and composition: (1) anthropometry, including a description both of perimetric and frame size, (2) densitometry, (3) caliper-measured skinfolds, and (4) radiogrammetry, limited to the arm for the purpose of rapid, routine survey. In support of primary procedures, data will include radioisotopic analysis of body compartments and determinations of total body potassium (^{40}K).

Professional football players of a previous generation will be compared with those of today. New concepts of height-weight relationships will be outlined in conjunction with specific tabular data. Body composition will be described in relation to sex differences, growth, and aging. A final section will deal with exercise and dietary regulation of body composition. Throughout, the text indicates promising lines for future investigation.

The presentation by the authors, one a physician, the other a physiologist, although closely integrated, is arranged to permit individual expression and interpretation. In effect, readers will have, from two individually-manned lecterns, alternate expositions covering the research experience of the authors.

In our highly industrialized and automated society, obesity and cardiovascular deterioration are closely associated with inactivity, overnutrition, and compulsive emotional stresses. Accumulative data now support the thesis that a major advance

1

is imminent in preventive medicine—namely curtailment, if not control, of the deterioration manifest in atherosclerosis and coronary heart disease. Yet, apart from the limited application of somatotype and skinfold assessment, diagnostic tools have not been routinely employed to appraise the gross deterioration manifest in excess fat and the loss of muscular tissue. A national program to combat hunger, for example, is not bolstered by substantive data to quantify secular deterioration (if any) in the needy. Even minimal evaluation of weight relative to increments of stature is not available for any community. It is therefore with tempered enthusiasm that we present highlights of two decades of research directed to quantitative evaluation of body build and composition which can be applied in routine examinations by qualified personnel.

Orientation

Body Composition

GAS DISSOLVED IN LEAN-FAT TISSUES. The elementary concept of the body as a two-component system comprising lean and fat tissue evolved from early tests (1932–1935) in which measurements were made of "air" nitrogen (N_2) which diffused from body tissues into a closed system during the course of oxygen inhalation. Except for a small quantity of N_2 dissolved or loosely combined with hemoglobin and other proteins, all of the gaseous N_2 is dissolved in "fluids" and in body fat in the ratio of about one to five. It is apparent from the projected and experimental N_2 elimination curves for man (Fig. 1.1) that collection of N_2 affords a simple but somewhat tedious method for "direct" assessment of body fat. The chief deterrent in the procedure at the time was inability to determine total body water. It would be rewarding to repeat these tests; as early as 30 minutes during the course of oxygen inhalation, the difference in the cumulative amount of N_2 collected from lean and fat subjects is striking. Further, in the altitude chamber at 0.25 atmospheres, the reduced partial pressure renders oxygen nonirritating, and small quantities of N_2 can be measured since the percentage of oxygen is increased by a multiple of four.

ABSORPTION OF LIPOPHILIC GASES. Lesser, Blumberg, and Steele (78) developed an accurate method for measurement of body fat in vivo in the small mammal by employing the inhalation and subsequent recovery of cyclopropane. Since this anesthetic gas has a high affinity for lipid (fat/fluid ratio in the body is 26 to 1), wide variation in estimates of total body water have little influence on the accuracy of results. Essentially, this method is independent of the composition of the fat-free body mass. In adapting this

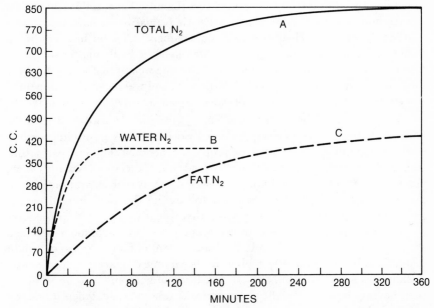

Fig. 1.1 Nitrogen elimination from the body during the course of O_2 inhalation. *A* curve is experimental and is the average cumulative N_2 from three lean men at normal pressure. Water N_2 (*B*) and Fat N_2 (*C*) project the elimination of N_2 from body solvents. (From *U.S. Nav. Med. Bull.*, 35, 1937, 219.)

method to man, Lesser, Perl, and Steele (79) combined krypton (another lipophilic gas) with cyclopropane, The results of an eight-hour test on Subject Z (weight: 96.4 kg) follow.

> Body fat (krypton uptake): 20.9 kg
> Body fat (cyclopropane uptake): 23.3 kg

The hourly metabolic rate which served to monitor the integrity of the closed system for recirculation of the lipophilic gases was 14.7, 14.8, 14.5, 15.2, 14.8, 15.2, and 14.9 liters per hour (STP). When this promising technique is standardized (and incorporates N_2 elimination as well), we shall have an unequivocal procedure for evaluating the accuracy of all in vivo techniques for assessment of body fat.

THE SPECIFIC GRAVITY (DENSITY) OF THE BODY. In 1939, following rescue and salvage operations in connection with the U.S.S. Squalus disaster, there was renewed interest in the Navy in development of a practical method to assess fat in divers who were then engaged in test dives to 500 feet. Since volume displacement of a submarine and buoyancy were matters of daily discussion, it was a logical step to measure the volume of the human body in diving tanks, and to reintroduce the basic parameter of volume as a "third dimension" in addition to weight and stature (Behnke, Feen, and Welham, 22).

Archimedes, some 2000 years earlier, is primarily responsible for Proposition 7 from T.L. Heath's classic (66), namely, "A solid heavier than a fluid will, if placed in it, descend to the bottom of the fluid, and the solid will, when weighed in the fluid, be lighter than its true weight by the weight of the fluid displaced." We may either determine loss of weight of the submerged body, or may measure the volume of water displaced as in Allen's volumeter (4).

The solution of the wreath problem by Archimedes associated with the above-stated hydrostatic principle allegedly originated as an intuitive deduction while bathing. The celebrated problem concerned the matter of substitution of a certain amount of silver for gold in a consecrated wreath which, being a sacred object, could not be subjected to physical separation of components (66). This problem, directed to Archimedes by King Hieron, is pertinent to current methodology in that the two reported procedures employed by Archimedes for extraneous analysis of a two-component system are currently in use, namely volume displacement of fluid and loss of weight determined by underwater weighing. In the volume displacement procedure, Archimedes is reported to have taken a lump of gold and a lump of silver, each having the same weight as the wreath; subsequently, when immersed in a vessel full of water, the materials caused different amounts of water overflow. When the wreath was tested, it caused more water to overflow than the gold had, and less than the silver. In the other procedure, equal weights (in air) of silver and gold were attached to the arms of a balance and suspended underwater; the difference in weight of silver and gold was then compared with the underwater weight of the wreath.

In 1945 at the Naval Medical Research Institute at Bethesda, the rectangular hyperbolic equation formulated by Morales et al. (90) was employed for the calculation of the weight of silver allegedly substituted for gold in King Hieron's consecrated wreath.

$$\text{Fat/Weight} = \frac{\dfrac{1}{D(\text{Body})} - \dfrac{1}{D(\text{Lean Mass})}}{\dfrac{1}{D(\text{Fat})} - \dfrac{1}{D(\text{Lean Mass})}}$$

The wreath of the king is reputed to have weighed 20 pounds in air, and to have lost 1.25 pounds when weighed underwater. From these values, together with 16 as the specific gravity of the wreath, we can substitute in the formulation of Morales, the density of silver (10.5) for $D(\text{Fat})$, and that of gold (19.3) for $D(\text{Lean})$.

$$\text{Then, } \frac{F(\text{silver})}{W(\text{wreath})} = 23.01/\text{sp.gr.(wreath)} - 1.192.$$

From this formula it appears that the wreath was adulterated with 24.6%, that is, approximately four pounds of its weight as silver.

COMMENTS ON INITIAL PROCEDURE (CIRCA 1939–1940). The prime measurement, that of net body volume, was ascertained as the difference between weight in air and weight in water, corrected for residual air volume. At the time it was sufficiently accurate for the purpose of the test not to correct for density of water ($\cong 0.995$), the temperature of which was usually close to that of the subject's skin surface (31–32°C). Two weights were recorded with the body immersed in water, one at the end of full inspiration, the other at the end of full expiration. The difference between the two weighings measured hydrostatic vital capacity, which, when corrected for the effect of mean hydrostatic pressure on thoracic volume, gave a value for vital capacity comparable to that obtained by standard spirometry. For the essential determination of residual volume (unless only mean group estimates or serial estimates of fat on the same individual are desired) Willmon and Behnke (142) first employed helium or nitrogen washout techniques, and occasionally a somewhat heroic method of pressure reduction consisting of complete exhalation to residual volume when the subject was in a chamber at four atmospheres, followed by precipitous reduction of pressure (within 15 seconds) to one atmosphere. The exhaled gas, collected in a closed system, represented approximately four times the residual air volume determined by the washout techniques. It was failure to correct to net body volume that vitiated numerous earlier attempts to determine true body specific gravity, notably as reported in analysis of data on 787 individuals by Dr. Edith Boyd. (33).

SOURCES OF ERROR. Failure to exhale to the same residual volume and the resultant variation in analysis when it is subsequently determined is perhaps the chief variable affecting the accuracy of estimates of net body volume. With proper hygiene, the amount of gas in the alimentary tract is negligible. One interesting source of error is the variable time taken for underwater weighing at the end of complete exhalation to residual volume. Thus, during the period that respiration is suspended underwater, oxygen is absorbed without commensurate replacement by metabolic carbon dioxide which is largely dissolved in blood and body fluids. One may obtain, in fact, a rough measure of metabolism from the progressive decrease in scale weight (about 75 grams for every 15 seconds underwater) during the course of breath-holding. Refinements in proper preparation of subjects and in procedure by von Döbeln (136) and Katch (73) make possible the determination of body volume with an error no greater than ± 1 ml per 1000 ml of volume measured.

COMMENTS ON EXPERIMENTAL DATA. In a group of 180 Navy men (average age: 29 yrs), specific gravity values were in the range of 1.021 (obese) to 1.100 (extremely lean). The range of body density was approximately 0.005 units lower than specific gravity. This range of values has been consistently found to apply to adult males in the 20–40 age group. Subsequently, densitometric values as high as 1.110 were recorded by Siri* for Berkeley males (age 16 years), and values well below 1.000 are obtained on obese women.

In the early Navy data, an inverse relationship generally existed between specific gravity and body weight. Thus, if subjects are divided into high and low density groups, the difference in mean weights of the two groups can be equated with tissue in the densitometric range of 0.92 to 0.94, as shown by the following data.

Date	No. Subjects	h	Density	Weight	Volume	$\dfrac{\Delta W}{\Delta V}$	LBW[c]
1942[a]	28	175.3	1.051	80.0	76.12		63.2
	38	177.0	1.076	67.6	62.83		60.8
				12.4	13.29	0.933	
1963[b]	16	176.5	1.0318	95.23	92.30		66.9
	21	176.5	1.0798	66.88	61.02		60.7
				29.35	31.28	0.938	

[a]*Behnke, Feen, and Welham (22).*
[b]*Brožek et al. (37).*
[c]*Lean body weight (25), Fat-free weight (118).*

Adult adipose tissue is usually in the densitometric range of 0.92 to 0.96, so that the weight difference between higher and lower density groups, as shown in the tabular data, is equivalent to adipose tissue. This inverse relationship between density and body weight led to the surmise by Welham and Behnke (139) that "If obesity and not weight *per se* is the chief factor tending to produce low values for specific gravity, then conversely a group of heavy but lean men should possess a high average value for specific gravity." They then examined a group of professional football players (the "Redskins" of Sammy Baugh's day), the majority of whom had been selected for All-American teams. It was found that the football players (average weight: 90.9 kg) had an average specific gravity of 1.080 (10% fat) and an estimated lean body weight some 20 kg higher than that of the Navy men. Here indeed was a presumptive demonstration that fat could be separated from bone and muscle in vivo or the "silver from the gold" by application of a principle renowned in antiquity.

INTERPRETATION OF DENSITOMETRIC DATA. The accurate assessment of body fat from a single number substituted in an equation depends in large measure upon the degree of constancy of the density of the dichotomous fractions, fat, and lean tissue. Lipid extracted from adipose tissue at a specified temperature is remarkably constant in composition in man and animals. Fidanza et al. (52) have provided a firm value of 0.90 for density of lipid (gm/ml at 36°C) extracted from human adipose tissue.

*Personal communication.

The density of the lean mass, which includes an undetermined percentage (probably in the range of 2 to 5% of lean body weight) of essential fat in bone marrow, spinal cord, brain, and other tissues, is influenced by body hydration, by the ratio of muscle to skeletal mass, and, during the course of aging, by involutionary changes in bone and supportive tissue. A clarifying distinction is the difference between the homogeneous composition of inbred strains of small mammals reared under controlled conditions, and the more variable composition of the "free-choice" large mammals, including man.

The density of fat-free aliquots of homogenized whole body tissues of small mammals is approximately the rounded value of 1.100 initially determined by Rathbun and Pace (107), Pace and Rathbun (99), and Morales et al. (90). In young adult males, the highest densitometric values are also about 1.100, and may be somewhat higher (1.110) for male adolescents.

VALIDATION OF DENSITOMETRY. These initial investigations established an inverse relationship between the fat fraction of body mass and specific gravity ($r \cong -.97$), and demonstrated the direct proportionality between specific gravity and total body water. Certainly the large body of data from animal husbandry bolsters the conclusion that in the "chemically-mature" mammal, fat is the diluent, if not of lean body mass, then assuredly of body water. The inverse correlation between percentage of body water and percentage of fat relative to body weight, is one of the highest in biology ($r \cong -.99$). Relative to total body protein, chemical analysis reveals a less striking but nevertheless substantial diluent effect of accumulative fat ($r \cong -.94$).

In 1971, Kodama (76) reported that the body composition in vivo and in vitro of the hamster confirmed the basic assumption of relative homogeneity of gross body components and the validity of techniques for the estimate of body fat from density, total body water, or combined parameters. The fraction of water, for example, found in the fat-free body of the hamster (73.3%) is nearly identical to the 73.2% which Pace and his associates established earlier.

> Although the two compartment representation of a body would seem to be an oversimplification, and the assumptions employed in this approach limit its usefulness under certain conditions, numerous variants of the above equations have been used by many investigators with apparently considerable success in predicting fatness in animals and man. Earlier criticisms of the basic approach pioneered by the Navy workers concerned second-order refinements in theory and technique, and have not substantially improved the predictive value of the estimating equations based on body density and specific gravity.[76]

ESTIMATION OF LBW FROM TOTAL BODY WATER. Although mean values for gross components of healthy persons who are capable of physical work reflect compositional homogeneity, it is necessary to measure total body water and even to partition the water (e.g., into sodium and potassium or extra- and intracellular spaces) if an individual is not in fluid balance or it he is exceptionally obese. It was an important advance, therefore, when Soberman et al. (122) introduced the antipyrine technique for determination of total body water (TBW) in man. The technique was employed by Osserman et al. (97) in conjunction with densitometry for compositional examination of 81 healthy and, for the most part, young, adult males. The percentage of water in the lean body mass (LBM) assessed by densitometry was $71.8 \pm 2.9\%$ (range 66.9 to 79.0% of lean body mass). Body fat was in the range of 2 to 35% of body weight. The correlation between percentage fat (densitometric) and fat estimated from the difference (weight—lean body weight from total body water) was only moderately high ($r \cong .91$, standard error of estimate 4.4%).

In an investigation of 31 males from a Navy Laboratory (23), Dr. William Siri determined total body water by dilution with tritiated (HTO) water, as well as body density in his helium dilution chamber at the Donner Laboratory of Medical Physics, University of California at Berkeley. Some wide discrepancies were apparent in estimates of body fat or lean body weight from density of total body weight singly, which will be discussed in Chapter 2. Variability in the estimation of the percentage of fat is reduced by a factor of two when both total body water and density are determined, as Siri (117, 118) has pointed out in his excellent analysis.

Isotope-Dilution, ^{40}K Methodology. In the period from 1958 to 1960, Dr. Eldon Boling applied his advanced and meticulously executed radio-isotopic techniques to assess total body water (HTO), total body potassium ($^{42}K_e$) and exchangeable chloride (utilizing ^{82}Br) in an examination of 37 males at the U.S. Radiological Defense Laboratory (San Francisco) where Dr. Siri previously examined personnel. Since about 98% of K_e is intracellular, it follows that this determination, which requires some 40 hours for equilibration, affords an estimate of body cell mass. On some subjects it was possible to combine the radioisotopic analysis with determinations of body density (Siri), ^{40}K measurement in the 4π scintillation counter at Los Alamos as well as in the heavily shielded 2π "human counter" in the Navy laboratory. The estimate of total body potassium from gamma emission of the naturally present ^{40}K in the body is less accurate (standard error of estimate, 3 to 5%) than the $^{42}K_e$ determinations, but the rapid (200 second) analysis affords group data on large numbers of persons.

From 1962 to 1966, in the Berkeley Nutritional-Anthropometric Survey (N-A S), under the direction of Dr. Ruth Huenemann, multi-parameter data were obtained on 16-year-old adolescents, male and female. This survey inaugurated a comparison of densitometric (underwater weighing), kaliometric (^{40}K), and anthropometric techniques for assessment of gross body composition. An additional contribution to the adolescent study was Dr. Siri's densitometric analysis of a subsample of males.

External Form—Anthropometry

The classical description of body form includes evaluation, chiefly from photographs, of fat, muscle, and bone. In the established procedure of Sheldon et al. (113), photoscopic somatotyping is employed to rate components on a seven-point scale in accord with the generic terms *endomorphy*, *mesomorphy*, and *ectomorphy*. Somatotyping, however, is a particular system attended by rigorous rules for posing subjects for photography, and requires an expert's experience for grading and interpretation. The value of the system, apart from convenient classification of body build with numerical rating of components, is photographic visualization of the examinee. In our experience, a posterior view of the examinee, who is wearing a basic garment, is usually adequate in conjunction with comprehensive anthropometry. There is no question, however, as to the value of Sheldon's system as described by H. Harrison Clarke (40) in the Medford Boys' Growth project, in which authoritative photoscopic evaluation was performed by Barbara Honeyman Heath.

It has been our objective to quantify body build by perimetric (girth) and bimetric (frame size) measurements. Such procedure has been challenged not only in regard to yield, for example, in nutritional assessment, but also in regard to the need for recording multiple, intercorrelated measurements—which is contrary to biostatistical parsimony.

In our experience, anthropometric surveys have incorporated too few measurements to provide other than a fragmentary picture derived from perhaps two diameters and usually not more than several girths. This endeavor was described over two centuries ago by Jonathan Swift in his narrative of Gulliver's travels. Thus in Lilliput,

> "Two hundred seamstresses were employed to make me shirts, and linen for my bed and table.... The seamstresses took my measure as I lay on the ground, one standing at my neck, and another at my mid-leg, with a strong cord extended that each held by the end, while the third measured the length of the cord with a rule an inch long (author's note: essentially a measure of trunk length). They then measured my right thumb, and desired no more; for by a mathematical computation, that twice round the thumb is once round the wrist, and by the help of my old shirt, which was displayed on the ground before them for a pattern, they fitted me exactly."

Admittedly, many measurements have been taken to comply with human engineering and clothing requirements, but the voluminous data recorded, neatly packaged in percentile form, are not related to description or integration of biologic structure. Certainly little usage has been made of these data directed to evaluation of body build, and a great deal of painstaking work lies buried in the potter's field of scientific data. A prime consideration is whether or not there are unifying principles that render such data meaningful for detailed description of body structure.

The formulations of Matiegka (84) and Willoughby (143) elucidate relationships underlying individual assessment of body build and partially support Harrison Clarke's concept of "Totality of Man." A model with wide clinical application is the Wetzel grid (140). Although limited to parameters of height and weight, the grid depicts physique channels and developmental levels from birth to maturity on an individual basis. Our effort is to extend this type of analysis to include multiple measurements which relate regional development to the body as a whole.

During the past 15 years, we have measured several thousand persons of widely different build, both male and female, and over a wide age range beginning with adolescence and extending beyond 90 years of age. Specific data such as those pertaining to Berkeley adolescents, university students, longshoremen, and athletes were analyzed in some detail. From these examinations were found consistent relationships which, in elementary terms, were amenable to routine application and uniform interpretation. Essentially, in the anthropometric phase of our endeavor, multiple girths and stature describe perimetric size which can be substituted for body weight ($r > .98$). In effect, the complex entity weight is converted to linear (stature) and girth components. Skeletal diameters and stature define frame size, which we extrapolate to reference weight or, employing another conversion factor, to lean body weight. The estimates of lean body weight from frame size are less accurate than those deduced from densitometry ($r \cong 0.80$ to 0.90), but nevertheless are useful for presumptive assessments. Further explanations of these relationships follow.

MODULES OF BODY BUILD. The stature-weight module (F) is the quotient of the square root of weight (kg) divided by height (dm). D is the module of perimetric size defined as the sum of 11 girths (two abdominal perimeters are averaged to comprise one of the 11 girths), divided by 100 (i.e., $D = 11c/100$). During late adolescence and adult life,

$$D = 3F, F = \sqrt{W/h}$$

During the growth period from age four years and throughout adult life as well,

$$D = 1.95 \, F\text{-}h^{0.7} \text{ (males)}$$
$$D = 1.98 \, F\text{-}h^{0.7} \text{ (females)}$$

$F\text{-}h^{0.7}$ is the square root of weight (kg) divided by $h^{0.7}$ (dm). The altered power of h reduced from 1.0 to 0.7 serves to compensate for diminishing head size relative to body size during growth from age four years.

THE PROBLEM OF HEAD SIZE. It is essential to include head circumference (*c*) in measurements of infants and small children if dimensions are to be closely identified with body weight. Head *c* was not routinely measured in the Berkeley N-A Survey, because this dimension has a coefficient of variation of about 3.5% (similar to stature), in contrast to trunk-extremity girths characterized by variation of about 6 to 10 percent. The head girth is therefore not readily integrated in the various combinations of girths employed in our analysis of dimensions unless we consider mean values only. In Fig. 1.2,

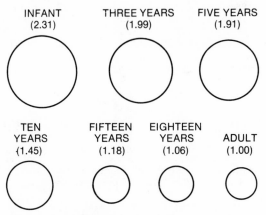

INFANT   THREE YEARS   FIVE YEARS
(2.31)   (1.99)   (1.91)

TEN   FIFTEEN   EIGHTEEN
YEARS   YEARS   YEARS   ADULT
(1.45)   (1.18)   (1.06)   (1.00)

Fig. 1.2 Decrease in relative head size during the growth period. The diminishing circumferences reflect the ratio,

$$\frac{(\text{Head } c/3F)^2, \text{ Age Specific}}{(\text{Head } c/3F)^2, \text{ Reference Man}}$$

$3F$ is the 'module' of unit size $(3\sqrt{W/h})$.

the infant's head relative to $3F$ is 2.31 times larger than that of the adult when body weight is scaled to unit stature.

$$\text{Relative Head Size} = \frac{(\text{Head } c/3F)^2 \text{ Age specific}}{(\text{Head } c/3F)^2 \text{ Reference Man}}$$

where $3F$ $(3\sqrt{W/h})$ is age specific.

COMMUNALITY OF ANTHROPOMETRIC RELATIONSHIPS. With reference to mean values, the same constant can be employed to convert dimensions which include head girth into ponderal equivalents for the infant, child, adolescent, and adult populations. For example, Bayley and Davis (6) recorded four measurements which can be used reliably for infants and young children, namely: head and chest girths, and bideltoid and bitrochanteric widths. Since the technique in taking these measurements is amenable to standardization, we are able to compare data of Bayley and Davis with similar dimensions recorded for such diverse groups as Berkeley adolescent males and Greek military personnel. In Table 1.1, the conversion constant

Table 1.1

IDENTITY OF THE DIMENSIONAL D' MODULE AND THE STATURE–WEIGHT
FACTOR ($3F$) FOR DIVERSE GROUPS OF MALES

Age	Length or Stature cm	Dimensions[a] cm	D'[b]	$3F$	Scale W kg	Calc. W[c] kg
Bayley and Davis (6)						
1 mos	55.5	100.9	2.67	2.66	4.37	4.39
6	68.5	123.1	3.26	3.27	8.12	8.07
12	76.9	134.5	3.56	3.59	11.0	10.8
24	88.4	142.1	3.76	3.71	13.5	13.9
36	97.4	145.3	3.84	3.82	15.8	16.0
Berkeley N-A S (63)						
17.2 yrs	178.1	224.3[d]	5.94	5.92	69.3	69.8
U.C. Berkeley (148)						
22 yrs	177.3	235.4	6.23	6.19	75.6	76.4
Greek Military (68)						
—	170.5	224.5	5.94	5.95	67.0	66.8
Reference Man (Chapter 4)						
20–24	174	226.8	6.00	6.00	69.6	69.6

[a]*Sum of head, chest girths, and bideltoid, bitrochanteric widths.*
[b]*D' = Dimension/37.8, where 37.8 is 226.8/6.00 (reference man)*
[c]*Calculated W (kg) = $(D')^2 \times h_{dm} \times 0.111$*
[d]*Head c taken from matched samples of Denver males.*

(37.8) is the sum of the proportionality constants for the four dimensions of the reference man (Chapter 4). This constant serves to convert the four measurements to a D' value which is nearly identical with $3F$, the stature-weight module for the respective groups.

The same type of analysis can be made for females in which the single conversion constant (37.7) from the reference woman (Chapter 4) is not significantly different from the male constant (37.8).

CONCERNING WIDTH MEASUREMENTS. An objective not always achieved was the measurement of eight skeletal diameters (biacromial, chest width, bi-iliac, bitrochanteric, both wrists, ankles, knees, and elbows). Together with stature, these diameters constitute frame size, from which reference (C) weight, lean body weight (male), and minimal weight (female) are projected. The ponderal equivalents of the diameters are calculated from the same formulas applicable to girths. Thus $D(C)$, Ref W, D(LBW), for LBW (males), and D(Min W) for Minimal Weight (females) are substituted for D in the formulas.

Helen Pryor (106), Leona Bayer and Nancy Bayley (8), and Robert White (141) relate weight standards to frame size comprising a limited number of diameters, usually not more than two. From Wilmore's analysis (Chapter 4), it is not statistically evident that it is advantageous to employ more than two diameters, e.g., biacromial and bi-iliac, or biacromial and bitrochanteric widths. However, it is my experience that a battery of trunk-extremity measurements is required for comprehensive evaluation of an individual. The extremity widths, for example, mature earlier in the growth period than those of the trunk. Pertinent deductions may be made concerning skeletal maturation from the ratio of extremity to trunk widths. During growth, this ratio decreases progressively to a plateau in young adults. In professional ballet dancers, the ratio of extremity (notably knee width) to trunk widths is smaller than it is for a matched age, height, weight sample of Berkeley girls.

Reference (C) weight is meaningful because, in the absence of excess fat or muscular hypertrophy, we can compute body weight from diameters as well as from girths. During the growth period, which is the relatively lean part of life span, mean width size advances concomitantly with perimetric size. Thus, from ages four through 17 years, the sum of the mean values of four trunk diameters (4 TD) is approximately 42 times the factor $(F\text{-}h^{0.7})$ derived from mean weight and stature both for males and females in the Brush Foundation (Simmons) study (115). This remarkable relationship was also evident in the Berkeley N-A Survey of adolescents in their progress from ninth to twelfth grades. There are racial differences, notably in the decreased bi-iliac and, to a lesser degree, bitrochanteric widths, of Negro males and females.

Distribution of Dimensions

Morphologic and physiologic parameters may be apportioned to two sharply separated groups with reference to their coefficients of variation. On the one hand are anthropometric surface dimensions, surface area, skeletal and heart diameters, basal metabolism, cardiac output, and even the cross section of the aorta and other blood vessels, with coefficients of variation in the range usually of 5 to 7%. On the other hand are lean body weights (or body weights with constant percentage of fat) and weights of such organs as the heart, liver, kidney, and tissue masses referrable to muscle and the skeleton, with coefficients of variation in the range of 10 to 14%, or about twice the coefficients of variation values of the first group. Thus, if we know only the mean or preferably median values of weight (free of excess fat) and of the various anthropometric dimensions, we can be fairly certain of their percentile distribution.

In regard to weight, which incorporates variable quantities of fat, as well as surface dimensions, which reflect fat gain, it is excess fat ("the fat blanket") which distorts the symmetry of the mathematically computed distribution curve. When skewness is marked because of excess fat, anthropometric values to the right of the mean are not accurately predictable.

The distribution of lean body weight for given stature, computed from the squared values of anthropometric dimensions, is depicted in the upper curve (Fig. 1.3). Thus, if a dimension or dimensional entity lies 6% to the right or 6% to the left of the median value, as the case may be, the ponderal equivalent on the upper curve will be 12.36% to the right or −11.44% to the left of the median value for lean body weight. This follows from the formulations,

$$(\text{Mean} + 0.06)^2 = \text{Mean}^2 + 0.1236\ \text{Mean}^2$$

and

$$(\text{Mean} - 0.06)^2 = \text{Mean}^2 - 0.1164\ \text{Mean}^2$$

It is evident from Fig. 1.3 that the small lean man has endowed advantages over the large lean man. Relative to weight, the small man has larger blood vessels (e.g., coronary arteries), higher metabolism, greater cardiac output, and better blood perfusion of those tissues proportional to lean body weight than the less well-endowed large lean man. Incidentally, with reference to head size (coefficient of variation of girth, 3.5%), the small man will have a larger ("academic") head relative to body mass than the large lean man.

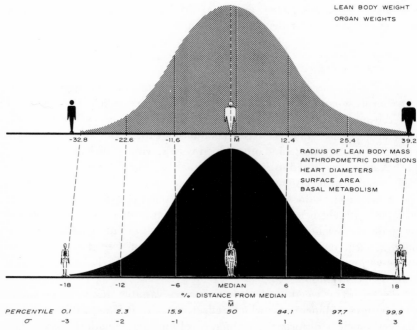

Fig. 1.3 Distribution of lean body weight and organ weights based on the squared values of the coefficients of variation of anthropometric and other parameters (lower curve). (From Behnke, Guttentag, Brodsky, *Hum. Biol.* Sept. 1959, p. 215.)

SAMPLE POPULATION DISTRIBUTION OF VALUES. In Table 1.2, the percentage deviation from the mean is shown for anthropometric parameters (Berkeley N-A S) at the 2.5 and 97.5 percentiles. The distribution of the

Table 1.2
PERCENTAGE DEVIATION FROM THE MEAN OF ANTHROPOMETRIC PARAMETERS AT THE 2.5 AND 97.5 PERCENTILES FOR BERKELEY MALES AND FEMALES (AGE 17.2 YEARS).

Girths	*Percentile*				*Component*[a]	*Percentile*			
	2.5		97.5			2.5		97.5	
	M	*F*	*M*	*F*		*M*	*F*	*M*	*F*
Shoulder	11.9	10.3	14.0	15.5	*A'*	13.9	12.9	22.8	22.5
Chest	12.6	11.0	16.1	16.1	*A*	13.0	12.7	20.6	20.4
Hips	11.4	12.8	17.5	18.5	*B*	12.7	13.1	16.0	18.0
Forearm	11.7	12.2	14.0	14.7	*B'*	12.0	13.1	16.2	16.7
Wrist	9.6	10.0	10.3	9.7	WFCA	11.7	12.5	15.8	11.1
Knee	10.4	12.5	14.7	19.1	C(6 Diam)	10.0	11.4	11.4	12.5
Calf	12.5	13.5	15.9	17.4					
Ankle	11.8	13.1	13.6	13.6					
Abdominal average	15.4	13.0	27.8	23.5	Weight	26.7	25.0	37.9	43.4
Thigh	15.8	17.4	26.6	23.8	√Weight	16.3	15.8	19.5	20.8
Biceps	14.6	16.0	20.2	24.3					

[a]*Trunk (A', A), extremity (B + Shoulder/4, B', WFCA), C(6 Diam): biac., chest W., bi-iliac, bitroch., ankles, wrists.*

dimensions generally (and components) is skewed, with the exception of width measurements. Notably out of line are girths of the abdomen, thigh, and biceps, as well as trunk components (*A'* and *A*) and body weight. The square root of the percentage deviations has been calculated for weight in order to afford a direct comparison with the perimetric and bi-metric dimensions.

SOMATOGRAPHIC DISTRIBUTION OF DIMENSIONS. A plot (somatogram) of single dimensions and components is shown as percentage deviation from the mean at the 2.5 (tenth value) and 97.5 (394th value) percentiles for the entire twelfth grade of the Berkeley N-A Group, from whom the data in Table 1.2 were compiled. It is evident that the girths of the abdomen, thigh, and biceps form a cluster markedly out of alignment at the 97.5 percentile. In the case of the abdominal girths (abdominal average), divergence to the right from central alignment may be attributed to increased thickness of the fat blanket as well as accumulation of internal fat. In the case of the thigh and arm, skewed alignment could be due both to fat and muscle or to muscle primarily.

From Fig. 1.4, it is apparent that the somatogram of an obese person

CIRCUMFERENCE

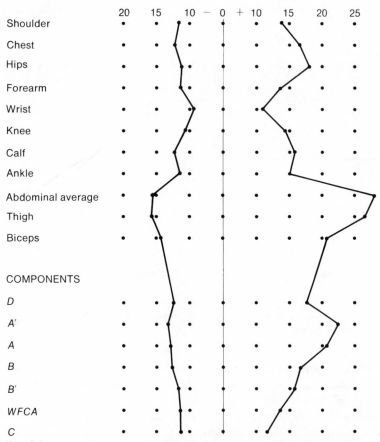

Fig. 1.4 Somatogram showing the percentage deviation of single and component dimensions from mean values, at the 2.5 and 97.5 percentiles for Berkeley tri-racial males. Age: 17.2 yrs; weight: 67.9 kg; stature: 17.65 dm.

would reveal relatively large abdominal, thigh, and arm girths; the lean person (2.5 percentile) would show an exaggerated decrease of the three aberrant girths.

CONCEPTUAL: VOLUME AND WEIGHT. Basic in our analysis is the resolution of the entity *weight* into a perimetric (girth) and a linear (stature) component. Although the direct relationship between perimetric size (together with stature) and weight may be challenged as geometrically untenable since the density of the body has been excluded as a variable, this omission is acceptable because our formulations provide ponderal and not volumetric values. Thus, the difference in volume of two large men of the same weight, e.g., 100 kg, may be six liters greater in a fat (low density) man compared with a lean (high density) man.

If the body did not alter its shape as fat accumulated, we would grossly overestimate the weight of fat men deduced from perimetric size. Actually the reverse is true, and we tend to underestimate the weight of the obese, and overestimate the weight of lean persons. It seems reasonable that the change in shape from linearity to rotundity is analogous to the geometrical representation in Fig. 1.5. Our data support the postulate that a summation

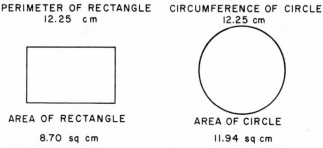

PERIMETER OF RECTANGLE
12.25 cm

CIRCUMFERENCE OF CIRCLE
12.25 cm

AREA OF RECTANGLE
8.70 sq cm

AREA OF CIRCLE
11.94 sq cm

Fig. 1.5 Geometric representation to show the influence of shape on surface area depicted by the circle and rectangle, both of which have the same perimetric measurement.

of girths, each encompassing tissues with wide variation in density (e.g., the chest encloses a pneumatic space, the ankle comprises essentially bone and ligaments), provides an accurate estimate, not of volume but of weight.

Radiogrammetry

Surface measurements of both girths and widths, no matter how well integrated into quantitative patterns of body build, require in-depth verification. The complementary examination which adequately fulfills this need is radiographic visualization of fat, bone, and muscle. In an initial study with Carlstein (unpublished), radiography of the arm was directed to an unequivocal assessment of the relative amount of fat tissue in compressed-air workers (fat tissue has long been associated with increased susceptibility to decompression sickness). The strikingly clear differentiation by Carlstein of bone, muscle, and fat shadows obtained in a fractional second x-ray exposure has proved to be an opportune extension of technique routinely utilized by Maresh (83), Garn (58), Tanner (130), and Johnston and Malina (71).

However, a barrier to routine fat-shadow radiography is conversion of the measured widths (and this applies to skin-folds as well) to individual estimates of body fat. Heretofore, over a period of some 40 years, radiographic analysis of data has been restricted to statistical vagary, to logarithmic manipulation (with dubious results), and to circuitous estimates of body density. This failure to provide an unambiguous and direct linkage between highly reliable measurements and individual percentages or weights of body fat, is reflected in the vapid "escape clause" that regression constants derived for a given population sample should not be applied to other groups without due caution.

In the effort to circumvent this unwarranted stricture, we have implemented a principle formulated by Matiegka (84) in 1921 with reference to skin-folds, namely that the weight of body fat could be computed as a product of surface area and skin-fold thickness. In application to radiogrammetry, we can state,

$$W(\text{Fat}) = \text{Fat widths} \times \text{Surface Area} \times k$$

and

$$\% \text{ Fat} = W(\text{Fat})/\text{Weight} \times 100.$$

Surface area is closely approximated from,

$$3F \text{ or } D \times h \times k,$$

and it will be shown further in the text,

$$\% \text{ Fat} = \frac{\text{Fat widths (radiogrammetric)}}{3F \text{ or } D \times k}$$

Summary

The objectives outlined for this monograph contain highlights of long-term investigations in the effort to implement the application of anthropometry, densitometry, and radiogrammetry for routine evaluation of individual and group studies of body build, muscular development, and assessment of fat. The feasibility and validity of these procedures have been tested on population samples which differ widely in age and physical characteristics. Collaborative work has extended the scope of the studies to include determinations of total body water, exchangeable potassium ($^{42}K_e$), and total body potassium estimated from ^{40}K gamma emission as detected in heavily shielded chambers or liquid scintillation counters.

The routine procedures comprise a multiparameter assessment of body build and gross composition featured by (1) comprehensive examinations suitable for large population samples, (2) conversion of anthropometric girths and diameters into equivalents of weight and lean body weight, (3) anthropometric analysis of regional body components and their synthesis into unified patterns, (4) diagrammatic representation of body build, (5) densitometric analysis of males and females including outstanding athletes, and (6) establishment of communality with similar data of other investigators.

The essential role of physiologist, physician, and physical educator will be evident in the outline of diagnostic measures to detect early deterioration, and in conservation measures to extend the productive period of life span. The authors will present independent but coordinated data and analyses in accord with objectives.

Chapter 2 / Laboratory Methods

A fundamental knowledge of the various methods used in the assessment of body build and composition is essential to even a basic understanding of this broad area of study. Because of the many problems inherent in the compositional dissection of the intact living human, science has been forced to turn almost exclusively to animal experimentation and indirect human analysis to gain the knowledge which is presently available. Consequently, each of the methods to be discussed contains certain basic errors which limit its use and applicability. Likewise, these methods vary considerably with regard to validity, reproducibility, and ease of administration. It is important, therefore, that the researcher and the individual interpreting the research literature be well aware of the limitations of each research study on the basis of the laboratory methods selected.

Laboratory methods for assessing body composition range from the relatively simple measurement of body volume to the more complex biochemical methods of isotopic dilution or inert gas absorption. Each of these will be discussed individually in some detail in this chapter.

Direct Cadaver Analysis

The direct compositional analysis of the human body can only be undertaken through the dissection of fresh human cadavers. The problems here are too numerous to mention. The efforts involved are enormous and the resulting data are questionable with respect to the generality of their applicability. Consequently, very few complete dissections have been performed on human cadavers (75,104). Much more extensive work has been performed on small laboratory animals, but how closely the resulting data matches comparable data on humans remains unknown. Consequently, the majority of research on body composition has been conducted through indirect means, with indirect methods usually being validated against other more widely accepted indirect methods.

Body Density

It is possible to determine the density of any object through the simple relationship of weight to volume:

$$\text{Density} = \text{Weight/Volume} \tag{1}$$

or

$$D = W/V$$

Assuming the body is divided into two compartments—lean tissue and fat tissue—it is possible to estimate the body fat and lean body weight from the calculated body density. When a system is composed of two intermixed components of different densities, the density of the whole system can be determined by the proportions of the two components in the system (75). In a system comprised of components A and B with respective densities of a and b, the density of the whole system (D) is as follows:

$$D = \frac{A + B}{(A/a) + (B/b)} \tag{2}$$

When working in proportions, if the whole system equals unity, the proportional contribution of B $(B = 1 - A)$, would be:

$$B = \frac{1}{D} \times \frac{ab}{(a - b)} - \frac{b}{(a - b)} \tag{3}$$

If, in equation 2, A is the proportion of lean body tissue and B represents fat, the relative and absolute fat and lean components can be calculated quite easily.

Using this approach, Rathbun and Pace (107), Brožek et al. (37), and Siri (117) have derived basic equations for estimating relative body fat which are very similar, differing only in that different values were used to estimate the densities of the fat and lean tissues components. These equations are as follows:

Rathbun and Pace (107) % body fat $= \left(\dfrac{5.548}{\text{specific gravity}} - 5.044\right) \times 100$

Brožek et al. (37)   % body fat $= \left(\dfrac{\text{density}}{4.570} - 4.142\right) \times 100$

Siri (117)   % body fat $= \left(\dfrac{4.950}{\text{density}} - 4.500\right) \times 100$

The fact that these equations result in similar values for calculated relative fat is illustrated by the correlations between these equations ($r = 0.995$ to $r = 0.999$) found in a sample of 54 college males (147).

The absolute fat weight is calculated simply by the equation:

$$\text{Fat weight} = \text{Body weight} \times \% \text{ body fat}/100 \tag{4}$$

and lean body weight (LBW) by the equation:

$$\text{LBW} = \text{Weight} - \text{Fat weight} \tag{5}$$

To estimate the body density for the subsequent calculation of body fat and lean body weight, it is necessary to first measure the volume of the body to satisfy equation 1. This has been done in several different ways: (a) hydrostatic weighing; (b) direct volume by water displacement; and (c) helium dilution.

Hydrostatic Weighing

One of the most accurate and widely used methods for assessing body volume—hydrostatic weighing—utilizes Archimedes' basic physical principle that a body immersed in a fluid is acted on by a buoyancy force, which is evidenced by a loss of weight equal to the weight of the displaced fluid. Thus, when an individual is weighed underwater, while totally submerged, his total body volume is equal to his loss of weight in water, corrected for the density of water (D_w) corresponding to the water temperature at the time of the underwater weighing. Thus, the volume (V) is simply derived from the equation:

$$V = \frac{W_A - W_w}{D_w} \tag{6}$$

where W_A and W_w are the individual's weight in air and water respectively. Equation 1 then becomes:

$$D = \frac{W_A}{\dfrac{(W_A - W_w)}{D_w}} \text{ or Specific Gravity} = \frac{W_A}{W_A - W_w} \tag{7}$$

Behnke (22) was the first to make adequate estimates of total body volume using this technique in the late 1930s.

Two extraneous volumes are necessarily included in the total volume calculated in equation 6, one of which must be taken into account in a revised estimate of the total body volume. Providing the underwater weight is recorded when the subject is in the full or maximal expiratory position, a correction must be provided for the air remaining in the lungs, i.e., the residual volume (RV). The residual volume makes a sizable contribution in the estimate of the total body volume, and since it is highly variable, it is essential to obtain a close approximation of the individual's actual residual volume. The second volume, gas bubbles or flatus in the gastrointestinal tract, is of a considerably smaller magnitude and is seldom if ever measured. Buskirk (39) has proposed the use of a constant correction of 100 ml (BTPS) to approximate the air volume of the gastrointestinal tract.

The residual volume, being a much larger volume, presents more of a problem. It has been shown, however, that for screening purposes, the use of a constant, assumed average residual volume or the estimate of residual volume from the vital capacity provides an acceptable substitute for the actual, determined residual volume (144). The differences in the mean densities for both males and females calculated from the actual, the estimated (from vital capacity), and assumed average residual volume, were less than 0.001 gm/cc (see Table 2.1). When observing changes in individuals over

Table 2.1

DIFFERENCES IN BODY COMPOSITION CALCULATED USING ACTUAL, ESTIMATED AND ASSUMED AVERAGE RESIDUAL LUNG VOLUMES[a]

Variable	Con- dition[d]	Males[b] $(N = 69)$				Females[c] $(N = 128)$			
		Mean	*S.D.*	*r*	*t*	*Mean*	*S.D.*	*r*	*t*
Density, gm/cc	1	1.0635	.0131			1.0406	.0098		
	2	1.0631	.0129			1.0405	.0105		
	3	1.0632	.0124			1.0407	.0102		
	1–2	0.0004	.0042	.948	.784	0.0001	.0051	.875	.220
	1–3	0.0003	.0044	.942	.563	−0.0001	.0047	.889	.306
Percent Fat[e]	1	15.51	5.78			25.73	4.50		
	2	15.71	5.67			25.80	4.79		
	3	15.64	5.49			25.71	4.65		
	1–2	−0.20	1.82	.949	.901	−0.07	2.33	.876	.306
	1–3	−0.13	1.92	.944	.563	0.02	2.16	.889	.104
Lean Body Weight, kg	1	64.24	8.76			43.37	4.73		
	2	64.11	8.86			43.36	5.05		
	3	64.11	8.34			43.37	4.67		
	1–2	0.13	1.30	.989	.817	0.01	1.32	.966	.086
	1–3	0.13	1.43	.987	.742	0.00	1.22	.966	.000

[a]*Adapted from Wilmore (144).*
[b]*A t-ratio of 1.98 and an r = 0.234 are needed for significance at the 0.05 level.*
[c]*A t-ratio of 2.00 and an r = 0.172 are needed for significance at the 0.05 level.*
[d]*Conditions: (1) actual residual volume; (2) residual volume estimated from vital capacity; (3) assumed average constant residual volume.*
[e]*Calculated through Siri's (117) equation: Percent Fat = (495/Density − 450).*

time, however, it is essential to obtain the highest degree of accuracy possible and, therefore, the residual volume should be measured. The actual measurement presents somewhat of a problem since indirect techniques must be used.

The open circuit nitrogen dilution technique, the helium dilution technique, and the hyperbaric technique have been used successfully (142). However, there does appear to be an advantage to using the closed circuit oxygen dilution technique as it is a very rapid technique (6–10 breaths) and has a small standard error of measurement (145). The residual volume measurement should probably be made in the water at the time of the underwater weighing, however, it appears that the difference between the residual volume measured in and out of water is small and variable (43). Additional research is certainly needed in this area.

With the correction for the residual volume and gastrointestinal tract volume taken into account, equation 7 becomes:

$$D = \frac{W_A}{\dfrac{(W_A - W_w)}{D_w} - (RV + 100 \text{ ml})} \tag{8}$$

The actual weighing of the individual underwater is easily accomplished by having the individual sit on a chair supported by a scale in a closed body of water as illustrated in Fig. 2.1. Katch (73) has demonstrated that there is a learning curve associated with successive trials of underwater weighing. His data support the contention that a mean of the eighth, ninth, and tenth trial gives an accurate approximation of the "true" underwater weight. Wilmore and Behnke have adopted the practice of making at least ten determinations per subject (144) but their selection of the "best" underwater weight differs significantly from Katch's findings. They select (1) the highest obtained weight if it is observed more than twice; (2) the second highest weight if it is observed more than once and if the first criterion is not attained; (3) the third highest weight if neither the first nor the second criterion are attained. This method of selection was used to reduce the possibility of underestimating the actual underwater weight on the subject who attained his highest values during the first 5–7 trials.

Water Displacement with a Body Volumeter

A second method for assessing body volume uses the actual water displacement technique with a body volumeter. The technique is nearly identical to that of hydrostatic weighing except that the actual volume of water displaced by the subject is measured rather than the loss of weight in water. The water displacement is assessed by submerging the subject underwater and then measuring the increase in the water level in the pool or tank by using a fine bore burette connected to the tank, which has been previously calibrated by placing objects or water of different but known volumes into the tank and noting the corresponding readings. It is also necessary in this technique to measure the residual lung volume, to account for its influence in the final determination of the body density. The equation for calculating body

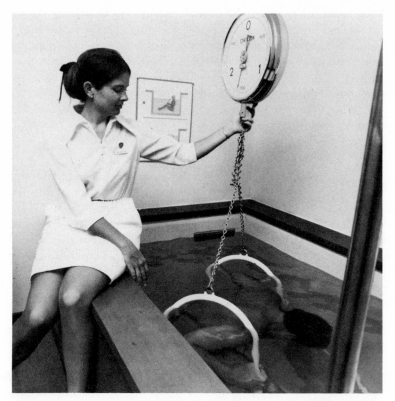

Fig. 2.1 Illustration of the hydrostatic weighing technique. As the subject expires to complete maximal expiration, the weighing chair will submerge below the water level. The subject's underwater weight is determined by subtracting the weight of the chair and the weight belt, if a weight belt is used, from the observed underwater weight. Preventive Medicine Center, Palo Alto, California.

density would be as follows:

$$D = \frac{W_{\text{air}}}{\dfrac{V}{D_w} - (RV + 100 \text{ ml})} \tag{9}$$

It has been estimated that this technique is less precise than either the hydrostatic weighing technique or the helium dilution technique (42) because of the difficulties inherent in distinguishing the changes in the volume in the tank to an accuracy necessary to obtain the same degree of discrimination found in the other two techniques. The technique does have certain advantages, however, which make it appropriate and desirable for certain applications.

The water displacement technique works exceptionally well when the purpose is to assess segmental volumes of the body. The volume of nearly any body segment can be determined rather accurately by having the subject assume various positions in the water. For example, if the intent is to assess the volume of the trunk, the investigator first defines the anatomical landmarks describing the superior and inferior boundaries. He then submerges the subject to the level of the superior boundary and obtains the volume reading and submerges him to the inferior boundary and obtains the volume reading. The difference between the two volume readings reflects the estimated volume of the trunk.

Helium Dilution

An ingenious method for determining body volume through gas dilution using helium as the inert tracer gas, was first proposed by Walser and Stein (137) in 1953, and greatly improved by Siri in 1956 (117). The subject enters a small, closed chamber of a constant volume (V_C). A known volume of helium (V_{He}) contained in a second chamber is then allowed to mix freely with the air in the first chamber. When an equilibrium is established, the concentration of helium at the point of equilibrium (C_{He}) is measured and applied to the subsequent calculation of body volume. The volume actually being assessed is the volume of the difference (ΔV) between the chamber volume (V_C) and subject volume (V_S) or:

$$\Delta V = \frac{V_{He}(1 - C_{He})}{d \times C_{He}} \tag{10}$$

where d is the ratio of the absolute temperature of the helium to the chamber air, measured just prior to mixing the two volumes. Substituting $V_C - V_S$ for V in equation 10,

$$V_S = V_C - \frac{V_{He}(1 - C_{He})}{d \times C_{He}} \tag{11}$$

The accuracy of this technique is dependent on several critical factors. First, the volume of the chamber should be adequate for the largest subject to be measured, yet small enough to ensure sufficient discrimination between subjects of varying volumes. For adults, Siri has used a chamber volume of about 400 liters and a helium volume of about 15 liters (119). With such volumes, a 50-liter subject would have a C_{He} of $\cong 4.0\%$ while a 150-liter subject would have $\cong 5.4\%$ C_{He}. Thus, there is a difference in helium concentrations of only 1.40% for 100 liters difference in volume. This points to a second factor of major importance, the resolution or degree of accuracy of the helium analyzer. Siri has approximated that it is necessary to be able to sense differences in helium concentration of about 0.001% in order to maintain a standard error no greater than ± 0.1 liter in the estimate of the subject's volume (119). While this is a somewhat difficult requirement to meet, it is not as restrictive as might first appear, since the range of helium values to be measured is relatively low, probably less than 2%.

This technique offers several distinct advantages over the hydrostatic techniques. First, it is not necessary to measure the residual lung volume since the lungs become a part of the ΔV. Secondly, this technique is applicable to individuals from infancy through old age, whether healthy or ambulatory. It can also be used on animals of varying sizes. It doesn't require nearly the degree of subject intelligence or cooperation necessary for the hydrostatic techniques. The helium dilution technique is basically more complex, however, and requires continous calibration checks. The initial expense is also somewhat high, but the operational costs are relatively low.

The validity of this technique appears to be quite high. Fomon, et al. (55) in an extensive series of calibration checks on aluminum blocks of various sizes found that the error in determined volume ranged from 0.65 to 8.46 ml/1,000 ml, with a mean error of 4.2 ml/1,000 ml, or less than 0.5% error. Comparisons between the hydrostatic weighing technique and the helium dilution technique have been made on only a few subjects. On the basis of these few subjects, the two techniques appear to compare quite favorably (Behnke: unpublished data).

Radiographic Analysis

Radiography has an ideal application in the area of body composition assessment since it is possible to use soft tissue x-ray to differentiate between the various layers of skin, fat, bone, and muscle. The use of x-rays for this purpose started in the late 1920s and has progressed to a sophisticated technique over the years. Garn, who pioneered much of the original work in this area, has provided an excellent summary of the research on radiographic analysis of body composition up through 1959 (59).

Behnke has recently developed an approach to radiographic analysis which offers a great deal of promise. His radiographic analysis of the upper arm evolved from a need to assess fat with its high absorption coefficient for nitrogen, in compressed-air tunnel workers, and as an additional application of an advanced high PKV technique developed by Carlstein (unpublished) to reveal frequently missed, incipient lesions of avascular bone necrosis which afflict these workers. The x-rays provided a strikingly clear differentiation in the upper arm between bone, muscle, and fat, attained in a 1/30th second exposure (3.33 MAS, 120 PKV). The most important aspect of this new approach to body composition assessment through radiography is the attempt to provide an unambiguous and direct linkage between the highly reliable radiogrammetric measurement and individual ponderal or percentage values for body fat.

RADIOLOGIC EXAMINATION. Features of the technique are use of high kilovoltage (120 PKV), short exposure time (1/30th second, 3.33 MAS), employment of a high-speed screen, and rapid (90 second) film processing. The high PKV is twofold greater and the MAS exposure is less by a factor of three than earlier recommended values from Garn (58) and Tanner (130). The objective in the examination is visualization of the arm (upper limb

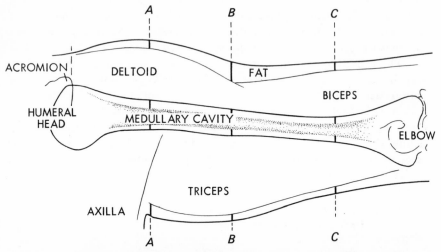

Fig. 2.2 Measurement sites for the radiogrammetric technique

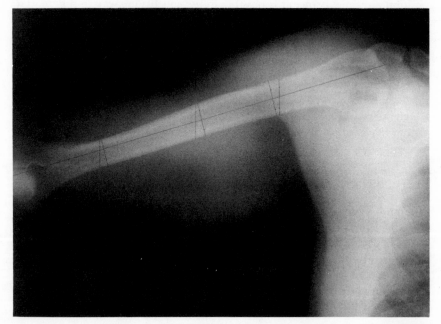

Fig. 2.3 Illustration of the measurement sites on the x-ray of a male shotputter

from shoulder to elbow, Figs. 2.2 and 2.3). With the subject erect, the left arm is brought to the anatomical position, then the free portion of the limb is abducted to a level parallel with the floor, in front of and with the humeral epicondyles parallel to the cassette. This position provides an anterior-posterior (A-P) visualization of the arm which is 90° clockwise from the lateral-medial exposure of Tanner's subjects. Anode-film separation is six feet to minimize magnification. The focal point of the x-ray beam is directed to the vertical and horizontal midpoint of the arm. It is essential that the long axis of the humerus be parallel to the horizontal film edge, otherwise a "slanting" error is introduced by the method of measurement. In 50 radiographic examinations the initial procedure was followed; all films were satisfactory without retakes.

The technique can be improved to attain more uniform positioning by provision of support for the forearm and of a vertical rod for the hand to grasp. Radiographs of both arms would afford better representation of arm tissue than that from a single film. A better assessment of muscular development may be provided by a position of 90° flexion of the forearm and maximal tension of the muscles.

The dosage of ionizing radiation received by the examinee when the arm alone is exposed, is minute, and hence there is no age restriction to the procedure. Even without shielding, it is evident from the assessment by Garn (58) that the dosage of radiation received from this type of exposure is only a fraction of yearly background average and not more than the radiation emission received from the TV screen during the football season.

MEASUREMENTS. The film is placed on a suitably illuminated screen and pencil lines are drawn at right angles to the film (and long axis of the humerus) for the breadths to be measured at the designated levels, A, B, and C (Fig. 2.2). The objective at the three levels is to obtain representative values for arm fat (six widths) and to measure maximal widths of deltoid, triceps, and biceps musculature. The axillary (A) level is about one-half the distance from the lateral border of the acromium process to the "deltoid pocket" (B); mid-biceps (C) is about one-half the distance from (B) to the elbow joint and proximal to flaring of cortical bone toward the distal cancellous portion of the humerus. Total bone and medullary widths are measured at sites A, B, and C where the cortex is compact and consistently uniform in young adults, but not necessarily so in older men. The skin-subcutaneous layer measured as six FAT widths from surface to muscularis contains in addition to ether-extractable fat ($d = 0.90$), vascular, nervous, and supporting tissues. Any correction for change in density of these tissues appears to be an unnecessary refinement at this time. Width measurements are made with a dial caliper calibrated to 0.05 mm and read usually to 0.10 mm.

Three arm girths are measured at A, B, and C (Fig. 2.2) with the arm positioned for x-ray visualization. The girth measurements afford a potential correction of any appreciable discrepancy from the mean ratio of x-ray widths to arm girths. Table 2.2 illustrates the measurements for the left arm of a shotputter (referred to as Subject 1 in Table 2.3).

Table 2.2

X-RAY DETERMINATION OF FAT, MUSCLE, AND
BONE IN A SHOTPUTTER[a]

Level	Girths, cm	*Radiogrammetric Widths (mm × 10)*			
		Fat	*Muscle*	*Bone*	*(Medullary)*
A. Axillary	47.8	84.0 125.5	500.0 698.0	277.0	125.0
B. Deltoid	40.8	300.0 44.5	109.5 761.0	288.5	92.0
C. Mid-biceps	37.1	125.0 94.0	368.5 403.0	232.0	83.5
Sum	125.7	773.0	2840.0	798.0	301.0

[a]27 years of age, h = 188.5 cm, W = 130 kg.

CALCULATION OF BODY FAT, ABSOLUTE AND RELATIVE. Matiegka (84) proposed that the amount of body fat could be computed from the product of surface area (SA), one-half of the thickness of double layered skinfolds, and a constant. The following formulation embodies Matiegka's concept modified only in the substitution of six radiographic widths (FAT) for skinfolds,

$$\text{Fat, kg} = SA \times FAT \times k \tag{12}$$

Surface area initially measured by DuBois and DuBois (48) on a few subjects, involves a tedious and exacting technique. Subsequently DuBois (47) reported that surface area could be calculated from perimetric size and length of body segments, and finally from weight and stature alone,

$$SA, \text{cm}^2 = W^{0.425} \times h^{0.725} \times 71.84. \tag{13}$$

However, "the formula, $SA = W^{0.5} \times H^{0.5} \times k$ was almost as good." Since $W = (D \text{ or } 3F) \times h \times 0.111$,* then with appropriate substitution,

$$SA, \text{m}^2 = 3F \times h, \text{dm} \times 0.01762 \tag{14}$$

and

$$\text{Fat, kg} = SA(3F) \times FAT \times 0.134 \tag{15}$$

The derivation of the constant (0.134) will be discussed in the chapter on radiogrammetric applications (Chapter 8).

*See equation 7, Chapter 4.

These equations have been validated against the traditional hydrostatic weighing in a small, but highly variable, sample of subjects. The data presented in Table 2.3 pertain to four examinees—two are exceptional athletes,

Table 2.3

COMPARISON OF DENSITOMETRIC AND RADIOGRAMMETRIC ESTIMATES
OF BODY FAT FOR EXAMINEES WHO DIFFER WIDELY IN BODY BUILD

Exa-minee	Age	h	W^a	Density	LBW	Weight^b	% Fat Density	% Fat SA	% Fat 3F	% Fat D
1	27	188.5	130.5	1.049	102.1	130.0	21.5	20.4	20.8	20.5
2	24	194.7	121.9	1.060	101.2	122.8	17.6	17.1	17.3	17.1
3	67	178.8	87.9	1.043	66.1	91.8	28.0	27.9	28.2	28.0
4	26	180.3	77.8	1.071	68.3	77.8	12.2	12.5	12.5	12.5

^{a}*Body weight when density was determined.*
^{b}*Body weight at the time of the radiogrammetric examination.*

a third is an old physician who has lost about 5 kg of *LBW* during the past 30 years, and the fourth is a well-proportioned, athletic Army officer.

Relative fat (%) can be estimated from the following equations,

$$\text{Relative Fat } (\%) = \frac{FAT}{3F \times k} \times 100, \, k = 4.71 \tag{16}$$

$$\text{Relative Fat } (\%) = \frac{0.94 \, FAT}{B + M} \times 100, \text{ where } B + M \tag{17}$$

are the radiogrammetric Bone + Muscle widths of the arm. This remarkable relationship will be analyzed subsequently. Table 2.4 illustrates the calcula-

Table 2.4

AN EXAMPLE OF THE BEHNKE RADIOGRAMMETRIC TECHNIQUE

Subject 1	$F = \sqrt{130.0/18.85} = 2.626$
Stature 18.85 dm	$3F = 7.88$
Weight 130.0 kg	$SA(3F) = 3F \times h \times 0.01762 = 2.617$ meters
FAT 77.3 mm	Fat, kg $= 2.617 \times 77.3 \times 0.134 = 27.1$ kg
B + M 36.38 cm	Fat, % = 20.8%

$$\text{(using equation 16) Fat, } \% = \frac{7.73}{7.88 \times 4.71} \times 100 = 20.8\%$$

$$\text{(using equation 17) Fat, } \% = \frac{0.94 \times 7.73}{36.38} \times 100 = 20.0\%$$

From the hydrostatic weighing, absolute fat = 28.4 kg and relative fat = 21.5%

tion of the absolute and relative quantities of fat derived from the formulations for the shot-putter.

Biochemical Approaches

A number of biochemical approaches exist for determining the basic fat and lean components of the body. These vary considerably in complexity and validity, but each technique makes a unique and valuable contribution to the gaining of a better understanding of the basic composition of the body.

Potassium-40 (^{40}K)

The body emits naturally occurring gamma radiation in the form of ^{40}K. Since ^{40}K does represent, proportionally, the total body potassium content, and since the lean body tissue has a fairly constant potassium content and constitutes the primary source of potassium, the ability to measure ^{40}K is of great practical significance relative to body composition assessment. The ^{40}K content of the body is assessed by radioactive counting. The counting is accomplished with either NaI crystals as the detector, or in a liquid scintillation counter (see Fig. 2.4).

Using the liquid scintillation counter for illustrative purposes, the subject assumes a supine position on a canvas sling which is aligned to connect directly to the trough leading into the well of the counter. The sling, with the subject in position, is moved along the trough into the counter. Inside the well of the counter, the subject is surrounded by a layer of liquid scintillator solution. This solution converts the photon energies of the gamma rays from ^{40}K into light impulses. The intensity of these impulses is proportional to the energies of the intersecting photon. These light impulses are referred to as scintillations and are detected by photomultiplier tubes mounted around the outer wall of the chamber. The photomultiplier tubes amplify and convert the scintillations into proportional voltages (108).

The accurate calibration of the counter is of extreme importance. By placing different objects or containers of known ^{40}K count into the chamber, it is possible to convert the actual counts into a meaningful assessment of the potassium content of the body. It is necessary to assess this counting efficiency for each test, as it will vary somewhat. Likewise, it is essential to measure the background count frequently so that the total count can be corrected for the influence of the background, i.e., subject count = total count − background count.

The length of time the subject remains in the counter varies with the type of counter being used, but can range from several minutes to several hours. Using the liquid scintillation counter, a common pattern of counting involves an initial calibration period with reference standards, a preliminary background count, two or three subject counts of 180–200 seconds in duration, and a final background count. Once the potassium content is determined,

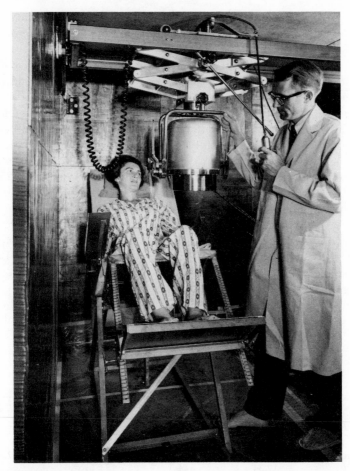

Fig. 2.4 Radioactive counter for detecting the ^{40}K content of the body

following the various corrections for background count, counting efficiency and background depression, the fat-free (FFW) or lean body weight (LBW) is calculated. The equation of Forbes and Lewis (57),

$$FFW \text{ or } LBW = \frac{^{40}\text{K (gms)}}{2.66 \text{ gms of } ^{40}\text{K/kg of } LBW \text{ or } FFW} \qquad (18)$$

was based on the assumption that there are 2.66 gms of ^{40}K/kg of FFW. Boling et al. (31) derived a new set of constants based on the high correlation between potassium and total body water $(r > 0.95)$. On the assumption that water comprises 72% of the fat-free weight or lean body weight, and that 87.3 mEq (male) and 81.0 mEq (female) of potassium are present in each liter or kilogram of total body water, Behnke calculated factors for converting total potassium to lean body weight to be 62.8 mEq (2.46 gms) and 58.3 mEq

(2.28 gms) for males and females, respectively. These values are substantially lower than the single constant derived by Forbes and Lewis from cadaver data.

Using the body density measurement as the criterion, several investigators have attempted to validate the ^{40}K counting technique. Myhre and Kessler (92) found a correlation of $r = 0.87$ between these two techniques, although the mean difference between the methods for all of the groups studied was statistically significant. Of their 100 subjects, 82 had higher fat content as a result of the ^{40}K technique. With the moderately high correlation coefficient between the two techniques, this would seem to indicate the possible influence of a constant error. Murphy et al. (91) in a similar study of men 25 to 45 years of age, found a correlation of $r = 0.88$ between the body density and body potassium techniques. They found the standard error of estimate to be ± 3.07 % relative fat. Their mean values for the two estimates were nearly identical (18.29% fat from density, and 18.55% fat from ^{40}K), and their subjects showed a fairly even distribution around the regression line. Behnke, in several unpublished studies, reported data on several different groups relating the lean body weight calculated from density to the lean body weight calculated from ^{40}K. In a group of 30 boys and 30 girls 16 years of age, he found correlations of $r = 0.938$ and $r = 0.745$, respectively. Table 2.5

Table 2.5

RELATIONSHIP OF ^{40}K AND SPECIFIC GRAVITY CALCULATIONS OF LEAN BODY WEIGHT IN ADOLESCENT MALES AND FEMALES[a]

Group N	Stature, dm	Weight, Kg	Lean Body Weight, Kg.	
			^{40}K	Specific Gravity
Caucasion Males				
10	17.55	66.1	55.9	57.1
10	17.34	60.1	52.7	52.2
10	17.63	66.3	55.5	57.3
Negro Males				
10	17.96	68.6	61.3	61.0
Oriental Males				
10	16.44	55.4	50.3	50.0
Lean Males				
10	17.11	51.9	48.3	49.0
Lean Females				
10	16.00	47.0	35.7	34.9

[a]*Unpublished data of A. R. Behnke, Jr.*

illustrates additional unpublished data collected by Behnke relating ^{40}K to specific gravity measurements. Judging from all of the data available, there appears to be a substantially high relationship between the ^{40}K and density-specific gravity techniques.

Isotopic Dilution

The biological "constant" for water in the lean body tissue has been established as 73.2%. Thus, it is possible to estimate lean body weight from a measurement of total body water, i.e.,

$$LBW = \text{Total body water} \times \frac{100}{73.2} \tag{19}$$

Total body water can be measured through one of several techniques of isotopic dilution. The tracers most commonly used include antipyrine, deuterium oxide, and tritium oxide. The typical procedure for any one of these tracers includes either an oral ingestion or the injection of a specified quantity of the tracer into the venous blood, an equilibration period, and a sampling period. The technique is based on the assumption that there is a uniform distribution of the tracer throughout the body fluids. While the tracer can be either ingested or injected, the sampling can also be either from the blood or urine or both. The calculation of the total body water volume is based on the following simplified relationship:

$$C_1 \times V_1 = C_2 \times V_2 \tag{20}$$

or

$$V_2 = C_1 \times V_1/C_2 \tag{21}$$

where

$C_1 =$ initial concentration of ingested or injected tracer

$V_1 =$ initial volume of ingested or injected tracer

$C_2 =$ final concentration of tracer in blood or urine

$V_2 =$ volume of total body water

A number of studies have shown high correlations between the isotopic tracer techniques and body specific gravity, body density, and direct biochemical techniques (64). Unfortunately, these studies were all performed on farm animals ranging from swine to cattle. Behnke and Siri in an unpublished report illustrated the relationship between fat-free weight calculated from density and from total body water for 31 Navy personnel (Fig. 2.5). The differences are quite large in certain individuals probably due to excessive variability in the degree of hydration. For this group, the standard error of the difference was 8.2%. In a study of 81 males, Osserman et al. (97) found a much closer agreement between lean weight calculated from density and that calculated from total body water. The standard error was only 3.5% and the correlation was $r = 0.900$.

Inert Gas Absorption

The inert gases cyclopropane and krypton are highly fat soluble and are readily absorbed by the body fat. Thus, it is possible to estimate the

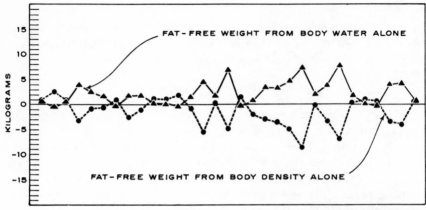

Fig. 2.5 The relationship between fat-free weight calculated from density and total body water

amount of body fat on the basis of the absorption or uptake of the inert gas. In small animals this technique works quite well as an equilibrium is established between the body tissues and the breathing chamber, and no further uptake occurs. In humans, however, the period of equilibration is quite lengthy and the usual experimental protocol necessitates stopping short of the period of equilibrium and estimating through extrapolation the equilibrium value. A simplified equation for the calculation of total body fat (*TBF*) from inert gas absorption is as follows:

$$TBF \text{ (gms)} = \frac{\text{quantity of gas dissolved in lipids}}{\begin{array}{c}\text{solubility coefficient/grams of fat at}\\ \text{equilibrium condition of experiment}\end{array}} \tag{22}$$

Lesser and Zak (80) have shown a relatively close agreement between fat estimated from inert gas absorption and fat estimated from total body water. They report a mean difference of 0.83 kg of fat between the two techniques with a maximum difference of 4.5 kg. This represents a mean error of 1.74%. While the technique is fairly straightforward and accurate, it is rather cumbersome and requires extreme subject and experimenter cooperation. It is therefore primarily intended as a laboratory research tool.

Ultrasound

Because muscle, bone, and fat have different density and acoustical properties, it is possible to use high frequency sound waves to differentiate between tissue types. Sound waves, generated by a special transducer, pass into the tissue and, when a change in density is encountered, a portion of these waves are reflected, picked up, and converted to an electrical impulse, then passed on to a detecting device for amplification and recording (125). The thickness and density of the tissue through which the ultrasonic waves pass determine the characteristics of the reflected sound waves.

The majority of the work using ultrasound to assess body composition has been performed on animals, since it is a rather simple way of obtaining estimates of body fat when compared to other existing techniques. Work with humans has been quite limited. Sloan (120) has reported a relatively high multiple correlation $(r = 0.81)$ between body density as determined by hydrostatic weighing and a regression equation estimate of density based on several ultrasonic measurements of body fat. While these results look encouraging, considerably more data is needed to assess both its practicability as well as its validity. Since the ultrasonic technique is assessing primarily subcutaneous fat, it is subject to many of the same limitations that influence total body fat estimations through skin-fold thickness measurements.

Summary

The various laboratory methods for assessing body composition have been discussed. While cadaver analysis is the only direct way of assessing absolute and relative fat and lean weight, indirect methods have been demonstrated to provide an accurate estimate of these parameters. Body density measurement through hydrostatic weighing is probably the most widely used and accepted indirect method. However, helium dilution and ^{40}K techniques are accurate and have certain advantages which will undoubtedly lead to their greater use in future research.

Chapter 3 / Field Methods

While the accuracy of precise laboratory evaluations of body composition is desirable, it is highly impractial to bring large segments of various populations into the laboratory for mass evaluations or screening. Because of this, and because of the belief that assessments of body composition are valuable and of interest and importance for the general population, methods have been proposed which are applicable to field testing. The validity and reliability of these methods vary considerably. They do, however, appear to approach the accuracy needed for meaningful mass screening. Whether they meet the requirements necessary for the application to research is open to debate at this time.

The present chapter is dedicated solely to describing the techniques and defining the various anatomical landmarks of the sites used in various anthropometric assessments. Chapter 4 will then be devoted to a detailed review of how these various anthropometric measurements can actually be applied to provide a valid and reliable estimate of body fat and lean body weight.

Anthropometry

The human body can be described quite accurately through a series of measurements of the external morphology of the body. Anthropometry, as described in this monograph, will be limited to the measurements of bone and general body diameters, girths or circumferences, and skin-fold thickness. Each of these will be discussed separately.

Bone and General Body Diameters

The diameters of the body can be measured rather accurately and with a high degree of reliability because of the nature of the measurement. In almost all instances, the measurements are made with a bone-to-bone contact, i.e., the soft tissue is compressed. This greatly reduces the degree of variability within a subject and facilitates accurate measurements. Diameters are typically measured with either a broad or narrow blade anthropometer, or with a small precision caliper (see Fig. 3.1). It is important to use the fingers of both

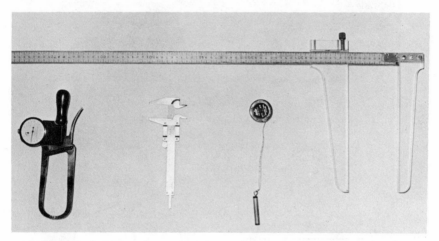

Fig. 3.1 Instruments for determining anthropometric measurements: broad blade anthropometer, Gulick cloth tape, Fisher precision caliper, and Harpenden skinfold caliper

hands to locate the precise bony landmarks, placing the blade of the anthropometer immediately over the identified landmark (see Fig. 3.2).

The anatomical landmarks for the various sites are illustrated in Figs. 3.3 to 3.9, and are described as follows:

HEAD LENGTH. Anterior-posterior diameter at the level of the eyebrow and occipital protuberance (Fig. 3.4).

HEAD WIDTH. Lateral diameter at the widest point of the skull (Fig. 3.3).

BIACROMIAL DIAMETER. Distance between the most lateral projections of the acromial processes with the elbows next to the body and the hands resting on the thighs (Fig. 3.3).

BIDELTOID DIAMETER. Distance between the outermost protrusions of the shoulder with the anthropometer making only light contact with the skin (Fig. 3.3).

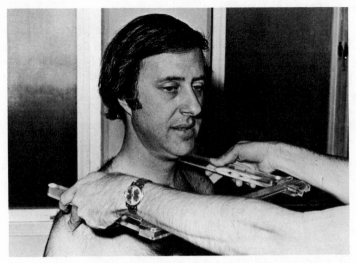

Fig. 3.2 Placement technique with the broad blade anthropometer

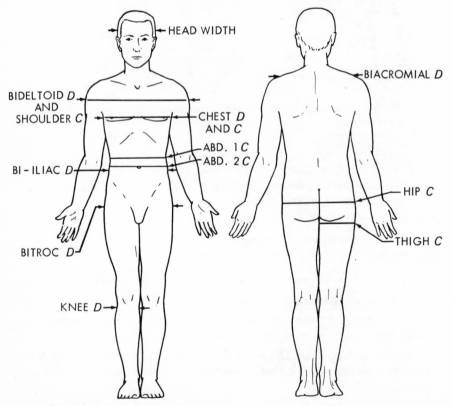

HEAD WIDTH

BIACROMIAL *D*

BIDELTOID *D*
AND
SHOULDER *C*

CHEST *D*
AND *C*

ABD. 1 *C*
ABD. 2 *C*

BI - ILIAC *D*

HIP *C*

BITROC *D*

THIGH *C*

KNEE *D*

Fig. 3.3 Anthropometric landmarks

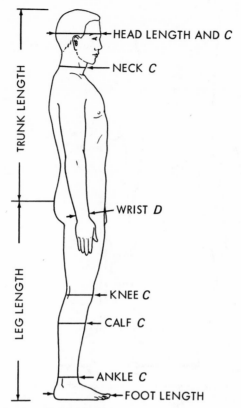

Fig. 3.4 Anthropometric landmarks

CHEST WIDTH. Arms abducted slightly for placement of the anthropometer at the level of the fifth to sixth ribs (nipple line in men). Arms adducted back to the side of the body for the measurement (Fig. 3.3).

BI-ILIAC DIAMETER. Distance between the most lateral projections of the iliac crests (Fig. 3.3).

BITROCHANTERIC DIAMETER. Distance between the most lateral projections of the greater trochanters (Fig. 3.3).

KNEE. Distance between the outermost projections of the tibial condyles, with the knee flexed to 90° (Fig. 3.3).

ANKLE. Distance between the malleoli with the anthropometer pointed upward at a 45° angle (Fig. 3.5).

ELBOW. Distance between the condyles of the humerus with the elbow flexed and hand supinated (Fig. 3.6).

WRIST. Distance between the styloid processes of the radius and ulna (Fig. 3.4).

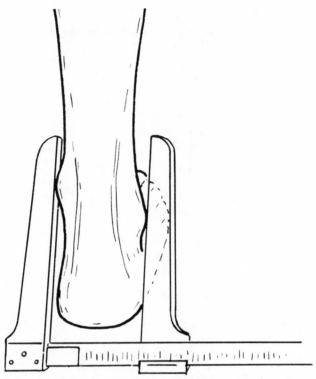

Fig. 3.5 Technique for measuring the ankle diameter with the anthropometer pointing up at a 45° angle

ARM SPAN. The greatest distance between the outstretched fingers of the right and left hand with the arms and forearms extended horizontally sidewards, and the back pressed against a flat surface (Fig. 3.7).

HAND LENGTH. Distance between the tip of the most distal phalange and the point of the most proximal carpal bone (Fig. 3.8).

FOOT LENGTH. Distance between the tip of the most distal phalange and the most posterior part of the calcaneus (Fig. 3.4).

LEG LENGTH. Distance between the floor and the coccyx, while the subject is standing. This closely approximates the level of the greatest height of the femur (Fig. 3.4).

TRUNK LENGTH. The difference between stature and leg length (Fig. 3.4).

STATURE. The height of the individual standing with his back against a wall. The height is recorded from a calibrated wall chart using a 90° projec-

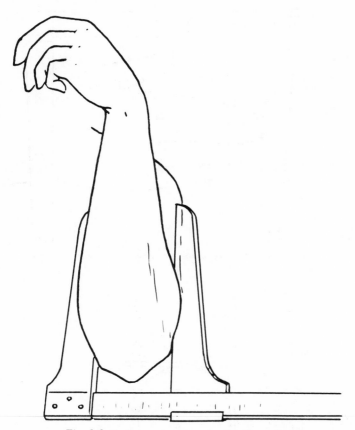

Fig. 3.6 Technique for measuring the elbow diameter

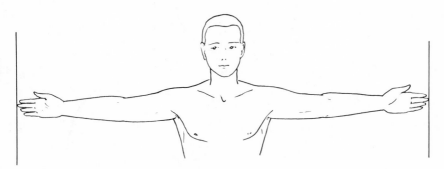

Fig. 3.7 Technique for measuring the arm span

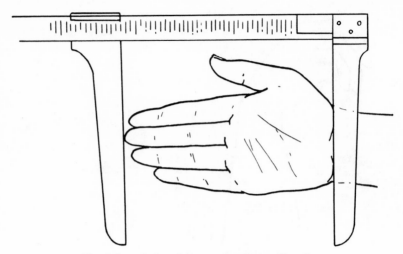

Fig. 3.8 Technique for measuring the hand length

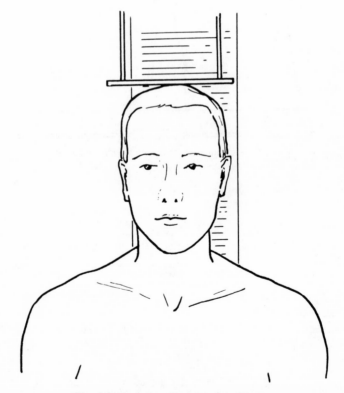

Fig. 3.9 Technique for measuring stature

tion from the wall to assure accuracy (Fig. 3.9). Of the above measurements, all except the chest, bitrochanteric, ankle, arm span, foot length, leg length, and stature are measured with the subject in the seated position.

Body Circumferences

Circumferential measurements are somewhat more difficult to obtain accurately. Whether using a cloth or steel tape, the compression of soft tissue presents a real problem relative to obtaining accurate data. The Gulick tape (see Fig. 3.1) was developed with a spring-loaded handle, allowing the application of a constant tension throughout all measurement sites. Without constant tension there can be considerable variability in the values for any one site. Another potential problem is in the placement of the tape. If the tape isn't placed carefully in a horizontal plane, or at right angles to the length of the segment, considerable error can result. Also, cloth tapes should be calibrated frequently, as they do stretch with use.

The anatomical landmarks for the various circumferential sites are illustrated in Figs. 3.3, 3.4, and 3.10 to 3.12, and are described as follows:

HEAD. Just superior to the eyebrow line and encompassing the occipital protuberance (Fig. 3.4).

NECK. Just inferior to the larynx (Fig. 3.4).

SHOULDERS. Laterally, at the maximal protrusion of the deltoid muscles and anteriorly, at the articular prominence of the sternum and second rib (Fig. 3.3).

CHEST. Nipple line at mid-tidal volume in the males. Just above the breast tissue in females (Fig. 3.3).

ABDOMEN 1. Laterally, midway between the lowest lateral portion of the rib cage and the iliac crest, and anteriorly, midway between the xyphoid process of the sternum and the umbilicus. This level is the natural waist and is readily identified as the level of minimal adbominal width when the side profiles are slightly concave (Fig. 3.3).

ABDOMEN 2. Laterally, at the level of the iliac crests, and anteriorly, at the umbilicus (Fig. 3.3).

ABDOMINAL AVERAGE. The average of the abdominal 1 and 2 measurements.

HIPS. Anteriorly, at the level of the symphysis pubis, and posteriorly, at the maximal protrusion of the gluteal muscles (Fig. 3.3).

THIGH. Just below the gluteal fold or maximal thigh girth (Fig. 3.3).

KNEE. Mid-patellar level, slightly flexed, weight transferred to opposite leg (Fig. 3.4).

CALF. Maximal girth (Fig. 3.4).

ANKLE. Minimal girth, superior to the malleoli (Fig. 3.4).

DELTOID. Maximal girth at the level of the axillae with the arm abducted 90° from the side of the body (Fig. 3.10).

BICEPS FLEXED. Maximal girth of the mid-arm when flexed to the greatest angle with the underlying muscles fully contracted (Fig. 3.11).

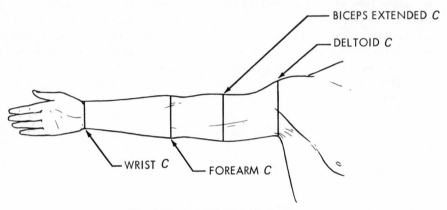

Fig. 3.10 Anthropometric landmarks, arm

Fig. 3.11 Technique for measuring the flexed biceps

BICEPS EXTENDED. Maximal girth of the mid-arm when the elbow is locked in maximal extension with the underlying muscles fully contracted (Fig. 3.10).

FOREARM. Maximal girth with the elbow extended and the hand supinated (Fig. 3.10).

WRIST. Minimal girth just distal to the styloid processes of the radius and ulna (Fig. 3.10).

For women, the following measurements are also sometimes taken.

BREAST. Maximum circumference of the thorax at the level of the breasts, including the material of the unpadded top of a two-piece bathing suit, at mid-tidal volume (Fig. 3.12).

BELOW BREASTS. Immediately below the breasts at mid-tidal volume (Fig. 3.12).

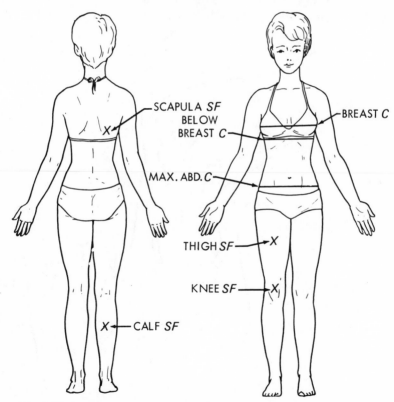

Fig. 3.12 Anthropometric landmarks, female. This figure was redrawn with permission from an original illustration drawn by M. Pritchard, and provided by Dr. Wayne Sinning, Springfield College, Springfield, Mass.

MAXIMUM ABDOMEN. Maximal abdominal girth (Fig. 3.12). All circumferences, with the exception of the upper extremity, are measured with the subject in a standing position.

Skin-folds

The assessment of subcutaneous body fat is accomplished by using special calipers which are calibrated to provide a constant tension throughout their range of motion. The calipers are actually measuring the thickness of a double layer of skin and the interposed layer of fat. There are only slight differences between individuals in the thickness of skin, so the resulting value is an indirect estimate of individual differences in the thickness of subcutaneous fat. When measuring skin-fold thickness, it is essential to determine precisely the location of the site. Likewise, it is important to grasp the skin-fold firmly and maintain a constant distance between the caliper, and the thumb and finger holding the site (refer to Fig. 3.13).

The anatomical landmarks describing the various skin-fold sites are illustrated in Figs. 3.12 to 3.15 and are defined as follows:

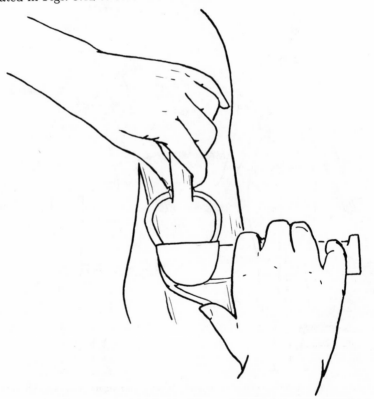

Fig. 3.13 Technique for obtaining the triceps skinfold thickness

CHIN. Under the mandible, fold running between the chin and neck (Fig. 3.13).

CHEST. Over the lateral border of the pectoralis major, just medial to the axilla, fold running diagonally between the shoulder and the opposite hip (Fig. 3.14).

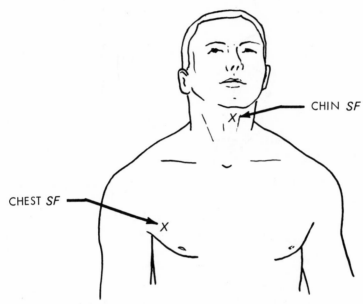

CHIN *SF*

CHEST *SF*

Fig. 3.14 Anthropometric landmarks

SCAPULA. Inferior angle of the scapula with the fold running parallel to the axillary border (Fig. 3.12).

TRICEPS. Midway between the acromion and olecranon processes on the posterior aspect of the arm, the arm held vertically, with the fold running parallel to the length of the arm (Fig. 3.13).

MIDAXILLARY. Vertical fold on the midaxillary line approximately at the level of the fifth rib (Fig. 3.15).

WAIST. Vertical fold on the midaxillary line midway between the twelfth rib and the iliac crest (Fig. 3.15).

SUPRA-ILIAC. Vertical fold on the crest of the ilium at the midaxillary line (Fig. 3.15).

ABDOMINAL. Horizontal fold adjacent to the umbilicus (Fig. 3.15).

THIGH. Vertical fold on the anterior aspect of the thigh midway between the hip and knee joints (Fig. 3.12).

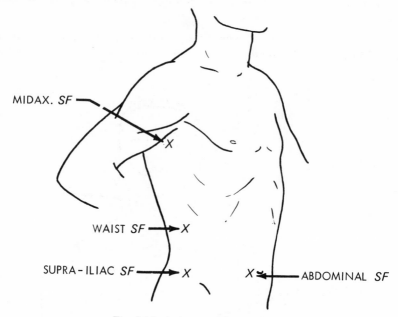

MIDAX. *SF*

WAIST *SF*

SUPRA-ILIAC *SF*

ABDOMINAL *SF*

Fig. 3.15 Anthropometric landmarks

KNEE. Vertical fold at the midpoint of the patella (Fig. 3.12).

CALF. Vertical fold on the posterior calf at the level of the maximal circumference (Fig. 3.12). All measurements are made with the subject in the standing position and are normally taken on the right side of the body.

General Considerations

The biggest problem associated with anthropometry is the inability to obtain reproducible results. To counteract this, several factors must be considered. First, it is important that the individual performing the analysis be properly trained. This implies a thorough understanding of the anatomical landmarks, familiarity with the testing equipment, and sufficient practice under close supervision. An effective way to determine if the individual is properly prepared to perform an anthropometric analysis is to compare his analyses of a group of test subjects to those of a highly trained anthropometrist. In addition, it is always desirable to measure the same site at least twice. If there is greater than 1% discrepancy between the first two values, it is advisable to take a third measurement. To eliminate the possibility of experimenter bias, it is important to complete the full series of measurements prior to starting the second series of measurements. It is essential that the experimenter not have a recollection of his previous measurements for any one site.

When dealing with a group of highly trained anthropometrists, the reliability of the measurements is quite high. In a study of 133 males, 17–37 years of age, the reliability coefficients for two trials on 44 measurement sites ranged from $r = 0.917$ to $r = 0.997$ (148). In a similar study of 128 females, 48 of the 55 measured sites exhibited reliability coefficients in excess of $r = 0.930$ (149). In both studies, however, six and seven of the measurement sites respectively, exhibited statistically significant differences between the first and second trials. This indicates the importance of replicate measures and suggests that a third assessment be made if the discrepancy is greater than 1% of the original value.

The examiner should be provided with a recorder. The job of the recorder is extremely important, particularly in reducing measurement errors. He or she is responsible not only for writing down the correct measurements as they are called out by the examiner, but also for carefully checking the position of the tape, anthropometer, or skin-fold caliper in relation to the specified landmarks for each site. This includes checking to see if the tape and anthropometer are maintained in a horizontal plane. Attention should also be given to the comfort of the examiner and the recorder, as well as of the subject. The recorder should be provided with a chair and desk which is situated to give the best possible observation point for inspecting the examiner. It is useful to construct a 12–15 inch high box for the subject to stand on when assessing the lower limbs. Since several measurements require a sitting rather than a standing position, a chair is also needed for the subject. Factors such as proper lighting, privacy, and the use of a monitor when working with groups of children, are also important.

Lastly, Behnke (20) has employed a simplified system for the estimation of body type. Using visual inspection, the subject is rated on a scale of from one to six for leanness–obesity, with values over three designating corpulence–obesity, and values below three denoting leanness. Accentuated muscular development is indicated by an asterisk (*). If the primary development is over the upper part of the body, a ^{u} is placed in the upper right quadrant of the asterisk ($*^u$). If the lower extremities are muscular, and the arms are relatively underdeveloped, an $_l$ is placed in the lower right quadrant of the asterisk ($*_l$). This system allows a quick classification of subjects into groups on the basis of their outward appearance relative to fatness and muscularity. It also provides a good cross-check in later analyses of the data if there are apparent inconsistencies between various measurements.

Summary

Realizing the value of body composition assessment for the entire population, but recognizing the limitations of laboratory-type analyses for mass testing, a section on field testing techniques has been included. The importance of proper techniques and an accurate location of the various sites cannot be overemphasized. Minor measurement errors may well lead to substantial errors in the estimation of the body composition parameters when these measurements are used in the various predictive regression equations.

Chapter 4 / Application of the Various Field Methods

While basic anthropometric data is of value and interest in itself, the application of this data to the prediction and estimation of various body composition components has far broader significance. To be able to accurately predict or estimate density, weight, relative and absolute body fat, or lean body weight from a few simple anthropometric diameters, circumferences, or skin-folds is of great practical significance. But, just as importantly, it shows that a basic relationship exists between external and internal measures of body composition, and thus allows the construction of theoretical models. These models, in turn, can then be used to gain an understanding of those factors which exert influence on patterns of growth, development, and aging, as well as to gain insight into the etiology of obesity.

While an extensive amount of work has been conducted in this area, this chapter will necessarily be limited to a discussion of the work accomplished by the authors. This chapter doesn't even begin to account for all of the fine research that has been completed in this area.

Estimation of Body Weight

In 1959, Behnke, Guttentag, and Brodsky (24) demonstrated that body weight can be calculated with remarkable accuracy from a few simple anthropometric measurements. It may seem somewhat ludicrous to even attempt to calculate one's body weight when it takes but a second to actually weigh the individual. The theoretical, however, rather than the practical aspect makes this basic finding so important. These authors demonstrated that a basic relationship exists between body dimensions and weight, which allows the description of body configuration in quantitative terms. Indeed, this was the beginning of Behnke's continued attempts to quantify body build.

In their original article, Behnke, Guttentag, and Brodsky used the cylinder as the geometrical analog of the body, although it was also shown that both volume and surface area relationships characteristic of the human body can be represented by von Schelling's double cone model. Weight (W) was described as:

$$W = \pi R^2 h \tag{1}$$

where R is the "body radius" and h is stature or height. They calculated the body radius for each of their 31 subjects from their respective body weights and stature.

$$R = \sqrt{W/\pi h} \tag{2}$$

The mean body radius $(\bar{R})$ was then calculated for the group and was used to convert the mean values for each anthropometric measurement $(\bar{D}_1, \bar{D}_2, \bar{D}_3, \ldots, \bar{D}_n)$ into conversion constants $(k_1, k_2, k_3, \ldots, k_n)$ as follows:

$$k_n = \bar{D}_n/\bar{R} \tag{3}$$

The whole body radius was then calculated for each individual (R) by the following equation:

$$R = \Sigma D/\Sigma k \tag{4}$$

Thus, to determine individual body radius values, it was necessary to know the mean body radius for the group, which was calculated from their mean height $(\bar{h})$ and weight $(\bar{W})$.

$$\bar{R} = \sqrt{\bar{W}/\pi \bar{h}} \tag{5}$$

$\bar{R}$ was then used to calculate the individual conversion constants (k values) for each site. As an example, if the $\bar{R}$ for the group was 1.178 dm and the chest circumference for a particular individual was 95.9 cm, the k value for that individual's chest circumference would be 81.4 (95.9/1.178). Table 4.1 illustrates the actual computation of an individual's body radius and weight from six body circumferences.

This theory was tested on a group of 31 Navy personnel. The correlation between the calculated weight and scale weight was reported to approach unity ($r = 0.99$). The standard error of estimate was ± 1.64 kg.

In 1961, Behnke reported data confirming his original work (15). In addition, he refined and simplified his method of analysis on the basis of

Table 4.1

COMPUTATION OF *R* AND *W* FROM BODY CIRCUMFERENCES

Site	Measurement (D) cm	Conversion Constant (k) $D/\bar{R}^a$
Chest	93.2	79.1
Biceps	31.0	26.3
Forearm	28.2	23.9
Hips	96.0	81.5
Thigh	57.5	48.8
Calf	39.2	33.3
	$\Sigma D = 345.1$	$\Sigma k = 292.9$

Height = 17.6 dm
Weight = 77.70 kg
$R = \Sigma D / \Sigma k = 345.1/292.9 = 1.178$
Calculated $W = \pi R^2 h = 3.14 \times 1.178^2 \times 17.6 = 76.69$ kg.

^{a}*Assuming an $\bar{R} = 1.178$.*

additional data and insight. In this refinement he was able to eliminate the constant π and the concept of the body radius. On the basis of this new method, weight was calculated as follows.

$$W = D^2 h \qquad (6)$$

where : W = weight; h = height and $D = C/K$. Additional symbols were used to represent the basic anthropometric measurements and their respective conversion constants. These include:

c = a specific circumference, e.g., c (biceps)
C = the sum of all 11 circumferences*
k = a conversion constant specific for a given circumference, e.g., k (biceps)
K = the sum of the 11 k values, equal to 300 for both men and women
d = the quotient, c/k, e.g., c(biceps)$/k$(biceps) = d(biceps)
D = the mean of the d values or the quotient, C/K.
$F = \sqrt{W/h}$

Behnke demonstrated in this paper a remarkable relationship between the group mean values for F (indicated as $\bar{F}$) and D (indicated as $\bar{D}$). For a group of 31 Navy men the two values were indentical, with a group mean of 2.087. The values were nearly identical for a group of 33 men and 24 women at Lankenau Hospital, with $\bar{F}$ and $\bar{D}$ values of 2.056 and 2.052 for the men, and 1.854 and 1.860 for the women, respectively. Thus, a basic relationship was revealed, indicating the equivalence of F, $\bar{F}$, derived from weight and stature, and D, $\bar{D}$, respectively, derived from the anthropometric circumferences.

*The eleven circumferences include shoulders, chest, abdomen, hips, thigh, flexed biceps, forearm, wrist, knee, calf, and ankle.

The concept of a body radius had been used previously to develop the geometrical analog of the body as a cylinder or a double cone arrangement. With the refinement in his technique of assessing body weight, $W = D^2h$, Behnke proposed that the geometrical analogue of the body may be looked upon as a rectangular prism with D representing a dimension of the square base.

Using this relationship, body weight was predicted with an accuracy of $\pm 2\%$ ($r = 0.98$). On a separate group of 488 heavy-duty workmen reported in the same study, the standard error of measurement tended to be somewhat higher. However, the weights were calculated on the basis of only nine circumferences, with the hips and thigh measurements excluded.

In order to estimate the stability of the conversion constants for each circumference (k values) among different population samples, data was obtained from five independent groups of males and five independent groups of females. This data is illustrated in Table 4.2. As a result of the relatively

Table 4.2

COMPARISON OF k VALUES COMPUTED FOR VARIOUS GROUPS
OF MEN AND WOMEN

Group and Number of Subjects		k Values		Abdominal Average
	Hips	*Thigh*	*Calf*	
Men				
Army, 25,000	46.5	27.3	17.9	38.9
Air Force, 4000	46.9	27.8	17.9	39.8
Air Force, 3000	47.3	27.9	18.1	39.5
Willoughby athletes, 52	45.9	27.3	18.3	37.9
Navy, 31	46.7	27.4	17.9	39.9
Women				
WAF, 852	50.8	30.1	18.5	36.4
USDA, 10,041	51.0	29.1	17.6	38.3
USDA, 2771	51.0	29.5	18.4	35.7
Willoughby, 20	51.1	29.9	18.4	35.7
Lankenau, 24	51.4	30.7	18.2	35.1

Adapted from A. R. Behnke (13).

small variation between groups, it is possible to establish k values for a reference man and a reference woman (see Table 4.3). The k values presented in this table are reduced to one-third of the original value, as Behnke in a later paper (17) redefined K as equal to 100, instead of 300.

In 1963 (17), Behnke further refined his technique for estimating body weight. The k values were reduced to percentages, thus $K = 100$. This revision necessitated a change in the basic equation for estimating body weight.

Table 4.3

BODY PROPORTIONS (*k* values) DERIVED FROM GIRTHS FOR A
REFERENCE MAN AND WOMAN, AGE 20–24

	Body Proportions			
	Reference Man		*Reference Woman*	
Stature	*17.40 dm*	*68.5 in.*	*16.38 dm*	*64.5 in.*
Weight	*70 kg*	*154 lb*	*56.8 kg*	*125 lb*
Anatomical Site	*Girth*		*Girth*	
	cm	k	cm	k
Shoulder	110.8	18.47	97.4	17.51
Chest	91.8	15.30	82.5	14.85
Abdominal 1	(77.0)	(12.84)	(65.6)	(11.83)
Abdominal 2	(79.8)	(13.30)	(77.8)	(13.95)
Abdominal Average	78.4	13.07	71.7	12.90
Hips	93.4	15.57	94.2	16.93
Thigh	54.8	9.13	55.8	10.03
Biceps	31.7	5.29	26.7	4.80
Forearm	26.9	4.47	23.1	4.15
Wrist	17.3	2.88	15.2	2.73
Knee	36.6	6.10	34.9	6.27
Calf	35.8	5.97	34.1	6.13
Ankle	22.5	3.75	20.6	3.70
	600.0 cm	100.00	556.0 cm	100.00

*Abdominal 1 and 2 values in parenthesis are not included in the totals. These measurements
represent the basic 11 circumferences.*

$$W = D^2 h \times 0.111 \tag{7}$$

Since $D = C/K$, and K was reduced to one-third of its initial value, it became
necessary to multiply $(D^2 h)$ by 0.111 to correct for this reduction. In addition,
in children and adolescents it may be necessary to employ a fractional power
of stature $(h^{0.7})$. This resulted in the following formulas:

$$W_{\text{females}} = (C/K)^2 \times h^{0.7} \times 0.255 \tag{8}$$

$$W_{\text{males}} = (C/K)^2 \times h^{0.7} \times 0.263 \tag{9}$$

Both formulas were found to be applicable to adults as well.

In 1968, Wilmore and Behnke, in an unpublished study, took a comprehensive series of anthropometric measurements on 54 college-age males.
Using equation 9 above, they found a correlation of $r = 0.98$ between actual
and predicted body weight. In a similar study conducted by the same authors
in 1969 on 133 young men and 128 young women comparable results were
found but have not been published. For the men, the correlation between
predicted and actual body weight was $r = 0.976$, with a mean difference of
only 2.31 kg. For the females, the correlation was $r = 0.975$, and the mean
difference was only 1.44 kg.

Estimation of Lean Body Weight

Lean body weight (*LBW*) is the weight of the lean body mass and is considered to be divisible into biologically constant proportions. These would include water (70–72%), mineral (7%), and organic substances including an undetermined but probably constant percentage (2–3%) of essential lipids in bone marrow, the central nervous system, and other organs (15). For a more definitive breakdown, refer to Table 4.4. The concept of fat-free weight is different from that of lean body weight, which includes the weight of the essential fat.

Table 4.4

THE ORGAN-TISSUE COMPOSITION OF THE LEAN BODY MASS AS REFLECTED BY DATA ON THE STANDARD MAN, AGE 20 TO 30 YEARS WEIGHT 70,000 gms.[a]

Organ	Total Weight	% of Body Weight
Muscles	30.000	42.86
Skin and subcutaneous tissues	8.500	12.14
Skeleton without bone marrow	7.000	10.00
Bone marrow "Red"	1.500	2.14
Bone marrow "Yellow"	1.500	2.14
Blood	5.400	7.71
Gastro-Intestinal Tract	2.300	3.29
Liver	1.700	2.43
Brain	1.400	2.00
Lung (2)	0.950	1.36
Lymphoid Tissue	0.700	1.00
Heart	0.350	0.50
Kidney	0.300	0.43
Spleen	0.150	0.21
Urinary bladder	0.150	0.21
Pancreas	0.065	0.09
Salivary glands	0.050	0.07
Testis	0.040	0.06
Thyroid	0.025	0.04
Eye (2)	0.030	0.04
Spinal cord	0.030	0.04
Teeth	0.023	0.03
Prostate	0.016	0.02
Adrenal (2)	0.014	0.02
Thymus	0.010	0.01
Total	62.203	88.84
Miscellaneous (Blood vessels, fat tissue, cartilage, nerves, etc.)	7.797	11.14
Total	*70,000 gm*	*99.98*

[a]*Data in this table have been proposed by Lisco of the Argonne National Laboratory on the basis of a careful evaluation of many sources.*

The anthropometric estimation of lean body weight is based on the principle that a constant proportion of lean tissue is associated with a given skeletal size (17). In 1959, Behnke (12) proposed the concept that the measurement of bone diameters be used as a basis for the estimation of skeletal weight and, in turn, lean body weight. The fat-free body weight was estimated through the Siri technique using body density and total body water measurements in 31 Navy personnel. Using the figure of 3% to estimate the essential fat, the mean fat-free weight of the group was 61.6 kg, or 63.4 kg of lean body weight. The mean radius of the lean body weight, $\bar{R}(LBW)$, was determined by the following formula:

$$\bar{R}(LBW) = \sqrt{LBW/\pi h} \tag{10}$$

where h represents height in dm. For this Navy group, the mean radius was calculated to be 1.064 dm. The k values were obtained for the group by dividing the mean group skeletal measurements by 1.064 dm. The radius of the lean body weight for any individual, $R(LBW)$, was calculated by dividing the sum of the skeletal measurements for each individual by the sum of the k values for the group, which was 181 for this particular group. The lean body weight was then calculated from the following equation:

$$LBW = \pi R(LBW)^2 h \tag{11}$$

In this same study, Behnke also used radiographic techniques to predict skeletal or lean body weight on the basis of eight transverse diameters, following the earlier work of Matiegka (84) and Trotter (133). The eight diameters included paired measurements of the ankles, knees, wrists, and elbows. Lean body weight was calculated according to equation 11, with the transverse diameter measurements being converted first to k values and then to a calculation of $R(LBW)$.

When compared to the densitometric and total body water techniques for estimating lean body weight, the anthropometric and x-ray techniques correlated approximately the same, $r = 0.83$ and $r = 0.81$ respectively. However, when the anthropometric assessment was made using three paired extremity widths (wrist, knee, and ankle) and three trunk (biacromial, chest, and bitrochanteric) measurements, the correlation increased to $r = 0.89$, and the standard error of estimate was reduced by nearly 40%. The relationship is shown in Fig. 4.1. Using these six specific sites, the following equation was proposed:

$$LBW, \text{gm} = 16.52 \, D^2 h \tag{12}$$

where h is height in dm.

The following formula provides an estimate of mean lean body weight and is derived from some eight group studies of total body water and density chiefly on military men.

$$LBW_{\text{males}} = 0.204 \, h^2 \tag{13}$$

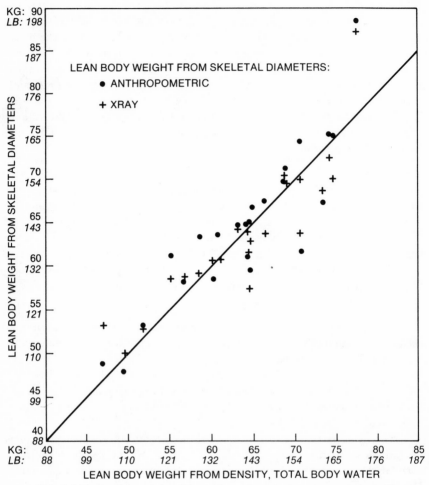

Fig. 4.1 Comparison of lean body weight values calculated from density–total body water, and from skeletal diameters.

At the time, lean body weights of females were indeterminate and the following estimate was made from skeletal diameters based on the male conversion constant for derivation of lean body weight (Table 4.5).

$$LBW_{\text{females}} = 0.18 \, h^2 \qquad (14)$$

Subsequently, it was ascertained that this formula predicted *minimal* weight of females (Table 4.5) and that the constant for prediction of female mean lean body weight in equation 14 was approximately 0.16.

In 1961, Behnke (15) reformulated equation 11 by substituting D for πR,

$$LBW = D(LBW)^2 h \qquad (15)$$

Table 4.5

DERIVATION OF GROUP CONSTANTS (*k* VALUES) FROM SKELETAL
DIAMETERS OF A REFERENCE MAN AND WOMAN AND FROM SIMILAR
MEASUREMENTS ON A NAVY GROUP AND ON BERKELEY (U.C.) MALES
AND FEMALES

	Ref Man	*Navy*[a]	*U.C.*[b]	*Ref Woman*	*U.C.*[b]
n	—	31	133	—	128
Age	20–24	22–52	22	20–24	21.4
h cm	174.0	177.8	177.3	163.8	164.9
W kg	70	78.3	75.6	56.8	58.6
LBW kg	61.8	63.4	64.3	42	43.4
3*F(LBW)*	5.655	5.66	5.70	4.802	4.857
3*F(RW)*	6.00	6.07	6.06	5.56	5.60
Diameters cm					
Biacromial	40.6	40.6	40.4	35.0	36.5
Chest width	30.0	29.9	29.3	25.5	25.8
Bi-iliac	28.6	29.4	28.4	28.6	28.4
Bitroch.	32.8	32.9	32.9	32.0	32.2
Wrists	11.1	11.2	11.2	9.6	9.80
Ankles	13.9	13.9	14.2	12.7	12.58
Knees	18.5	18.4	19.0	17.7	17.88
Elbows	13.9	13.9	14.0	11.9	11.94
TOTAL	189.4	190.2	189.4	173.0	175.1

k Values	Lean Body Weight			Minimal Weight		Lean Body Weight	
	Ref Man	*Navy*	*U.C.*	*Ref Woman*[c]	*U.C.*[d]	*Ref Woman*	*U.C.*
4 Trunk d.	23.34	23.46	22.98	23.42	23.41	25.20	25.30
4 Extrem. d.	10.15	10.14	10.25	10.06	9.94	10.81	10.75
TOTAL	33.49	33.60	33.23	33.54	33.35	36.01	36.05
	Reference Weights (RW)[e]						
4 Trunk d.	22.01	21.88	21.61		21.95	21.77	
4 Extrem. d.	9.57	9.46	9.64		9.32	9.33	
TOTAL	31.58	31.34	31.25		31.27	31.10	

[a]Behnke (12).
[b]Wilmore, Behnke Univ. Calif. data (148, 149).
[c]Reference woman, Minimal W., 48.4 kg; 3*F*(Min *W*) = 5.16.
[d]U.C., Minimal W., 50.4 kg; 3*F*(Min *W*) = 5.25.
[e]*RW* (kg): Reference man, 70; Navy, 72.7; U.C., 72.3; Reference woman, 56.8; U.C., 57.5.

where $D(LBW)$ is the average of four d values for any individual derived from
two trunk and two extremity diameters. The diameters of the wrists and
ankles or the elbows and knees can be combined with the biacromial
and bi-iliac, biacromial and bitrochanteric, chest and bi-iliac, or chest and
bitrochanteric. Individual d values are obtained by dividing any one specific
measurement for an individual (c) by the conversion constant for that specific
measurement (k). The conversion constants specific for each diameter have
been calculated from the data comprising Behnke's reference man (15), but
probably should be calculated from the mean diameters for each group
evaluated. The equation for determining the conversion constants is as

follows:

$$k_i = \bar{c}_i/\sqrt{LBW/h} \tag{16}$$

where i refers to any one single diameter, $\bar{c}_i$ represents the group mean measurement for that diameter, and h represents height in dm. LBW in the above equation is estimated for the group from equations 13 and 14.

In 1963, Behnke (17) reported the following equations for calculation of lean body weight of children (from age 5 years upward), adolescents, and adults as well. In the formulations, the power of h (stature) was decreased from 1.0 to 0.7 to compensate during the growth period for the relative decrease in the size of the head which is not included in the skeletal widths.

$$LBW = D(LBW)^2 \times h^{0.7} \times 0.263 \text{ (males)} \tag{17}$$

$$LBW = D(LBW)^2 \times h^{0.7} \times 0.255 \text{ (females)}$$

where $D(LBW)$ is redefined as the sum of either six or eight diameters divided by the sum of their respective six or eight constants, i.e., $D(LBW) = (\Sigma$ of 6 or 8 c's$)/(\Sigma$ 6 or 8 k's). The constant, k, is then redefined as:

$$k_i = (\bar{c}_i/\sqrt{LBW/h})/3 \tag{18}$$

When eight diameters are used, they include biacromial, chest, bi-iliac, bitrochanteric, knees, ankles, elbows, and wrists. When six diameters are used, all of the above are included except the chest and bi-iliac diameters. It was felt that the use of six rather than eight diameters may be more meaningful when assessing obese individuals (26), since there is less fat over the extremities, and biacromial and bitrochanteric diameters, than over the bi-iliac and chest diameters in the obese. Similarly, these same six diameters should be used when assessing Negroes (26), since they generally have smaller bi-iliac diameters.

In 1968, Wilmore and Behnke (147), on an independent sample of 54 college males, attempted to validate the various techniques to estimate lean body weight proposed earlier by Behnke. Excellent agreement was found between the k values for Behnke's reference man (17) and those derived independently for this sample of men. These are illustrated in Table 4.6. It is important to note, however, that in assessing the lean body weights, differences of from 1.5 to 2.0 kg were noted when using the reference man k values as opposed to using the k values calculated specifically for this sample. In addition, the lean body weights calculated using the newly derived k values were within 0.09 to 0.59 kg of those calculated from the hydrostatic weighing. This suggests the importance of using k values specific to the group being evaluated to obtain the closest possible estimate of the true or actual lean body weight.

The anthropometric equations were validated against the hydrostatic weighing technique for determining lean body weight. The results of this analysis are presented in Table 4.7. The equation $LBW = 0.204h^2$ exhibited the lowest correlation with the hydrostatic determination, but the mean

Table 4.6

COMPARISON OF THE k VALUES FOR REFERENCE MAN WITH THOSE
FROM AN INDEPENDENT SAMPLE (N = 54)[a]

	Actual Measurements, cm		*k Values from Equation 16*		*k Values from Equation 18*	
Diameter	*Mean*	σ	*Reference man*[b]	*Present*	*Reference man*[b]	*Present*	*Reference man*[c]
1. Head length	19.8	0.68	—	10.5	—	3.50	—
2. Head width	15.3	0.55	—	8.1	—	2.71	—
3. Biacromial	40.2	2.28	40.6	21.3	21.6	7.10	7.18
4. Bideltoid	46.0	2.92	45.2	24.4	24.0	8.13	7.98
5. Chest	29.2	2.17	30.0	15.5	15.9	5.16	5.31
6. Bi-iliac	27.9	1.59	28.6	14.7	15.3	4.92	5.06
7. Bitrochanteric	32.6	1.43	32.8	17.3	17.4	5.76	5.79
8. Knee[d]	18.4	0.87	18.5	9.7	9.8	3.25	3.27
9. Ankle[d]	13.6	0.75	13.9	7.2	7.4	2.39	2.46
10. Elbow[d]	13.4	0.86	13.9	7.1	7.4	2.36	2.46
11. Wrist[d]	11.2	0.73	11.1	5.9	5.9	1.98	1.96

[a] *Adapted from Wilmore and Behnke (147).*
[b] *Behnke (15).*
[c] *Behnke (17).*
[d] *Sum of both right and left sides.*

Table 4.7

VALIDATION OF BEHNKE'S VARIOUS EQUATIONS FOR CALCULATING
LEAN BODY WEIGHT ON AN INDEPENDENT SAMPLE OF SUBJECTS
(N = 54)[a]

	Lean Body Weight		*Corelations with*[b]		
Equations	*Mean, kg*	σ, kg	*Rathbun-Pace (107)*	*Siri (117)*	*Brožek et al. (37)*
Density-specific gravity					
Rathbun-Pace	62.78	6.77	—	0.998	0.995
Siri	62.60	6.64	0.998	—	0.999
Brožek et al.	62.56	6.65	0.995	0.999	—
Anthropometric					
$LBW = 0.204 \times h^2$ (equation 13)	63.11	5.74	0.732	0.739	0.741
$LBW = D^2 \times h$ (equation 15)					
(1–9)[c]	62.98	7.55	0.906	0.919	0.924
(1, 3–9)	63.00	7.51	0.901	0.912	0.916
(1, 4, 7, 9)	63.15	7.79	0.879	0.886	0.887
(1, 5, 7, 9)	62.98	7.52	0.888	0.895	0.896
(3, 4, 7, 9)	63.15	8.23	0.879	0.889	0.891
(3, 5, 7, 9)	62.97	7.93	0.891	0.900	0.902
(1, 4, 6, 8)	63.05	7.42	0.870	0.883	0.888
(1, 5, 6, 8)	62.88	7.19	0.875	0.888	0.893
(3, 4, 6, 8)	63.04	7.89	0.867	0.882	0.888
(3, 5, 6, 8)	62.87	7.62	0.875	0.890	0.896
$LBW = D^2 \times h^{0.7} \times 0.263$ (equation 17)					
6 diameters (1, 5–9)[c]	62.91	6.49	0.864	0.875	0.879
8 diameters (1, 3–9)	62.92	6.73	0.878	0.893	0.898

[a] *Adapted from Wilmore and Behnke (147).*
[b] *Refer to Chapter 2 for the specific equations.*
[c] *The numbers refer to specific diameters: 1—biacromial; 2—bideltoid; 3—chest; 4—bi-iliac; 5—bitrochanteric; 6—knee; 7—ankle; 8—elbow; 9—wrist.*

value differed by only 0.33 kg. This equation was originally proposed for group estimates of a mean lean body weight, to be used primarily for calculating k values. The results substantiate this procedure. However, relative to the actual prediction of an individual's lean body weight, this equation would result in far too gross an estimate to be of any significant or practical value.

The lean body weights calculated from the various combinations of body diameters correlated highly ($r = 0.879$ to $r = 0.924$) with the hydrostatically determined lean body weight. These coefficients were in agreement with the correlation of $r = 0.90$ originally reported by Behnke (12). The sample studied was relatively homogeneous in body composition, thus a substantially higher correlation would be anticipated in a more heterogeneous sample.

The anthropometrically determined values were very similar to the hydrostatically determined values, with nearly 60% of the subjects differing by less than ± 1 kg, with a standard error of estimate of only 2.54 kg. There appeared to be little difference as to which formula or which combination of sites was chosen for the anthropometric estimate. With this in mind, the authors recommended the use of equation 15 using the biacromial, bitrochanteric, wrist, and ankle diameters. This selection was predicated on the basis that this equation does not require height to be expressed exponentially or the use of a correction constant. Each dimension is also given equal weighting, which is not true in equation 17. In addition, the recommended sites are readily accessible and have well-defined landmarks. An illustration of the above technique using equation 15 and these four diameters is presented in Table 4.8.

Table 4.8

ILLUSTRATION OF THE ANTHROPOMETRIC TECHNIQUE FOR DETERMINING LEAN BODY WEIGHT FROM FOUR DIAMETERS[a]

Subject: THB Age: 27.4 yrs Height: 17.39 dm Weight: 76.00 kg		Densitometric Analysis Density: 1.053 Percentage fat: 19.60% Lean body weight: 61.10 kg	
Diameter	*c, cm*	*k*	*d*
Biacromial	39.3	21.3	1.85
Bitrochanteric	32.5	17.3	1.88
Ankle[b]	14.3	7.2	1.99
Wrist[b]	10.4	5.9	1.76
			$d = 7.48$
			$D = d/4 = 1.870$

LBW = D^2 × h = 1.870^2 × 17.39 = 3.497 × 17.39 = 60.81 kg.
Fat percentage = (body weight − LBW)/body weight = (76.00 − 60.81)/76.00.
*   = 15.19 kg/76.00 kg = 19.9% fat.*

[a]*Adapted from Wilmore and Behnke (147).*
[b]*Sum of right and left sides.*

In a later study, Wilmore and Behnke (148) evaluated the predictability of body density and lean body weight from a sizable number of anthropometric measurements, including skin-folds, diameters, and circumferences. Fifty-two anthropometric measurements were taken on a sample of 133 college-age males. These measurements were taken in duplicate, and whenever the difference between the two independent measurements for each site exceeded 1% of the initial value, a third measurement was taken. Reliability coefficients were reported in Chapter 3.

Using the hydrostatic weighing determination of body density and lean body weight as the criteria, the results from the anthropometric assessment were treated through a regression analysis, computing stepwise multiple linear-regression equations to predict body density and lean body weight. The results of this analysis are presented in Table 4.9. The analysis was performed in three stages: first, analyzing skin-folds alone; second, analyzing diameters and circumferences; and third, analyzing all of the variables combined. Predictive accuracy was not substantially enhanced by including more than five variables in any of the equations.

The results of this analysis indicate that both body density and lean body weight can be predicted rather accurately from a few simple anthropometric measurements. The anthropometric data from these 133 men was also used to compute lean body weight through the previous equations developed by Behnke (equations 15 and 17). The actual value differed by no more than 0.34 kg for the various combinations of diameters, but the correlations between the anthropometric and hydrostatic estimates were substantially lower than reported previously (17, 147), with the coefficients ranging from $r = 0.73$ to $r = 0.82$. This reduction in validity is difficult to interpret, but may be due to the possibility that predictive equations attain maximum predictive accuracy only when they are applied to samples similar to those from which the original equations were derived.

A similar study was performed on 128 young women (149). In addition to determining multiple regression equations to predict body density and lean body weight, an attempt was made to evaluate in young women the validity of Behnke's previous equations relating proportions of body diameters and height to the prediction of lean body weight. These equations had not been previously validated for women. Duplicate anthropometric measurements were obtained from 55 sites. A third measurement was taken when the difference between the first and second measurements exceeded 1%. The reliability coefficients were reported in Chapter 3.

A regression analysis was performed to determine the accuracy of predicting body density and lean body weight from a combination of skin-folds, diameters, and circumferences. The analysis was identical to that performed in the previously cited study. The results are presented in Table 4.10. They indicate that both body density and lean body weight can be

Table 4.9

DERIVATION OF PREDICTIVE EQUATIONS TO ESTIMATE BODY DENSITY AND LEAN BODY WEIGHT IN YOUNG MEN ($N = 133$)[a]

Predicted Variable	Anthropometric Measurement Used[b]	No. of Variables	Multiple Regression Equation[c]	R	Standard Error of Estimate
Density, g/ml	S	2	$D = 1.08543 - 0.00086V_2 - 0.00040V_3$	0.800	0.0076
		5	$D = 1.06671 + 0.00098ht - 0.00027V_1 - 0.00071V_2 - 0.00040V_3 + 0.00074V_4$	0.811	0.0075
	D, C	2	$D = 1.18351 + 0.00069wt - 0.00202V_9$	0.792	0.0078
		5	$D = 1.15114 + 0.00068wt + 0.00146V_5 + 0.00057V_7 - 0.00192V_9 - 0.00124V_{10}$	0.848	0.0068
	S, D, C	2	$D = 1.11847 - 0.00078V_2 - 0.00048V_9$	0.805	0.0075
		5	$D = 1.05721 - 0.00052V_2 + 0.00168V_5 + 0.00114V_6 + 0.00048V_7 - 0.00145V_9$	0.867	0.0064
Lean body weight, kg	S	2	$LBW = 10.260 + 0.7927wt - 0.3676V_2$	0.931	2.977
		5	$LBW = -6.481 + 1.1401ht + 0.7453wt - 0.2423V_2 - 0.2017V_3 + 0.2100V_4$	0.941	2.783
	D, C	2	$LBW = 44.636 + 1.0817wt - 0.7396V_9$	0.938	2.815
		5	$LBW = 39.652 + 1.0932wt + 0.8370V_5 + 0.3297V_8 - 1.0008V_9 - 0.6478V_{11}$	0.953	2.497
	S, D, C	2	$LBW = 44.636 + 1.0817wt - 0.7396V_9$	0.938	2.815
		5	$LBW = 10.138 + 0.9259wt - 0.1881V_3 + 0.6370V_5 + 0.4888V_6 - 0.5951V_9$	0.958	2.358

[a] Adapted from Wilmore and Behnke (148).
[b] S = skin-folds, D = diameters, C = circumferences.
[c] Key: V_1 = suprailiac skin-fold
V_2 = abdominal skin-fold
V_3 = thigh skin-fold
V_4 = knee skin-fold
V_5 = bi-iliac diameter
V_6 = neck circumference
V_7 = chest circumference
V_8 = abdomen 1 circumference
V_9 = abdomen 2 circumference
V_{10} = thigh circumference
V_{11} = knee circumference

Table 4.10

DERIVATION OF PREDICTIVE EQUATIONS TO ESTIMATE BODY DENSITY AND LEAN BODY WEIGHT IN YOUNG FEMALES $(N = 128)$[a]

Predicted Variable	Anthropometric Measurement Used[b]	Multiple Regression Equation[c]	R	Standard Error of Estimate
Density, g/ml	S	$D = 1.06234 - 0.00068X_2 - 0.00039X_3 - 0.00025X_4$	0.676	0.0074
	D, C	$D = 1.065551 + 0.01120X_6 - 0.00055X_9 - 0.00082X_{10} - 0.00159X_{11} + 0.00362X_{12}$	0.739	0.0068
	S, D, C	$D = 1.07685 - 0.00063X_2 - 0.00336X_5 + 0.00227X_7 - 0.00049X_8 - 0.00043X_9$	0.755	0.0066
Lean body weight, kg	S	$LBW = 8.629 + 0.680X_1 - 0.163X_2 - 0.100X_3 - 0.054X_4$	0.916	1.940
	D, C	$LBW = 8.987 + 0.732X_1 + 3.786X_6 - 0.157X_9 - 0.249X_{10} + 0.434X_{12}$	0.922	1.873
	S, D, C	$LBW = 1.661 + 0.668X_1 - 0.158X_2 - 0.081X_3 + 0.555X_7 - 0.141X_9$	0.929	1.792

[a] Adapted from Wilmore and Behnke (149).
[b] S = skin-folds, D = diameters, and C = circumferences.
[c] Key: X_1 = weight, kg
X_2 = scapula skin-fold, mm
X_3 = triceps skin-fold, mm
X_4 = thigh skin-fold, mm
X_5 = knee diameter, cm
X_6 = wrist diameter, cm

X_7 = neck circumference, cm
X_8 = minimum abdominal circumference, cm
X_9 = maximum abdominal circumference, cm
X_{10} = hip circumference, cm
X_{11} = extended biceps circumference, cm
X_{12} = forearm circumference, cm

predicted almost equally well from either skin-folds, circumferences and diameters, or a combination of these. The magnitude of the resulting multiple correlations was sufficiently high to suggest an acceptable level of predictive accuracy. In the evaluation of Behnke's previous equations, the correlations between the anthropometrically and hydrostatically determined lean body weights varied from $r = 0.77$ to $r = 0.80$. The mean values were quite close, differing by only -0.15 to -0.27 kg. In unpublished work conducted by Wessinger and Wilmore on 32 females of the same age, the correlations ranged from $r = 0.79$ to $r = 0.85$. These results are highly acceptable considering the results of previous and subsequent studies performed on women using other predictive equations.

In 1970, Wilmore, Girandola, and Moody (150) reported on the results of their investigation of the validity of using skin-fold and girth assessments for predicting changes in body composition. While the accuracy of the various equations for predicting density, specific gravity, fat, and lean body weight had been well established, no attempt had been made previously to determine whether these equations were sensitive to changes in body composition.

Two groups of subjects from independent studies were used. The first, a group of 55 adult males, were evaluated before and after a ten-week walk-jog-run program. The second group consisted of 23 high school females who were in a similar program covering a nine-month period. The men were evaluated anthropometrically and through hydrostatic weighing only at the beginning and conclusion of the training program. The girls were evaluated additionally at the midpoint of the nine-month study.

Predictive equations proposed by various authors in previous publications were evaluated relative to how closely they estimated the changes in body composition between the beginning and conclusion of the training programs. The results are illustrated in Table 4.11. Unfortunately, the changes in lean body weight and fat were relatively small, thus the low to moderate correlations between the actual and estimated change. It is anticipated that had greater changes been observed, these equations would have more accurately predicted these changes.

In this same study, the equations developed by Wilmore and Behnke for estimating density and lean body weight (from Tables 4.9 and 4.10) were evaluated for both of these groups. For the girls, the estimated density values for all three measurement periods were considerably higher than the actual values (0.014–0.017 gm/ml), while the correlation was higher than that reported in the original study ($r = 0.77$). The estimated lean body weights were likewise higher than the actual values (4.47–5.24 kg) while the correlations were nearly the same as those reported in the original study. This difference between the anthropometrically and hydrostatically determined

Table 4.11

ACCURACY OF PREDICTIVE EQUATIONS TO ESTIMATE CHANGES IN BODY
COMPOSITION RESULTING FROM PHYSICAL EXERCISE PROGRAMS[a]

Investigator	Interval[b]	ΔD_b^c	ΔSG^c	Fat, kg[c]	LBW[c]
Women					
Katch	I–M	0.321			
	M–F	0.594			
	I–F	0.646			
Sloan	I–M	0.398			
	M–F	0.400			
	I–F	0.531			
Wilmore	I–M	0.271			0.341
	M–F	0.591			0.707
	I–F	0.394			0.355
Allen	I–M			0.568	
	M–F			0.794	
	I–F			0.753	
Men					
Brožek	I–F		0.605		
Pascale	I–F	0.636			
Sloan	I–F	0.429			
Steinkamp	I–F			0.633	
Wilmore	I–F	0.543			0.317

[a]*Adapted from Wilmore, Girandola, and Moody (150).*
[b]*I–M = change between initial and midpoint values.*
M–F = change between midpoint and final values.
I–F = change between initial and final values.
[c]*Correlations between actual and predicted change.*

lean body weights can possibly be accounted for by Behnke's concept of minimal weight in women, which will be discussed in the next section of this
chapter.

The estimated mean values for the men were nearly identical to the
actual values, with density differing by only 0.001 gm/ml and lean body
weight by only 0.45 kg. The correlations were also high, approaching those
reported in the initial study. These results help validate and confirm the
results from the earlier studies.

Minimal Weight in Women

In the description of the female, Behnke (21) has proposed that it
is necessary to introduce the concept of *minimal weight* as an entity distinct
from lean body weight. In the male, minimal weight and lean body weight
may be identical. In the female, minimal weight associated with the leanest

individuals for a given stature incorporates, in addition to lean body weight, sex-specific "essential" fat in mammary and perhaps other tissues. In the male, lean body weight derived from skeletal diameters, ^{40}K, total body water, and body density, are interchangeable, excluding both the supramuscular and undeniably underweight individual. In the female, lean body weight derived from ^{40}K or body density is appreciably lower than the lean body weight calculated from the diameters, and lower than the weights of the leanest healthy females in a population. Behnke terms the anthropometrically calculated lean body weight in girls and women *minimal weight*. Examples of this difference between minimal weight and lean body weight are illustrated in Table 4.12. It is clear that the anthropometrically calculated *LBW* in these

Table 4.12

EXAMPLES OF DIFFERENCES BETWEEN LEAN BODY WEIGHT
AND MINIMAL WEIGHT IN MALES AND FEMALES[a]

| | | | Lean Body Weight, kg | | |
	Stature, cm	Weight, kg	Anthro.	^{40}K	Density
Males					
Caucasian (N = 54)	17.41	64.6	55.7	54.7	55.5
Negro (N = 24)	17.54	71.2	56.1	59.6	59.7
Oriental (N = 11)	16.61	56.0	50.0	51.0	50.9
Females					
Caucasian (N = 54)	16.47	57.0	47.9[b]	41.3	41.2
Negro (N = 25)	16.28	59.7	47.3[b]	42.2	42.7
Oriental (N = 9)	15.81	48.5	43.4[b]	35.0	37.0

[a]*Data from the Berkeley Nutritional-Anthropometric Program.*
[b]*Anthropometric lean body weight is defined as minimal weight in females.*

girls is substantially greater than that calculated through ^{40}K or specific gravity measurements.

Minimal weights were calculated from six diameters and stature for female ballet dancers who represent exceptionally lean girls accustomed to rigorous exercise and strict dietary control. Minimal weights were found to be higher than actual body weights in three of the 20 girls. By definition, these girls would be underweight. In the remaining 17 girls, minimum weight approached body weight. These results are presented in Table 4.13.

In an unpublished study of five chronically underweight young women, Wilmore found results similar to those for the ballet dancers. These are illustrated in Table 4.14. The three values for each girl represent the initial, midpoint, and final values throughout a 20-week moderate exercise program. The actual lean weights were higher than those calculated anthropometrically, indicating excessive leanness and underweight.

Table 4.13

ANTHROPOMETRIC EVALUATION OF BALLET DANCERS

Age, Years	Height, cm	Weight, kg		
		Actual	Reference[a]	Minimal[b]
19	163.0	54.1	54.2	46.7
30	166.4	50.5	58.1	50.1
19	165.7	55.0	56.1	48.4
22	170.2	50.0	58.7	50.6
20	164.2	49.1	53.6	46.2
22	172.2	53.9	59.7	51.4
21	163.5	47.3	56.1	48.4
24	173.0	56.1	59.8	51.6
26	161.5	49.1	50.4	43.4
23	164.4	48.9	52.3	45.1
17	163.6	44.1	51.4	44.5
22	159.0	46.1	49.1	42.4
22	154.6	47.7	48.1	41.5
27	155.1	48.2	49.3	42.5
18	160.2	51.6	51.0	43.9
18	168.2	51.8	54.7	47.1
15	169.8	52.5	60.7	52.3
18	171.5	53.4	57.2	49.3
22	165.4	54.5	54.6	47.1
16	171.0	57.0	58.9	50.8

[a]Defined in equation 19.
[b]Defined in equation 14.

Table 4.14

DIFFERENCE BETWEEN LEAN BODY WEIGHT AND MINIMAL WEIGHT IN CHRONICALLY UNDERWEIGHT YOUNG WOMEN

Subject	Hydrostatic Values		Anthropometric Values			
	Fat	LBW	LBW^a	LBW^b	LBW^c	LBW^d
	%	kg	kg	kg	kg	kg
LW	13.1	39.2	35.5	31.0	36.1	33.0
	13.2	39.8	35.6	31.2	36.6	33.3
	11.3	40.9	36.0	31.4	36.3	33.5
KL	19.2	42.2	39.1	36.7	42.3	40.1
	17.9	43.2	39.7	37.2	42.6	40.8
	20.3	43.7	40.4	37.0	42.3	40.2
KJ	5.7	40.8	35.0	36.1	39.7	37.9
	3.8	41.3	34.0	36.8	40.0	38.3
	6.0	40.6	35.3	35.9	39.6	37.6
MT	14.9	37.8	35.8	32.4	39.2	37.2
	12.6	39.3	36.1	31.6	38.1	35.8
	11.9	39.5	35.7	32.2	38.4	36.3
CN	17.8	48.2	45.3	38.1	45.6	41.3
	26.6	49.5	45.6	38.2	45.9	41.7
	16.3	49.1	44.8	39.0	46.0	42.4

[a]LBW calculated from last equation, Table 4.10.
[b]$LBW = D(LBW)^2 h$, equation 15.
[c]$LBW = D(LBW)^2 \times h^{0.7} \times 0.255$ (using eight diameters), equation 17.
[d]Same as [c] above except using six diameters.

Reference Weight

The reference weight is the median group weight for both age and sex computed from six or eight body diameters* and stature. The specific conversion constants for young adults, $k(RW)$, are derived by dividing the group mean for a specific diameter or summated diameters by $3F$ computed from stature and standard weight (see Chapter 6). The sum of the $k(RW)$ values for eight diameters is 31.58 for the reference man, 31.1 for the reference woman, and 31.3 for Berkeley males and females (Table 4.5). Standard weights are mean weights relative to stature for young adults in the age range of 20–24 years and are about 0.5 to 0.8 kg higher than median weights which afford a slightly more accurate calculation of the $3F$ factor.

Reference weights computed from individual diameters and stature are relatively stable over the adult life span and vary only with change in frame size and thickness of subcutaneous fat over the bony landmarks. Reference weight is calculated from the following equation:

$$\text{Reference weight} = D(RW)^2 \times h \times 0.111 \tag{19}$$

Fractional and Equivalent Weights

The relative size of various body segments can be estimated from the individual d values (d = measurement/conversion constant for that measurement). Since girth measurements can be used to calculate total body weight, it is possible to determine the relative contribution of each measurement to body weight. The d values for each dimension can be converted into an equivalent weight simply by using the equation:

$$\text{Equivalent weight}_i = d_i^2 \times h \tag{20}$$

where i represents any one circumferential site. Behnke (13), in 1961, illustrated the utility of this concept for an obese man and a young woman (see Table 4.15). For the obese man, the excess adiposity is obviously around the abdominal area, as the d (abdominal average) $= 3.42$, where the average or mean d value (D), is 2.83 and $F = 2.84$.†

The high correlation between anthropometric circumferences, stature, and body weight makes possible the partition of weight into components. Through the years, Behnke (20) has developed and refined the following method for this fractional analysis. The girths are allocated to the following categories: A, A', B, B', and $WFCA$. Diameters fall into categories $B–B$ and

---

*The same diameters used in equation 17.

†Subsequently, with conversion of k values to percentages (i.e., sum of $11k = 100$, not 300), d and D values are increased threefold.

Table 4.15

FRACTIONAL AND EQUIVALENT WEIGHTS FOR AN OBESE MAN
AND A NORMAL YOUNG WOMAN[a]

Percentages $(k/300 \times 100)$	*Circumferences*	*d Values*	*Equiv. Wt., kg*
A. Man—wt.: 150.9 kg; stature: 18.67 dm; F: 2.843[b]			
Navy k values			
55.4	18.47	Shoulder	2.57	123
45.9	15.30	Chest	3.07	176
40.6	13.53	Abdominal average	3.42	218
46.7	15.57	Buttocks	2.69	135
27.4	9.13	Thigh	3.04	173
15.4	5.13	Biceps	2.92	159
13.4	4.57	Forearm	2.56	122
8.2	2.73	Wrist	2.57	124
18.3	6.10	knee	2.59	125
17.9	5.97	Calf	2.49	115
10.8	3.60	Ankle	2.45	112
300.0	100.00			Average 143.8

B. Woman—wt.: 42.9 kg; stature: 15.80 dm; F: 1.648[c]			
Ref. k values			
52.0	17.33	Shoulder	1.72	47
44.5	14.83	Chest	1.74	48
38.7	12.90	Abdominal average	1.74	48
50.8	16.93	Buttocks	1.70	46
30.1	10.03	Thigh	1.67	44
14.4	4.80	Biceps	1.64	43
13.0	4.33	Forearm	1.54	37
8.2	2.73	Wrist	1.63	42
18.8	6.27	Knee	1.57	39
18.4	6.13	Calf	1.46	34
11.1	3.70	Ankle	1.55	38
300.0	99.98			Average 42.2

[a]*Adapted from Behnke (13).*
[b]*Sum of 11 circumferences = 850.1 cm; D = 2.834; D² × h = 149.9 kg.*
[c]*Sum of 11 circumferences = 501.7 cm; D = 1.672; D² × h = 44.2 kg.*

C, the latter representing frame size from which reference weight is computed.

A reflects fat accumulation in the obese. It consists of the girths of the chest, the average of the two abdominal girths, and hips. The chest girth is omitted when there is excessive muscular hypertrophy of the chest.

A' is the sum of the average of the abdominal girths and the hip girth.

B represents muscular development in the male and includes the girths of the shoulder (divided by four to give it equal weighting with the other dimensions in this category), flexed biceps, forearm, and calf. The flexed biceps are used to accentuate muscular development.

B' embraces body structure with more bone and less fat than is present in B. It includes the girths of the flexed biceps, forearm, wrist, knee, calf, and ankle.

$WFCA$ is comprised of the girths of the wrist, forearm, calf, and ankle. These sites are relatively fat-free and comprise bone, ligaments, and muscle, closely identified with frame size. Body weight computed from $WFCA$ and stature serves as a monitor weight which is considerably less than body weight in the obese and usually greater than scale weight in the lean.

B–B is the combination of the bideltoid and bitrochanteric diameters. This component is designed as a scanning procedure to reflect both skeletal and muscular development.

C comprises the anthropometric diameters from which reference weight is calculated.

Relative weights are calculated from these components by substituting the appropriate D values, e.g., $D(A)$, $D(A')$, $D(B)$, etc., into the equation:

$$W(x)_{male} = D(x)^2 \times h^{0.7} \times 0.263 \tag{21}$$

$$W(x)_{female} = D(x)^2 \times h^{0.7} \times 0.255 \tag{22}$$

where x represents one of the components: A, A', B, B', $WFCA$, B–B, or C. The D values simply reflect the sum of the C values for each of the specific sites divided by the sum of the appropriate k values. For $D(C)$ and $D(B$–$B)$ use the $k(RW)$ values and not the $k(LBW)$ values.

Body weights can also be calculated from these relative weights. For most adults, the average of $W(A)$ and $W(B)$, or $W(AB)$, closely approximates scale weight. In addition, a body weight can be derived from the three major components $W(A)$, $W(B)$, and $W(C)$ as follows:

$$W(ABC) = 0.30 \, W(A) + 0.55 \, W(B) + 0.15 \, W(C), \text{ where the} \tag{23}$$
muscular component $W(B) > W(A)$, or

$$W(ABC) = 0.30 \, W(B) + 0.55 \, W(A) + 0.15 \, W(C), \text{ where the} \tag{24}$$
obese component $W(A) > W(B)$.

Behnke has proposed a new concept to define the linearity of body build, which he refers to as Unit Size-Weight $(uS$–$W)$. uS–W is an expression of fractional body weight per unit of stature, i.e., uS–$W = k \times W/h^{1.7}$. In standard height-weight tables, uS–W is practically constant for age-specific mean weights for increments of stature between 145 and 178 cm for the female and between 159 and 195 cm for the male. For the reference man and woman, uS–W is arbitrarily set equal 100. Likewise, the uS–W for the mean weight per each inch of height, taken from standard height-weight tables, is equal to 100. To accomplish this, k in the above equation is 183.6 for males and 204.2 for females. Thus,

$$uS$–$W_{males} = 183.6 \times W/h^{1.7} \tag{25}$$

$$uS$–$W_{females} = 204.2 \times W/h^{1.7} \tag{26}$$

The normal range of uS–W in adults who are not excessively fat or muscular is 90–110 for about 95% of the population. In large athletes, e.g., shot-putters, $uS-W$ may be in the range of 115 to 120, but not higher unless excess fat is also present. This appears to be a more effective means of describing the linearity of body build than the conventional ponderal index ($\sqrt[3]{W}/h$).

The Somatogram

In 1959, Behnke, Guttentag, and Brodsky (24) proposed a concept which was later to be developed into what is now referred to as Behnke's Somatogram. They expressed the deviations of a single radius from the total body radius in terms of a percentage.

Through the years, Behnke has modified this somatogram to its present form. Each girth is divided by its respective k value to obtain the d value ($d = c/k$). D, which is the sum of the circumferences divided by the sum of the k values (normally 100), is used as the reference value. The percentage deviation of each d quotient from D is integrated into a pattern, the somatogram, which is a quantitative representation of the shape of the body. If the anthropometric proportions of an individual conform to group symmetry, then all of his deviation values fall on the same plane.

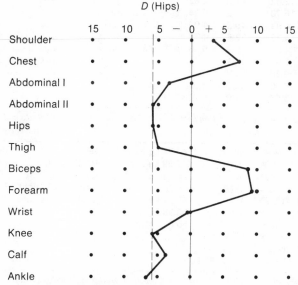

CIRCUMFERENCE   PERCENTAGE DEVIATION FROM D

D (Hips)

Fig. 4.2 Somatogram of a weight lifter. Age: 30 yrs; weight: 79.0 kg; stature: 17.4 dm. D = 6.51. D(Hips) = 6.12. (– – – vertical) is an estimate of D prior to muscular hypertrophy.

Fig. 4.2 illustrates the somatogram of a weightlifter. D(sum of $11c/100$) $= 6.51$; the average girth of the right and left arms (biceps) is 37.5; and $d = 37.5/5.29$, where 5.29 is the k(biceps) value for the reference man. The quotient, d(biceps) is 7.09, which is 8.9% greater than D ($7.09-6.51/6.51 = 8.9\%$). In a similar manner, all the other d values and their deviation from D are computed. The shape of the weightlifter is clearly abnormal compared with the proportions of the reference man.

It is observed in Fig. 4.2 that the deviation of the abdominal, hip, thigh, knee, calf, and ankle girths are in approximate alignment along a vertical axis about 5% to the left of D. We can now make an estimate of body weight if the development of the examinee had proceeded in a normal manner without benefit of induced muscular hypertrophy. "Natural" D would have been

Table 4.16

ANTHROPOMETRIC AND COMPOSITION DATA FOR AN
UNDERWEIGHT FEMALE, 21 YEARS OF AGE

Stature 16.67 dm, 65.60 inches				Weight 45.10 kg, 99.22 lbs			
$D = 5.100$	$3F = 4.934$		$uS-W = $ 77.08	Reference Weight = 50.42 kg			

	Anthropometric Girths					*Anthropometric Diameters*		
Site	k^a	c	d	Dev^b	*Site*	$k(RW)^a$	$k(LBW)^a$	c
Shoulder	17.73	91.3	5.15	+1.0	Biacromial	6.35	7.49	34.3
Chest	14.84	75.0	5.05	−1.0	Bideltoid	7.33	8.65	38.4
Abdominal					Chest	4.49	5.30	23.9
Average	13.32	61.5	4.62	−9.4	Bi-iliac	4.94	5.82	22.9
Hips	16.70	84.2	5.04	−1.2	Bitroch.	5.60	6.60	29.9
Thighs	9.92	49.2	4.96	−2.7	Knee	3.02	3.68	16.0^c
Biceps	4.73	22.6	4.78	−6.3	Ankle	2.20	2.58	11.6^c
Forearm	4.09	20.7	5.06	−0.8	Elbow	2.08	2.46	11.2^c
Wrist	2.59	14.1	5.44	+6.7	Wrist	1.70	2.00	10.0^c
Knee	6.28	32.8	5.22	+2.4				
Calf	6.10	30.9	5.07	−0.6				
Ankle	3.68	21.0	5.71	+12.0				

Anthropometric Fractionation of *Body Weight*				*Body Composition Through* *Hydrostatic Weighing*	
$D(A)$	4.92	$W(A)$	44.24 kg	Density	1.0690 gm/cc
$D(A')$	4.85	$W(A')$	42.99 kg	Relative Fat	13.06 %
$D(B)$	5.01	$W(B)$	45.87 kg	Fat Weight	5.89 kg
$D(B')$	5.17	$W(B')$	48.90 kg	Lean Body Weight	39.21 kg
$D(WFCA)$	5.27	$W(WFCA)$	50.71 kg	Total Body Weight	45.10 kg
$D(B-B)$	5.28	$W(B-B)$	50.99 kg		
$D(C)$	5.26	$W(C)$	50.57 kg		
		$W(AB)$ =	45.06 kg		
		$W(ABC)$ =	46.09 kg		
		LBW =	35.85 kg		

$^a k$ *values from study of 128 University of California, Berkeley females (149).*
^{b}*Percent deviation from D.*
^{c}*Sum of right and left sides.*

about 5% to the left of its present position and the presumptive value of D would be 6.18. By substitution of D in the equation, $W = D^2h$, the calculated weight is 73.8 kg compared with a calculated weight from actual D of 81.8 kg. The difference between these two calculated weights, 8 kg, represents an estimate of the weight of excess muscle.

The somatogram was intended primarily for comparing individuals with reference man and woman. However, it is also possible to compare any one individual with another, or one group with another by making a simple correction for height. D is altered by the following factors:

$$\text{Correction}_{males} = D \times (0.645/h^{0.5}) \tag{26}$$

$$\text{Correction}_{females} = D \times (0.728/h^{0.5}) \tag{27}$$

Table 4.17

ANTHROPOMETRIC AND COMPOSITION DATA FOR AN OBESE FEMALE, 16 YEARS OF AGE

Stature 16.02 dm, 63.10 inches					Weight 119.50 kg, 262.90 lbs			
$D = 8.039$	$3F = 8.194$		$uS{-}W = 218.52$		Reference Weight = 76.83 kg			

Site	\multicolumn{4}{c}{*Anthropometric Girths*}	*Site*	\multicolumn{3}{c}{*Anthropometric Diameters*}
	k^a	c	d	Dev^b		$k(RW)^a$	$k(LBW)^a$	c
Shoulder	17.52	120.3	6.87	−14.5	Biacromial	6.29	6.79	39.2
Chest	14.85	116.3	7.83	−2.6	Bideltoid	7.27	8.15	—
Abdominal					Chest	4.59	4.94	31.2
Average	12.90	119.9	9.29	+15.6	Bi-iliac	5.14	5.55	33.3
Hips	16.93	140.4	8.29	+3.1	Bitroch.	5.75	6.20	39.5
Thighs	10.03	95.4	9.51	+18.3	Knee	3.18	3.44	23.7^c
Biceps	4.80	42.7	8.90	+10.7	Ankle	2.28	2.46	13.0^c
Forearm	4.15	30.3	7.30	−9.2	Elbow	2.14	2.32	14.2^c
Wrist	2.73	17.4	6.37	−20.8	Wrist	1.74	1.86	10.4^c
Knee	6.27	48.4	7.72	−4.0				
Calf	6.13	47.0	7.67	−4.6				
Ankle	3.70	25.8	6.97	−13.3				

\multicolumn{3}{c}{*Anthropometric Fractionation of Body Weight*}	\multicolumn{2}{c}{*Body Composition Through Hydrostatic Weighing*}
$D(A)$	8.43	$W(A)$ 126.31 kg	Density	0.9750 gm/cc
$D(A')$	8.73	$W(A')$ 135.46 kg	Relative Fat	55.00 %
$D(B)$	7.71	$W(B)$ 105.65 kg	Fat Weight	65.73 kg
$D(B')$	7.62	$W(B')$ 103.20 kg	Lean Body Weight	53.77 kg
$D(WFCA)$	7.21	$W(WFCA)$ 92.39 kg	Total Body Weight	119.50 kg
$D(B{-}B)$	—	$W(B{-}B)$ —		
$D(C)$	6.573	$W(C)$ 76.80 kg		
		$W(AB)$ = 114.48 kg		
		$W(ABC)$ = 124.21 kg		
		LBW = 66.00 kg		

^{a}*k values from reference woman.*
^{b}*Percent deviation from D.*
^{c}*Sum of right and left sides.*

Case Studies

To illustrate the principles and techniques presented throughout this chapter, a complete work-up will be provided for three individuals: an extremely underweight young woman; an extremely obese young woman; and an older man. These are illustrated in Tables 4.16 through 4.18 and in Figs. 4.3 through 4.5.

The anthropometric evaluation of the underweight female agrees closely with both the hydrostatically determined analysis and the visual analysis of the subject. The fact that the d(abdominal average) and d(biceps) were 9.4% and 6.3% less than D respectively, indicates that she was deficient in both fat and muscle. Likewise, the high positive deviation of d(wrist) and d(ankle)

Table 4.18

ANTHROPOMETRIC AND COMPOSITION DATA FOR A
MALE, 67 YEARS OF AGE

Stature 17.88 dm, 70.39 inches Weight 84.30 kg, 185.5 lbs
$D = 6.546$ $3F = 6.541$ $uS-W = 115.0$ Reference Weight = 82.1 kg

Site	*Anthropometric Girths* k^a	c	d	Dev^b	Site	*Anthropometric Diameters* $k(RW)^a$	$k(LBW)^a$	c
Shoulder	18.47	116.6	6.31	−3.6	Biacromial	6.77	7.18	41.0
Chest	15.30	102.6	6.71	+2.5	Bideltoid	7.53	7.98	48.0
Abdominal					Chest	5.00	5.31	31.8
Average	13.07	90.1	6.89	+5.3	Bi-iliac	4.77	5.06	32.0
Hips	15.57	100.8	6.47	−1.2	Bitroch.	5.47	5.79	34.7
Thighs	9.13	55.6	6.09	−7.0	Knee	3.08	3.27	20.1^c
Biceps	5.29	36.3	6.86	+4.8	Ankle	2.32	2.46	14.8^c
Forearm	4.47	29.3	6.55	+0.1	Elbow	2.32	2.46	15.4^c
Wrist	2.88	19.1	6.63	+1.3	Wrist	1.85	1.96	13.2^c
Knee	6.10	41.4	6.79	+3.7				
Calf	5.97	39.5	6.62	+1.1				
Ankle	3.75	23.3	6.21	−5.1				

Anthropometric Fractionation of Body Weight				*Body Composition Through Hydrostatic Weighing*	
$D(A)$	6.68	$W(A)$	88.4 kg	Density	1.0493 gm/cc
$D(A')$	6.67	$W(A')$	88.0 kg	Relative Fat	21.74 %
$D(B)$	6.68	$W(B)$	88.4 kg	Fat Weight	18.36 kg
$D(B')$	6.64	$W(B')$	87.3 kg	Lean Body Weight	65.90 kg
$D(WFCA)$	6.51	$W(WFCA)$	84.0 kg	Total Body Weight	84.26 kg
$D(B-B)$	6.36	$W(B-B)$	80.1 kg		
$D(C)$	6.44	$W(C)$	82.1 kg		
		$W(AB) =$	88.4 kg		
		$W(ABC) =$	86.3 kg		
		$LBW =$	72.7 kg		

$^a k$ values from reference man.
^{b} Percent deviation from D.
^{c} Sum of right and left sides.

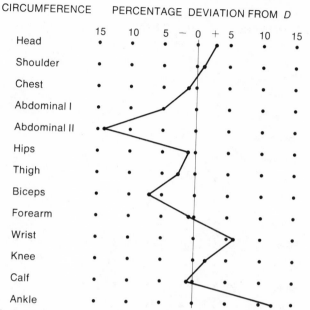

Fig. 4.3 Somatogram of a chronically underweight female. Age: 21 yrs; weight: 45.10 kg; stature: 16.67 dm. *D* = 5.10.

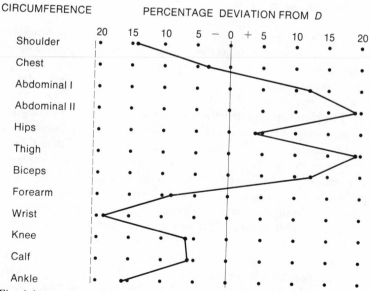

Fig. 4.4 Somatogram of an obese female. Age: 16 yrs; weight: 119.50 kg; stature: 16.02 dm. *D* = 8.04; *D*(Diam) = 6.61. (– – – vertical) indicates disparity between frame and girth size.

CIRCUMFERENCE   PERCENTAGE DEVIATION FROM *D*

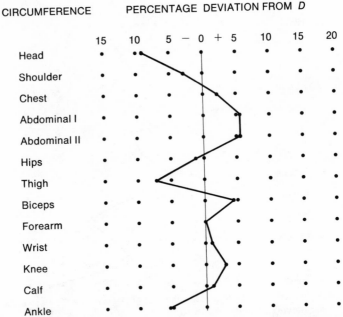

Fig. 4.5 Somatogram of an older adult male. Age: 67 yrs; weight: 84.30 kg; stature: 17.88 dm. *D* = 6.546.

indicates a preponderance of bone. $W(C)$ is also a reflection of skeletal development and indicates the subject could carry substantially more weight for her frame size.

The obese girl has a preponderance of fat and muscle over the abdominal, thigh, and biceps areas, as is indicated by their high percentage deviations from D. The high negative deviations of the wrist and ankle—predominantly bony areas—suggest that there is far too much mass for the supportive structure. $W(A)$ and $W(A')$ reflect fat accumulation and the relatively low value for $W(B)$ indicates a lack of musculature to support such a body size.

The pattern for the older man reflects the expected variation. With the exception of the head and thigh, the d values are all within $\pm 5\%$ of D. Likewise, there is little difference between the calculated weights. The fact that $W(C)$ and $W(B-B)$ are less than the actual body weight, while $W(A)$, $W(A')$, $W(B)$ and $W(B')$ are greater, indicates that there is an excess of both muscle and fat. The latter is confirmed by the hydrostatic weighing. The presence of excess muscle is suggested by the difference between $W(B)$ and $W(ABC)$ of 2.6 kg. If the subject was 17.5% body fat (close to the ideal relative fat for this age), at his present lean weight of 65.9 kg, he would weigh 80.0 kg. Adding 2.6 kg of excess muscle to this weight would result in a total body weight of 82.6 kg, which is very close to the calculated $W(C)$ and reference weight.

Summary

Through the use of various regression equations, or equations developed on the basis of intuitive models, it is possible to accurately predict body weight, lean body weight, body density, and relative and absolute body fat from selected anthropometric measurements. In addition, an anthropometric assessment enables the estimation of an entity known as minimal weight in women, which is comparable to lean body weight in men. Fractional and equivalent weights are used to determine the relative contribution of each measurement to the total body weight and the somatogram provides a quantitative representation of the shape of the body. With these tools, it is possible to conduct a refined analysis of the individual's body composition and constitution.

Chapter 5 / Variations in Body Build and Composition

The great differences in the shapes of individuals are apparent from inspection of boys and girls of the same age in a secondary school. Nine channels on the Wetzel grid are required to portray the wide variation in body bulk relative to stature alone. In this chapter we are concerned with the deviation of a comprehensive battery of anthropometric parameters from the mean proportions (k values) of the reference young male or female adult.

Pertinent data from other studies will be introduced to show the extended applicability of the relationships. Some population characteristics in three of these surveys follow. The United States Department of Agriculture (USDA) studies consisted of (1) a comprehensive report of measurements and statistical analysis of data on 147,000 American children by Ruth O'Brien, Meyer A. Girshick, and Eleanor P. Hunt (95), and (2) a scientific body of measurements on 10,042 Caucasian women by Ruth O'Brien and William C. Shelton (96) which provides, for the first time, standards for the manufacture of women's clothing. These superlative surveys and concomitant statistical analyses, exemplary in scope and execution, were made possible from 1937 to 1939 by the cooperation of the Works Progress Administration. In the second survey reported by Katherine Simmons in 1944 as "The Brush Foundation Study of Growth and Development" (115), cross-sectional data with longitudinal buffering were obtained on Cleveland children of North European ancestry and above average economic and educational status. There were ten to 200 individuals for each age group up to 16 and 17 years. The four trunk diameters measured (biacromial, chest width, bi-iliac, and bitrochan-teric) serve our purpose well, since we are interested in the consistency of mean values of these widths in relation to stature and weight at successive ages during the growth period. We convert these measurements to ponderal equivalents for comparison with the Berkeley N-A data. The results of a third program by Read Tuddenham and Margaret Snyder (134) was published in 1954 in a monograph on "Physical Growth of California Boys and Girls from Birth to Eighteen Years." In this longitudinal survey (usually referred to as the Berkeley survey) 66 boys and 70 girls (Caucasian) were examined. Apart from height (including stem length) and weight, only three anthropo-metric measurements were made, namely, biacromial and bi-iliac widths, and calf circumference. Valuable in this study was the somatotype evalua-tion.

Changes in Shape

USDA FEMALES DATA, AGES 4 TO 70 YEARS. Six girths were selected which can be reliably measured by trained personnel, although sites of measurement may not always be identical for thigh and knee girths.

Table 5.1

PERCENTAGE DEVIATION THROUGHOUT LIFE-SPAN OF SIX GIRTHS FROM THOSE OF A REFERENCE GROUP OF USDA YOUNG WOMEN, AGE GROUP, 20–24 YEARS

Number	Age	h	W	Chest	Waist	Circumferences[a] Hips	Thigh	Knee[b]	Calf	$6\,c/F{-}h^{0.7}$
100	4	104.4	17.1	2.0	16.4	−8.1	−7.8	2.8	0.8	131.5
2600	5	110.9	19.0	1.6	14.5	−7.4	−7.2	3.2	1.2	131.5
4600	6	116.8	21.1	1.3	12.7	−7.0	−7.1	3.7	1.6	131.2
6300	10	138.2	31.9	0.5	8.0	−5.2	−4.6	4.9	1.8	131.4
3600	14	157.9	48.3	−0.2	1.4	−1.6	−2.1	2.4	0.8	130.9
793	18	162.0	55.4	−0.9	0.0	0.0	0.2	−1.6	1.6	131.0

Reference Group						Proportionality Constants[c]				
1661	20–24	161.5	55.9	29.94	23.75	33.67	19.39	12.29	11.96	131.0

Number	Age	h	W	Chest	Waist	Hips	Thigh	Knee	Calf	
1368	25–29	160.9	56.7	0.0	2.4	0.2	−0.2	−1.1	−1.7	131.4
1285	30–34	160.9	58.9	0.1	4.3	0.0	0.0	−2.0	−2.8	131.3
933	45–49	159.7	66.3	0.3	10.0	−1.4	−1.8	−4.7	−5.5	131.6
517	55–59	158.6	66.5	0.2	13.2	−2.1	−4.0	−6.4	−4.1	131.3
317	60–64	157.3	64.8	0.2	13.5	−1.5	−4.4	−5.9	−3.0	131.6
115	65–69	157.7	65.8	−0.1	13.9	−2.1	−6.6	−6.6	−3.5	131.5

[a] Circumferences (cm) are each divided by group specific factor ($F{-}h^{0.7}$).
[b] Knee girth measured at tibiale, not at mid-patellar level.
[c] Each girth is divided by group specific ($F{-}h^{0.7}$) and all quotients ([a] above) are computed as % deviation from these reference values.

Deviation of the mean values of the six girths relate to reference proportions for USDA age group, 20–24 years (Table 5.1 and Fig. 5.1). Calculation of the deviations involved the conversion of each mean girth to a multiple of $F–h^{0.7}$ specific for age. The multiples (mean $c/F–h^{0.7}$) for the age-grouped dimensions were then expressed as percentages of the reference multiples, age 20–24 years. At age four, for example, mean waist girth is 50.22 cm and $F–h^{0.7}$ is 1.817; the multiple (50.22/1.817) is 27.64, which is 16.4% greater than the reference multiple (23.75) for waist girth, age 20–24 years.

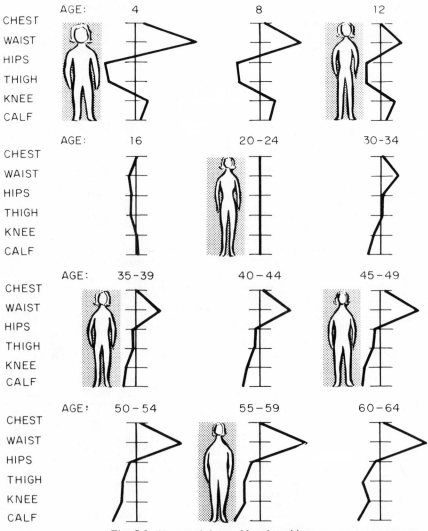

Fig. 5.1 Change of shape of females with age

We may also employ the sum of six girths in the calculation of percentage size of each girth. However, recourse to the factor, $F\!-\!h^{0.7}$, renders unnecessary the measurement of all six girths if we are interested in one or, at most, several girths. We have established previously the equivalence of the stature-weight module $(F\!-\!h^{0.7})$ and perimetric size, in this case six girths divided by a constant.

INTER-GROUP COMPARISON WITH USDA DATA. In Table 5.2, the comparative data pertain to Berkeley (N-A S) females comprising three racial groups, University of California (Berkeley) females, WAF Trainees (1953), Lankenau nurses, and the reference woman. The reference (USDA) proportions are in Table 5.1 for the age group 20–24 years. The mean proportions as represented by the girths measured, are similar for the different groups of young women except for girths of thigh and knee. In both the Berkeley N-A survey and the Lankenau examination the measurement of the thigh girth was at too high a level ("as high on the thigh as possible"), rather than the proper position around the maximal thigh perimeter but slightly below the gluteal fold to obviate inclusion of gluteal tissue. Knee girth in the USDA survey was at the lower (tibiale) and not mid-patellar level. These differences between groups illustrate the necessity for uniform procedure. In Table 5.2, the ratio of the sum of the six girths (SUM 6 c) to the Factor, $F\!-\!h^{0.7}$, is nearly identical for all groups with 131.0, the USDA ratio (Table 5.1).

EXCERPTS FROM TUDDENHAM-SNYDER DATA. The 1954 report of this extended longitudinal study is a standard reference (134). Although the measurements were limited, the somatotype ratings accorded the subjects from photographs at age 18, are highly useful in selection of "types" from the well-arranged columns of "static" measurements. In Table 5.3, the quotients, Diameters/Factor, are similar for males and females except at age 17 years. The lower quotient for the female (22.43) reflects fattening in contrast to the male quotient (22.66) in accord with leanness associated with weight of 68.7 kg relative to stature of 177.9 centimeters.

INDIVIDUAL ANALYSIS, TUDDENHAM-SNYDER DATA. Three growth records have been selected to compare ponderal equivalents of biacromial–bi-iliac diameters with scale weights from ages eight to 18 years. The data relating to females and their type of body build is indicated by the conventional somatotype. The conversion constant for the two diameters is the sum of the k values (11.43) for the reference woman multiplied by 1.98 to eliminate the constant (0.255) in the conversion formula. Therefore,

$$\text{Calculated weight} = (2 \text{ Diam}/22.63)^2 \times h^{0.7}.$$

Comments pertain to the following cases (Table 5.3).

SOMATOTYPE 4 3 4 (rated at about the age of skeletal maturation).

Table 5.2

PERCENTAGE DEVIATION OF THE PROPORTIONS OF VARIOUS FEMALE POPULATIONS
FROM THOSE OF A USDA REFERENCE GROUP, AGE 20-24 YEARS (Table 5.1)

Population (No. persons)	Age	h	W	Percentage Deviation of Girths (c)[a]						Sum 6 c $F-h^{0.7}$
				Chest	Waist	Hips	Thigh	Knee	Calf	
Berkeley N–A S										
Caucasian 164	15.1	163.7	56.9	-0.6	-0.8	-1.4	4.4	4.1	2.3	131.5
Negro 59	15.2	163.1	58.2	-1.5	-2.2	-2.4	3.9	3.8	0.2	131.1
Oriental 29	15.1	155.8	49.2	0.5	-0.6	-1.9	3.8	5.1	2.7	132.1
WAF Trainees[b]										
851	18–24	162.7	55.8	-2.7	-1.9	-1.2	1.7	—	1.1	129.8
Lankenau Nurses										
24	18–20	165.3	57.2	-2.5	-3.0	0.1	3.9	-0.3	-0.5	130.3
U. C. Berkeley										
128	21.4	164.9	58.6	-0.8	-0.4	-0.7	2.5	2.5	-0.4	131.5
Reference Woman	20–24	163.8	56.8	-2.7	-2.5	-1.2	1.6	0.2	0.7	130.2
USDA Reference Group[c] 1661	20–24	161.5	55.9							

[a]From the proportions of the USDA Ref Group, see Table 5.1, and text.
[b]Daniels, Meyers, and Worrall (45). WAF trainees provided basic proportions for the reference woman.
[c]Proportions: Chest (29.24), waist (23.75), hips (33.67), thigh (19.39), knee (12.29), calf (11.96), sum of the proportions = 131.0.

Table 5.3

RATIO OF BIACROMIAL–BI-ILIAC DIAMETERS TO FACTOR ($F-h^{0.7}$) AND THE CALCULATION OF INDIVIDUAL REFERENCE WEIGHTS FROM THESE DIAMETERS[a]

Group Data

Age	Males					Females				
	h	W	$F-h^{0.7}$	Diameter	Ratio	h	W	$F-h^{0.7}$	Diameter	Ratio
9	136.0	31.7	2.258	51.1	22.53	135.2	31.6	2.260	51.2	22.65
14	165.8	54.8	2.771	62.3	22.48	163.1	54.9	2.789	62.8	22.52
15	171.9	60.7	2.879	64.9	22.54	164.9	57.8	2.832	63.9	22.56
16	175.8	65.9	2.976	65.9	22.55	165.8	59.7	2.858	64.5	22.57
17	177.9	68.7	3.027	68.6	22.64	166.2	60.1	2.884	64.7	22.43

Individual Data

	Somatotype		Age	8	9	10	12	14	16	17	18
Normal Build	4 3 4		Scale	31.4	34.2	38.5	51.2	57.4	61.3	60.0	60.4
			Calc.	31.1	32.9	38.2	51.7	58.0	63.0	62.8	63.3
Obese	7 2.5 1.5		Scale	—	41.4	48.8	63.4	84.8	99.4	97.0	97.7
			Calc.	20.1	35.6	43.8	53.8	73.8	75.9	73.0	74.7
Underweight	3 3 6		Scale	26.2	22.8	24.8	33.5	43.4	45.6	46.5	
			Calc.	22.3	28.8	32.1	42.5	51.5	55.0	55.1	
	Minimal Weight			19.9	24.6	27.3	36.4	43.1	46.6	47.2	
	W (Calf Girth)				21.9	24.3	33.7	43.9	46.9	47.6	

[a]Analysis of data from Tuddenham and Snyder (133).

Scale weights and ponderal equivalents begin to diverge at age 14; at age 18 the calculated weight is 3 kg higher than the scale weight, which is interpreted as less than average weight for the examinee's frame size.

SOMATOTYPE 7 2.5 1.5. In this obese girl the scale weights are progressively higher beginning at age nine than are the equivalent weights, which tend to plateau at age 14 years.

SOMATOTYPE 3 3 6. This "underweight" girl is 6.1 kg below the scale weight at age eight yrs. Minimal weights were computed (conversion $k(\text{Min } W) = 12.34$ and multiplied by $1.98 = 24.4$) and reveal that scale weights during the observed growth period are consistently below minimal weight. Pertinent is the conversion of calf girth to an equivalent weight. For this conversion, age-specific constants were selected from the population data. It is observed that the calculated weights are closely identified with minimal (frame) size weights.

These cases illustrate principles underlying the anthropometric analysis in this monograph. Despite the paucity of measurements, it has been possible by means of a single conversion constant to convert width measurements into equivalents which can be compared directly with scale weight.

GROWTH OF A CHILD (AA). In Fig. 5.2, 12 girths were scaled to the proportions of the reference woman. The principal changes in shape as observed in the figure from ages 2.5 to 8.5 years, and (Fig. 5.3) in Table 5.4,

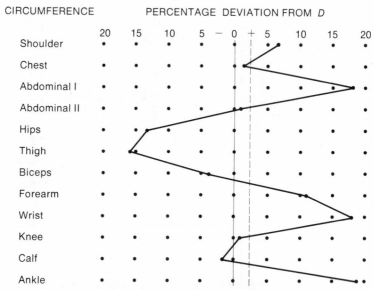

Fig. 5.2 Somatogram of female child (AA), progressive development. Age: 2.5 yrs; weight: 13.5 kg; stature: 9.42 dm. $D = 3.38$; $D(\text{Diam}) = 3.46$ (– – – vertical).

Table 5.4

CHANGE IN SHAPE DURING GROWTH OF A FEMALE CHILD (AA)
AND COMPARISON OF SELECTED DIMENSIONS WITH
USDA DATA

Examinee AA				Percentage Increase (4–12 years)	
				AA	USDA
Age yrs	2.5	4	12	AA	USDA
h cm	94.2	106.5	165.4	165	155
W kg	13.5	17.0	61.4	190[a]	168[a]
$1.98 \times F-h^{0.7}$	3.32	3.57	5.81	163	136
D	3.38	3.63	5.81	160	135 (6 girths)
D(C)[b]	3.46	3.73	5.58	150	—
Girths	% *Dev. of D from D axes*				
Shoulder	6.7	3.2	−0.4	154	—
Chest	1.6	2.1	−3.6	151	133
Abdominal 1	18.8	15.7	4.7	144	122
Abdominal 2	0.9	−0.1	7.7	172	—
Hips	−13.5	−11.0	−5.3	170	142
Thigh	−15.3	−12.0	1.9	189	142
Biceps	−4.5	−3.0	0.8	166	—
Forearm	10.5	3.2	1.1	149	—
Wrist	18.1	16.3	1.2	122	—
Knee	0.5	1.9	3.0	161	137
Calf	−1.5	−2.0	1.1	161	136
Ankle	19.2	17.7	10.6	149	—
Diameters					
4 *TD*	−3.1	−1.3	−5.9	153	—
4 *ED*	15.4	12.2	0.5	144	—

[a] *% increase of the square root of weight.*
[b] *Sum of 8 Diam (4 TD + 4 ED)/31.1 (K(C), Ref Woman).*

from 2.5 years to 12 years, are: relative decrease in size of the waist (abdominal 1), and enlargement of hips and thigh. Thus, development to maturity can be followed progressively as the deviations of the converted dimensions migrate to the midline, which is the *D*-axis. At age 12 (menarche at age 11.7 yrs), the development of this early-maturing girl is nearing completion as reflected by the somatograms specific for age 2.5 years (Fig. 5.3) and 12 years (Fig. 5.4).

In Table 5.4, the percentage gain in the factor $(F-h^{0.7})$ and selected dimensions (girths of the chest, waist, hips, thigh, knee, and calf) between ages four and 12 years are compared with gain in mean values taken from USDA data for the same ages. The accelerated growth of the girl is apparent. At ages 2.5, 4, and 12 years, the stature-weight factor $(F - h^{0.7})$ is interchangeable with *D* (11 girths/100). At age four, $D(C)$ from eight diameters was greater than *D*, which reflects less than average weight in relation to frame size. The child had a severe illness at this time.

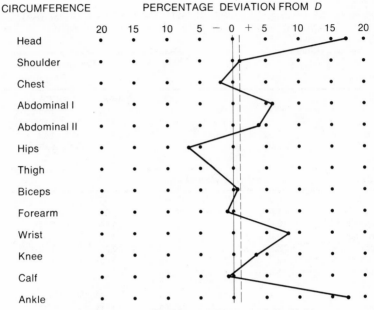

Fig. 5.3 Somatogram of growth (AA). Age: 8.5 yrs; weight: 33.9 kg; stature: 14.00 dm. D = 4.66; D(Diam) = 4.73 (– – – vertical).

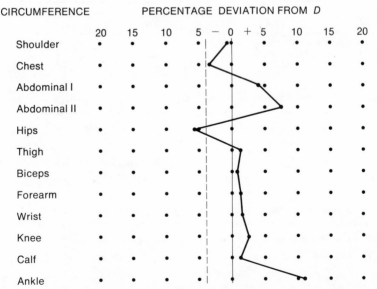

Fig. 5.4 Somatogram of growth (AA). Age: 12 yrs; weight: 61.4 kg; stature: 16.54 dm. D = 5.79: D(Diam) = 5.58 (– – – vertical).

Table 5.5

BI-METRIC GROWTH OF A CHILD (AA). PONDERAL EQUIVALENTS HAVE BEEN CALCULATED FROM DIAMETERS AND STATURE. FOR COMPARISON WITH INDIVIDUAL DATA, MEAN WEIGHTS HAVE BEEN CALCULATED FROM BRUSH FOUNDATION (SIMMONS) EXAMINEES

Age	Dimensions (AA)[a]				Ponderal Equivalents[b]				Simmons Data[c]		
	h	W	4(ED)	4(TD)	Ratio	W(4 ED)	W(4 TD)	W(8 Diam)	h	W	W(4 TD)
2.5	94.2	13.5	36.4	71.3	51.1	18.7	13.1	14.7	—	—	—
3	98.3	14.6	37.6	74.8	50.3	20.5	14.9	16.5	93.4	14.7	14.0
4	106.5	17.0	37.9	78.1	48.6	22.0	18.0	18.6	103.3	16.9	16.6
5	115.3	20.0	40.5	84.0	48.2	26.6	21.0	21.6	110.6	19.2	19.0
8	135.9	31.0	45.7	96.5	47.4	38.0	31.1	33.1	129.8	28.1	27.6
10	152.2	42.7	50.4	106.9	47.1	50.0	41.3	43.8	141.0	35.5	34.6
12	165.4	61.4	54.5	119.1	45.8	62.0	54.4	56.6	154.2	45.6	44.8
13	168.7	63.6	54.7	122.8	44.5	63.3	58.6	60.0	159.5	50.2	50.2

[a]4 ED: Wrists, ankles, knees, elbows; 4 TD: Biacromial, chest width, bi-iliac, bitrochanteric. Ratio: 4(ED)/4(TD).
[b]Conversion constants from reference woman: 4 ED(9.33), 4 TD(21.77), 8 Diam (31.1). Equivalent Weight = $(Dimensions/constant)^2 \times h^{0.7} \times 0.255$
[c]Conversion constant (all ages): 4 TD (21.31); $21.31 \times 1.98 = 42.2$
Males (all ages): 4 TD (21.64); $21.64 \times 1.95 = 42.2$.

In Table 5.5, the four trunk and four extremity diameters have been converted to ponderal equivalents from age 2.5 to 13 years. The conversion constants, 4 TD (21.77) and 4 ED (9.33), are from the reference woman. For comparison, mean weights computed from 4 TD in the Brush Foundation study have been included. The conversion constant derived from the Brush Foundation data was 21.31 for all ages, with minor variation as indicated by the agreement between calculated weights from the 4 TD and stature, and scale weights. With reference to the child, the extremity—but not trunk—diameters keep pace with scale weight. The serious illness between ages four and five years did not inhibit subsequent accelerated development and onset of early menarche at age 11.7 years.

The major changes in female body shape are evident from USDA and individual data. During the growth period, hips and thighs are relatively small, the head and waist (abdominal 1) are large. In adult life beginning at about age 30, the abdomen becomes relatively larger in contrast to the size of thigh and calf girths. This apparent loss of tissue (lean and fat) is relative to the body as a whole, which has gained fat. Data for estimate of frame size were not available to assess absolute gain of fat and loss of lean tissue.

Age Changes in Body Build of Adult Males

LONGSHOREMEN. These men, referred to again in Chapter 6, represent Caucasian and Negro races and exhibit the predominant characteristic of massive musculature. (In the Negro, however, calf and ankle girths are usually relatively small.) About 2300 examinees were measured as part of a "beltline" multiphasic screening examination which served to process as many as 100 men daily. Nine of the 11 girths were measured; the excluded girths (hip and thigh) were deliberate. Two additional general characteristics of these workmen were the average age of 55 years, and the generous accumulation of fat.

Anthropometric data are tabulated for four age groups embracing a span of less than 45 to greater than 74 years (Table 5.6). Group weight and stature decrease with age, while abdomen enlarges and muscular masses in the extremities reduce. The comparison of intergroup dimensions can be adjusted to the same scale if the girths are converted to d values and corrected for stature. Explanation of this correction follows.

Dimensions, unlike proportions, require a correction for stature for interindividual comparison. Both diameters and girths in our analysis are proportional to the square root of stature ($h^{0.5}$) and equated to a scale of 100 (reference man and woman). The correction for males is $69.5 \times D/h^{0.5}$

Table 5.6

MEAN AND COEFFICIENTS OF VARIATION OF BODY MEASUREMENTS
BY AGE GROUPS (LONGSHOREMEN STUDY, 1961[a])

	Number	485		648		325		65	
	Age	<45		45–54		65–74		>74	
	h cm	175.9		175.0		171.1		170.4	
	W kg	82.0		83.7		78.9		77.0	
Girths		cm	v	cm	v	cm	v	cm	v
Shoulder		117.5	6.1	117.4	6.1	112.6	5.9	110.2	6.0
Chest		99.6	8.1	101.8	7.9	101.1	8.0	100.4	8.1
Abdominal average		88.4	10.7	93.0	11.1	95.4	10.2	96.1	9.7
Hip (calc.)[b]		100.9	—	100.6	—	99.8	—	99.3	—
Biceps		35.9	8.9	35.7	9.0	32.4	9.3	31.1	7.7
Forearm		29.7	7.1	29.5	6.8	27.6	6.9	26.8	6.0
Wrist		17.7	6.2	17.9	5.6	17.9	5.0	18.0	6.3
Knee		37.6	6.4	37.8	6.6	37.4	7.0	37.4	6.4
Calf		36.8	7.9	36.7	8.2	35.4	8.5	35.2	8.8
Ankle		22.1	6.3	22.3	7.2	22.1	6.8	22.1	7.2
Sum		485		492		482		477	
$D(9c)$[c]		6.44		6.53		6.40		6.33	

[a]*California State Department of Health (statistical analysis by Robert Buechley, and H. Hechter, 32)*
[b]*Calc. hip c = 3F × 15.57, where 15.57 is k(Hip c), reference man.*
[c]*D(9c) = Sum 9c/75.3, where 75.3 is sum of k values (9c), reference man.*

(h in dm), and $72.8 \times D/h^{0.5}$ for females. The quotients, $69.5/h^{0.5}$ and $72.8/h^{0.5}$, designated q, thus serve to correct for differences in stature. In addition, q adjusts the individual d quotients (cm/k) to a reference value of 100. Thus the mean value for biceps girth (first group, Table 5.6) is 35.9 cm and the d conversion (35.9/5.29) is 6.786; the q multiple from group stature (17.59 dm) is 16.57; and the dq product for the biceps girth is 112.4. Therefore, the mean biceps girth (stature corrected) for this group of longshoremen is 12.4% greater than that of the reference man.

Fattening with age is observed (Table 5.7) in the increase of dq (abdominal average) from 112.1% to 123.5%. Loss of lean tissue is assessed by the decrements of the dq products for biceps, forearm, and calf girths.

Component analysis provides the overall picture of anthropometric change with age.

Component	Group I	Group II	Group IV	Group V
A'	85.3 kg	88.7 kg	88.2 kg	88.0 kg
B'	78.1	77.6	70.0	66.4
Average A', B'	81.7	83.2	79.1	77.2
Scale weight	82.0	83.7	78.9	77.0

Table 5.7

INTERGROUP COMPARISON OF DIMENSIONS OF LONGSHOREMEN
SCALED TO THE PROPORTIONS OF THE REFERENCE MAN ADJUSTED TO
100 BASELINE[a]

Number	485	648	325	65
Age Group	<45	45–54	65–74	>74
D^b	6.44	6.53	6.40	6.33
$D \times q^c$	106.9	108.5	107.5	106.2
Girths				
Shoulder	105.4	105.6	102.4	100.3
Chest	106.6	110.5	111.0	110.1
Abdominal average	112.1	118.2	123.5	123.3
Hip (calc.)	107.4 *A′*	107.3 *A′*	107.7 *A′*	107.0
Biceps	112.4	112.1	102.9	98.6
Forearm	110.1	109.7	103.7	100.6
Wrist	101.8	103.3	104.4	104.3
Knee	102.1 *B′*	103.0 *B′*	103.0 *B′*	102.9
Calf	106.9	102.1	99.6	98.9
Ankle	97.7	98.8	99.0	98.9

[a]*Reference man: (D × k)/h^0.5 = 100, k = 69.5*
[b]*D was calculated from 9 girths/K, where K = 75.3 (reference man).*
[c]*q corrects for differences in stature; q = 69.5/h^0.5.*

A measure of group fat accumulation is the difference between A' (trunk component) and the average of A', B'; presumptive loss of lean tissue is the difference between B' (extremity component) and the A', B' average. In the computation of the A' component (abdominal average and hip c), it was necessary to calculate hip c, which was not measured. This estimate introduces negligible error because hip girth constitutes a remarkably constant percentage of perimetric size in all populations we have examined. Of the various girths it is the one most highly correlated ($r = .93$ and higher) with body weight. In garment patterning, this girth is interchangeable with weight as a reference parameter.

BALTIMORE INDIGENTS. This group ($N = 20$), in the age range of 57 to 93 years (average 87 years), was composed of resident but ambulatory men confined to the hospital compound chiefly because of age and poverty. The group somatogram (Fig. 5.5) reveals the relative predominance of large abdominal girths. Notably, the size of the thighs were reduced to the extent that they corresponded to an average body weight of only 60.6 kg, or less than standard weight (62 kg) calculated from stature alone. Individual data are presented for six of the oldest males (Table 5.8). In all examinees the ponderal equivalents of A' are higher, and of thigh girth lower, than body weight. Reference (C) weight from frame size is, with one exception, greater than scale weight. Widely aberrant changes in body shape characterize these

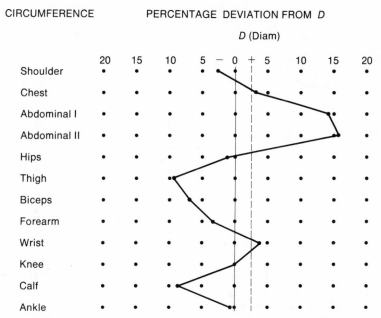

CIRCUMFERENCE   PERCENTAGE DEVIATION FROM *D*

D (Diam)

Fig. 5.5 Somatogram of composite of 10 aged males (Baltimore indigents). Age: 83 yrs; weight: 60.6 kg; stature: 16.19 dm. *D* = 5.80; *D*(Diam) = 5.95 (– – – vertical).

Table 5.8

COMPONENT ANALYSIS OF AGED BALTIMORE INDIGENTS

| | | | | Calculated Weights[a] (kg) | | | | | |
| | | | | Girths | | | | Diameters | |
No.	*Age*	*h*	*W*	*A'*	*Thigh*	*Hip*	*WFCA*	*Ref(C)*	*LBW*
1	82	164.3	60.9	63.7	49.1	61.1	58.4	64.4	57.2
2	93	154.0	57.0	64.3	46.1	54.7	54.0	57.8	51.3
3	90	158.7	53.3	56.8	41.6	53.7	53.1	60.2	63.4
4	83	165.1	53.7	64.9	41.3	55.1	61.8	67.3	59.7
5	90	164.0	70.0	85.8	66.1	70.5	59.3	62.6	55.6
6	82	168.5	65.5	76.6	60.8	62.1	61.1	70.6	62.7
average	87	162.4	60.1	68.7	50.8	59.5	58.0	63.8	56.3

[a]*Conversion constants from the reference man.*

aged "survivors" whose tissue bulk is less than average for frame size. Noteworthy are the nearly normal (reference man) proportions of one of the group, age 82 years, with the exception of reduced thigh girth (somatogram, Fig. 5.6).

CIRCUMFERENCE   PERCENTAGE DEVIATION FROM *D*

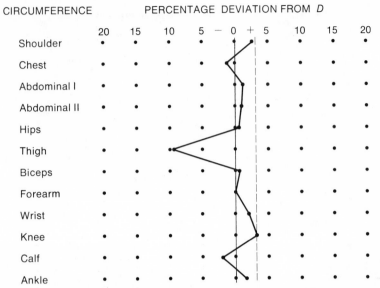

Fig. 5.6 Somatogram of aged male. Age: 82 yrs; weight: 60.9 kg; stature: 16.43 dm. *D* = 5.76; *D*(Diam) = 5.94 (– – – vertical).

Anthropometric Growth Data Berkeley N-A Survey

Group Data—Girths

In the Berkeley Nutritional-Anthropometric Survey (1961–1964) under the direction of Dr. Ruth Huenemann of the Department of Nutrition, School of Public Health, University of California, an entire class of adolescents (approximately 450 boys and 500 girls) were measured yearly in their progress from ninth to twelfth grades (mean ages were, 14.5, 15.2, 16.2, and 17.2 years). The longitudinal core of the survey was comprised of 227 males and 254 females. The boys were measured throughout the survey by one examiner with the aid of a recorder and a "master-at-arms." The measurements of the girls were made by several examiners who received on-the-job training.

Table 5.9 lists mean proportions for three racial groups of 17-year-old Berkeley adolescents. The dimensional values (not shown in the table) are the product of the proportionality constants (*k*) and *D* for specific groups. With the exception of the slightly larger abdominal and arm (contracted biceps) girths, the *k* values for Caucasian boys and the reference man are similar. The female proportions (Caucasian) also are consistently close to those of the reference woman. The relatively larger knee girth of the Cauca-

Table 5.9
PROPORTIONALITY CONSTANTS (*k* VALUES) FOR GIRTH DIMENSIONS OF BERKELEY N–A S ADOLESCENTS

	Males			Females		
	Caucasian	*Negro*	*Oriental*	*Caucasian*	*Negro*	*Oriental*
N	224	140	35	245	172	37
h cm	178.1	174.1	168.7	165.0	163.9	157.0
W kg	69.3	67.6	60.8	58.2	59.6	51.2
Age	17.2	17.4	17.2	17.2	17.2	17.2
D	5.88	5.83	5.62	5.67	5.70	5.44
Girths						
Shoulder	18.59	18.92	18.91	17.46	17.51	17.61
Chest	15.37	15.27	15.11	14.96	14.91	15.07
Abdominal 1	12.66	12.44	12.58	11.71	11.95	11.78
Abdominal 2	13.03	12.57	12.72	14.00	13.75	14.04
Abdominal average	12.66	12.50	12.65	12.86	12.86	12.90
Hips	15.58	15.28	15.50	16.75	16.68	16.54
Thigh	9.18	9.21	9.18	9.95	10.02	9.71
Biceps	5.19	5.42	5.20	4.74	4.75	4.76
Forearm	4.49	4.60	4.43	4.14	4.21	4.17
Wrist	2.82	2.96	2.79	2.68	2.72	2.68
Knee	6.09	6.09	6.12	6.40	6.47	6.42
Calf	6.05	6.02	6.25	6.21	6.12	6.21
Ankle	3.81	3.74	3.77	3.81	3.72	3.79

sian girl requires confirmation since it was considerably smaller ($k = 6.28$) in the ninth grade compared with $k = 6.40$ in the twelfth grade. There may have been procedural variation in this particular measurement, since the relative size of the knee after age 14 becomes smaller, as shown in the USDA data (Table 5.1).

RACIAL DIFFERENCES. In the Negro male, waist and hip girths are relatively smaller, and the girths of shoulders, biceps, and forearm larger compared with Caucasians. Calf girth of the Oriental (in the small sample) is relatively larger than that of Caucasian and Negro.

PROPORTIONS OF SUB-GROUPS. The single standard principle which applies to mean proportions of a young adult man or woman has much in its favor. However, as weights (or the unit-Size index, *uS–W*) of examinees approach either end of the Gaussian distribution curve, it is informative to depart from a gross reference scale and to apply the vernier proportions of a height-weight matched subgroup. Table 1.2 and Fig. 1.4 showed that deviation from mean proportions, notably those of abdomen, thigh, and biceps, was pronounced at the 2.5 and 97.5 percentile levels. It appears that specific types of leanness or obesity within lean or fat categories require comparison with an appropriate subgroup. Table 5.10 compares two groups of ballet dancers with a weight-matched group of Berkeley girls. Differences observed

Table 5.10

ANTHROPOMETRIC COMPARISON OF TWO GROUPS OF THE BALLET
WITH A LOW-WEIGHT GROUP OF BERKELEY N-A S GIRLS

Groups	Ballet I[a] N = 10	Ballet II N = 10	Berkeley[b] N = 10
Age	21.8	19.5	17.1
h cm	166.4	163.8	162.3
W kg	51.4	50.7	50.5
$D \times q^c$	94.2	94.4	97.6
$D(C) \times q^c$	99.0	97.7	99.0
Sum 6 Diam	143.0	140.2	141.2
6 Diam/D	27.1	26.7	26.2
Proportionality Constants $(k)^d$			
Shoulder	18.14	17.81	17.83
Chest	15.22	14.93	15.27
Abdominal 1	11.73	11.54	11.46
Abdominal 2	13.91	13.74	13.74
Hip	16.66	16.72	16.72
Thigh	9.88	9.77	9.61
Biceps	4.51	4.88	4.66
Forearm	4.05	4.13	4.15
Wrist	2.64	2.71	2.74
Knee	6.12	6.17	6.36
Calf	6.31	6.65	6.20
Ankle	3.77	4.00	3.85

[a]*Premier dancing group.*
[b]*Group III in a series of 13 groups aligned in order of descending weight.*
[c]$q = 72.8/h^{0.5}$, *D × q converts perimetric size to a scale of 100 (reference woman).*
[d]*Dimensions divided by respective D values.*

in this comparison focus on the relatively small knee girth in contrast to the larger calf circumference of the dancers and the Berkeley subgroup.

INTER-GROUP COMPARISON OF COMPONENT (k) VALUES. The tabular data (Table 5.11) are indicative of the restricted variation of the proportionality constants derived for summated dimensions as components and representative of the various male and female populations we have measured. Berkeley Caucasian male and reference man constants are interchangeable. Those for Negroes and Orientals are race-specific. But, with the exception of the Lankenau group and B', WFCA constants for University of California females, the k values for the five components are interchangeable.

It is this close consistency in the grouped proportions of males and females in the age range of 17 to 30 years which supports wide application of these data as standards of reference.

Group Data—Diameters

Four to eight body widths as measured with an anthropometer, together with stature, serve as a reference standard for evaluation of growth

Table 5.11

INTERGROUP COMPARISON OF COMPONENT (*k*) VALUES

Males

Group	Berkeley N-A S Caucasian	Negro	Oriental	U.C.	Oregon College	Navy Lab	Ref Man
N	224	140	35	133	100	31	+25,000
h cm	178.1	174.1	168.7	177.3	180.3	177.8	174
W kg	69.3	67.6	60.8	75.6	78.5	78.3	70
Age	17.2	17.4	17.2	22	18–22	20–52	20–24
D	5.88	5.83	5.62	6.28	6.27	6.26	6.00

Components	Conversion Constants (*k*)						
A	44.01	43.05	43.26	44.10	44.07	44.41	43.94
A'	28.42	27.78	28.15	28.58	28.49	29.10	28.64
B	20.38	20.77	20.61	20.27	20.42	20.18	20.35
B'	28.45	28.83	28.56	27.99	28.27	28.01	28.46
WFCA	17.17	17.32	17.24	16.70	16.99	16.77	17.07

Females

Group					Lankenau	Ref Woman
N	245	172	37	128	24	+800
h cm	165.0	163.9	157.0	164.9	165.3	163.8
W kg	58.2	59.6	51.2	58.6	56.8	56.8
D	5.67	5.70	5.44	5.72	5.58	5.56

Components	Conversion Constants					
A	44.57	44.45	44.51	44.59	44.51	44.68
A'	29.61	29.54	29.44	29.70	29.60	29.83
B	19.46	19.46	19.52	19.47	19.29	19.46
B'	27.98	27.99	28.01	27.61	27.47	27.96
WFCA	16.84	16.77	16.85	16.54	16.46	16.71

and as a guide for determination of an individual's optimal weight. During normal growth as observed in the Berkeley adolescents from ages 14.5 to 17.2 years, body diameters increased proportionately with perimetric size.

The comprehensive set of eight diameters (although all widths may not be routinely used) provides a differential appraisal in growth between trunk and extremity widths, e.g., in the child (AA), Table 5.5, Figs. 5.3, 5.4.

PROTOCOL DATA PERTAINING TO FRAME SIZE (MALES). In Table 5.12 are mean values for stature, weight, *D*, and skeletal diameters for the various groups of males which comprise our study. The bideltoid diameter is also included, but this dimension is treated as though it were a girth. In order to normalize the data for the purpose of intergroup comparison, it was expedient to compute *standard* weights from stature alone. The standard weights approximate mean weights for young adults and adolescents (age 17 years) in the Equitable Life Assurance tables, 1940 (65) and can be calculated also from data on Army recruits (1943) from the survey by Karpinos (72). It suffices

Table 5.12

DERIVATION OF PROPORTIONALITY CONSTANTS FOR CONVERSION OF DIAMETERS TO REFERENCE WEIGHTS (MALES)

Population	Berkeley N-A Survey			U.C. Berkeley	Oregon College	Navy Lab	Ref Man
	Caucasian	Negro	Oriental				
h cm	178.1	174.1	168.7	177.3	180.3	177.8	174.0
Scale W kg	69.3	67.6	60.8	75.6	78.5	78.3	70
D	5.88	5.83	5.62	6.28	6.27	6.27	6.00
Standard W	69.3	66.5	63.1	72.3	74.3	72.7	70
$1.95\ F\text{-}h^{0.7}$	5.92	5.85	5.76	6.06	6.11	6.07	6.00
Diameters cm							
Biacromial	39.7	40.4	39.3	40.4	41.8	40.6	40.6
Chest width	28.3	27.7	26.9	29.3	30.3	29.9	30.0
Bi-iliac	28.1	26.4	26.9	28.4	29.0	29.4	28.6
Bitrochanteric	32.6	31.4	31.1	32.9	33.2	32.8	32.8
Subtotal	128.7	125.9	124.2	131.0	134.3	132.7	132.0
Wrists	11.37	11.49	10.77	11.20	11.60	11.18	11.0
Ankles	14.36	14.38	13.77	14.20	14.20	13.88	13.9
Knees (tibiale)	18.48	18.44	18.04	19.00	19.00	18.42	18.5
Elbows	14.02	13.98	13.14	14.00	14.20	13.88	13.9
Subtotal	58.23	58.29	55.72	58.40	59.00	57.36	57.40
TOTAL (8 Diam)	186.9	184.2	179.9	189.4	193.3	190.1	189.4
Bideltoid	44.8	45.2	43.7	47.6	—	47.1	45.24

at this time to introduce the following formula, which will be discussed in Chapter 6 in connection with height-weight tables.

Young Male Adults, Standard Weight (kg) = 0.545 $h^{1.7}$, h in dm.

Standard weights (Table 5.12) for the Berkeley, Oregon College, and Navy Lab groups are appreciably lower than mean scale weights. For Caucasian adolescents, a scale weight of 69.3 kg is approximately mean weight for males age 17 years and 178.1 cm tall, in the Equitable tables. From these data, the constant (0.517) was derived for the calculation of mean weights for the Negro and Oriental groups (Berkeley Survey) of approximately the same age, and for males (age 17), Standard Weight (kg) = 0.517 $h^{1.7}$. The tabular data shows that scale weight for the Negro group is somewhat higher, and that of the Oriental group substantially lower than the calculated standard weights.

Table 5.13

PROPORTIONALITY CONSTANTS FOR CONVERSION OF
DIAMETERS TO REFERENCE WEIGHTS

Males	*Berkeley N-A Survey*			*U.C.*	*Reference*
Diameters k(C)	*Caucasian*	*Negro*	*Oriental*	*Berkeley*	*Man*
Biacromial	6.76	6.91	6.82	6.67	6.77
Chest width	4.78	4.73	4.67	4.84	5.00
Bi-iliac	4.75	4.51	4.67	4.69	4.77
Bitrochanteric	5.51	5.37	5.40	5.43	5.47
Subtotal	21.74	21.54	21.56	21.63	22.01
Wrists	1.92	1.96	1.87	1.85	1.85
Ankles	2.43	2.46	2.39	2.34	2.32
Knees (tibiale)	3.12	3.15	3.13	3.14	3.08
Elbows	2.37	2.39	2.28	2.31	2.32
Subtotal	9.84	9.96	9.67	9.64	9.57
TOTAL (8 Diam)	31.58	31.50	31.23	31.27	31.58
Females					*Reference Woman*
Biacromial	6.42	6.52	6.45	6.48	6.29
Chest width	4.43	4.42	4.43	4.58	4.59
Bi-iliac	5.05	4.83	5.02	5.05	5.14
Bitrochanteric	5.68	5.62	5.61	5.72	5.75
Subtotal	21.58	21.39	21.51	21.83	21.77
Wrists	1.80	1.84	1.77	1.74	1.73
Ankles	2.25	2.29	2.24	2.24	2.28
Knees (tibiale)[a]	3.10	3.14	3.20	3.18	3.18
Elbows[a]	2.11	2.14	2.15	2.12	2.14
Subtotal	9.26	9.41	9.36	9.28	9.33
TOTAL (8 Diam)	30.84	30.80	30.87	31.11	31.10

[a]*Constants for Berkeley N-A Survey were derived from a subsample.*

From these standard weights and stature, specific for each group, comes the factor, $1.95 F-h^{0.7}*$ as computed as $1.95\sqrt{W/h^{0.7}}$. The conversion constants (Table 5.13) are the quotients, Diameter/Specific Factor. Reference (frame size) weights can then be calculated from the eight diameters or any combination following their conversion to $D(C)$ quotients and substitution in the basic formulas.

PROTOCOL DATA PERTAINING TO FRAME SIZE (FEMALES). Standard weights for the Berkeley females and for the adolescents (age 17.2 years) were calculated from,

$$\text{Standard } W \text{ (kg)} = 0.49\, h^{1.7}, \; h \text{ in dm}$$

The constant (0.49) was derived from mean W (56.8 kg, 125 lbs) relative to stature (163.8 cm, 68.5 inches). In Table 5.14 are the mean skeletal diameters for the three racial groups in the Berkeley N-A Survey, and for the Berkeley females and the reference woman.

The Factor, $1.98 F-h^{0.7}†$ was calculated for each group (except reference

Table 5.14

DERIVATION OF PROPORTIONALITY CONSTANTS FOR CONVERSION OF DIAMETERS TO REFERENCE WEIGHTS (FEMALES)

Population	Berkeley N-A Survey			U.C. Berkeley	Reference Woman
	Caucasian	Negro	Oriental		
h cm	165.0	163.9	157.0	164.9	163.8
Scale *W* kg	58.2	59.6	51.2	58.6	56.8
D	5.57	5.70	5.44	5.72	5.56
Standard Weight	56.4	55.7	51.8	57.5	56.8
$1.98 F-h^{0.7}$	5.58	5.53	5.44	5.63 *(D)*	5.56
Diameters cm					
Biacromial	35.8	36.2	35.1	36.5	35.0
Chest width	24.7	24.5	24.1	25.8	25.5
Bi-iliac	28.2	26.8	27.3	28.4	28.6
Bitrochanteric	31.7	31.2	30.5	32.2	32.0
Subtotal	120.4	119.3	117.0	122.9	121.1
Wrists	10.02	10.22	9.62	9.80	9.6
Ankles	12.54	12.72	12.16	12.58	12.7
Knees	17.32	17.40	17.42	17.88	17.7
Elbows	11.76	11.86	11.70	11.94	11.9
Subtotal	51.64	52.20	50.90	52.20	51.9
TOTAL (8 Diam)	172.0	171.5	169.7	175.1	173.0
Bideltoid	—	—	—	42.1	40.4

*This factor, not $3\sqrt{W/h}$, is employed for comparative derivation of male adolescent and adult k values.

†See p. 10 and p. 127.

woman) from standard weight and stature. The conversion constants (Table 5.13) are the quotients (as calculated for the males), Diameter/Specific Factor. The conversion constant for bi-iliac width is low both for the Negro female and the male, and this appears to be a racial characteristic. The value of 5.00 for chest width (k), reference man, appears to be too high, and biacromial (k) reference woman, is too low. Otherwise, either set of constants from the Berkeley data and the reference man and woman can be employed for the calculation of reference (frame size) weights from diameters. If eight diameters are employed, a rounded constant of 31.3 would apply both to male and female young adults.

INTER-GROUP COMPARISON OF BI-METRIC DATA. If mean values of diameters are divided by the factor $(F-h^{0.7})$ without the multiples (1.95 or 1.98), then the quotients (conversion constants) are similar both for males and females for "complementary" dimensions. In Table 5.15, with reference to Simmons' Brush Foundation data, mean weights for males and females from ages four to 17 years, inclusive, can be calculated with small error from the four trunk diameters (4 TD) and stature.

$$\text{Mean weight (kg)} = (4\ TD/42)^2 \times h^{0.7}$$

Table 5.15

INTER-GROUP COMPARISON OF BI-METRIC GROWTH DATA

Population	Mean and Range of k Values[a]					
Brush Foundation (Simmons)	4 Trunk Diameters					
	Males			Females		
Ages 4–17 (incl.)	41.98 (41.2–42.3) *Biac.–Bitroch.*			42.02 (41.5–42.2)		
	23.30 (22.7–23.5) *Biac.–Bi-iliac*			23.29 (23.0–23.6)		
	22.33 (22.07–22.70)			22.36 (22.06–22.55)		
Tuddenham-Snyder Ages 9–18 (incl.)	22.55 (22.39–22.70)			22.44 (22.31–22.66)		
Olympic Athletes[b]	Males			Females		
	Caucasian	Negro	Oriental	Caucasian	Negro	Oriental
	22.42	21.97	22.64	—	—	—
Berkeley N-A S Age 17.2 yrs[c]	22.44	22.27[c]	22.41	22.71	22.47	22.71
		Biac.–Bitroch.				
Age 17.2 yrs[c]	23.93	24.04	23.83	23.96	24.04	23.88
		4 Trunk Diam				
Age 17.2 yrs[c]	42.39	42.00	42.04	42.73	42.35	42.59

[a]$k(Ref\ W) = Diameters/F-h^{0.7}$, where $F-h^{0.7}$ is $W/h^{0.7}$.
[b]Author's analysis of Tanner's data.
[c]Weight standardized for the calculation of $F-h^{0.7}$ (see text); a lower constant (22.16) is obtained if $F-h^{0.7}$ is calculated from scale weight.

The range of variation of the conversion constant calculated at yearly intervals (ages four to 17 years, inclusive) is 41.2 to 42.3 (males), and 41.5 to 42.2 (females). Likewise, in the Tuddenham-Snyder data, the range of variation of the constant for biacromial–bi-iliac widths is narrow for yearly intervals from nine through 18 years.

The generally higher Berkeley N-A S constants pertain to a leaner standardized weight at age 17 years. The constants, male and female, are remarkably similar for the biacromial-bitrochanteric widths. Constants have been calculated from mean values of biacromial–bi-iliac widths for Tanner's Olympic athletes (129) for comparison with the racial groups (Berkeley N-A S). The low value of the constant (Negro) is due to the relatively smaller bi-iliac width, as mentioned previously.

The data in the preceding paragraphs support the concept that constants of similar magnitude convert width dimensions to reference weights during the growth period from four years upward. Further, with small error, the same constant is applicable both to male and female widths which are complementary as biacromial–bitrochanteric diameters. Adjustment for racial difference is necessary, particularly if bi-iliac width is employed in the examination of Negroes. The wide usefulness of the four trunk widths (4 *TD*), which are conveniently measured, is evident.

A correlative finding is the constancy of mean values of body widths to regional girths during the growth period and early adult life when individuals are generally lean. The following examples support this remarkable relationship.

*4 Trunk Diam/Girth Component A**

Age	14.5	15.2	16.2	17.2	Reference man
Caucasian	49.7	50.2	50.0	50.0	50.1
Negro	49.6	50.0	50.0	50.2	
Oriental	51.2	51.3	50.9	51.0	

4 TD (biac., chest w., bi-iliac, bitroch.)/(chest, abdominal average, hip, c). The higher ratio in the Oriental reflects greater leanness in the sample measured.

Growth as an Expression of Perimetric–Bi-Metric Change

In the following paragraphs we shall combine width-girth measurements with the usual parameters of stature and weight in order to widen the scope of growth analysis.

GROWTH OF CAUCASIAN MALES. We may begin with a sample (Berkeley N-A S) of 100 boys divided into ten subgroups and aligned in order of ascending weight when the examinees were in the ninth grade. In Table 5.16, the mean values represent growth of each of the ten groups of boys from ninth to twelfth grades (14.5 to 17.2 years). The gains in absolute units are recorded

Table 5.16

GROWTH GAINS OF CAUCASIAN BOYS EXPRESSED AS GROUP
DIFFERENCES BETWEEN ANTHROPOMETRIC PARAMETERS AT AGES 14.6
AND 17.2 YEARS

Group	h^a	W^a	$uS–W$	Δh cm	ΔW kg	Δ Calculated Weights^b (kg)					
						D	C	$WFCA$	A	B	B'
I	155.1	42.2	73	17.8	17.3	17.5	17.6	11.9	16.9	18.5	16.3
II	164.0	48.1	76	12.2	13.4	13.5	14.2	11.9	12.5	15.0	12.2
III	163.9	50.1	79	14.2	14.6	13.5	14.9	13.0	13.0	15.8	13.3
IV	167.6	52.4	80	8.6	10.5	10.0	9.7	7.9	9.8	11.9	8.6
V	170.8	54.2	80	10.0	12.0	11.0	12.1	9.7	11.1	12.4	9.9
VI	170.7	56.5	83	6.9	9.6	8.9	9.4	8.1	8.1	7.0	7.2
VII	171.1	59.5	87	8.5	10.7	10.3	9.6	7.8	10.8	11.2	9.4
VIII	174.0	63.1	90	7.2	10.9	10.0	9.3	8.2	9.8	12.1	8.6
IX	174.2	68.5	98	5.0	8.2	7.9	6.3	5.7	7.8	9.3	6.5
X	176.8	86.2	121	4.7	9.6	9.5	7.3	5.8	10.9	10.8	6.5

^{a}*Height and weight at age 14.6 years.*
^{b}*Calculated weights from D(11 girths), D(C), 6 Diameters.*

for stature, scale weight, and relative weights computed from 11 c (D), six
Diam (C), and the regional girth components, A, B, B', and $WFCA$. A close
association is observed for the ponderal equivalent gains calculated either
from girths or diameters. A graphic representation of these gains is shown
(Fig. 5.7) for groups I, V, and X, which are Caucasian. A chart showing
similar gains could be prepared for the Negro examinees as well.

GROWTH OF CAUCASIAN FEMALES. In contrast with males, the growth
spurt of females is nearly complete at age 14.6 years (Fig. 5.8). The reduced
but fairly uniform differences in stature, weight, and calculated weights were
tabulated for 13 groups of Caucasian girls aligned in order of ascending
weight when they were in the ninth grade (age 14.6 years). Data in Table
5.17 have been extracted for seven of the 13 groups. The ponderal equivalents
of dimensional components ($WFCA$, A, B, and B') were computed from the
same type of formulation applied to measurements on males. The conversion
constants were k values from the reference woman. In the heaviest group
(XIII) there is substantial growth gain (increase in Ref(C)W) as well as
presumptive increase in fat, $W(D) > W(C)$. At age 17.2 years, frame size
weight is 8.0 kg greater than scale weight.

Individual Growth Data—Males

1. *Smallest boy (age 14.2 years) in the ninth grade.* This adolescent is
136.2 cm (53.6 inches) tall, and weighs 27.7 kg (60.9 lb). On inspection, he
was given a rating of 1 based on a lean-fat scale,

$$0 \quad 1 \quad 2 \quad \underline{3} \quad 4 \quad 5 \quad 6$$

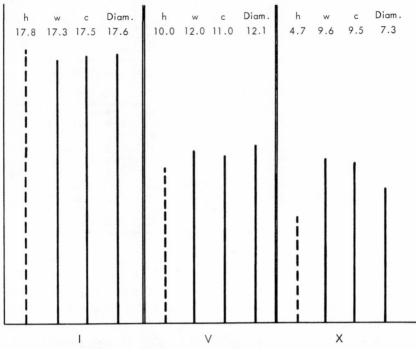

h	w	c	Diam.		h	w	c	Diam.		h	w	c	Diam.
17.8	17.3	17.5	17.6		10.0	12.0	11.0	12.1		4.7	9.6	9.5	7.3

I   V   X

Fig. 5.7 Growth of adolescent males, 14.4 to 17.2 yrs, over a period of 2.5 years is represented as gain in stature (*h*), weight (*w*), and in relative weights computed from 11 circumferences (*c*) and 6 diameters (Diam.). Data represent the average of Groups I, VII, and X of 100 boys aligned in order of ascending weight (*N* = 10 boys per group). Group I—age: 14.4 yrs; weight: 42.2 kg; stature: 15.51 dm. Group V—age: 14.7 yrs; weight: 54.2 kg; stature: 17.08 dm. Group X—age: 14.5 yrs; weight: 86.9 kg; stature: 17.68 dm.

Table 5.17
GROWTH GAINS OF CAUCASIAN GIRLS EXPRESSED AS GROUP DIFFERENCES BETWEEN ANTHROPOMETRIC PARAMETERS AT AGES 14.6 AND 17.2 YEARS

Group	h^a	W^a	uS–W	Δh cm	ΔW kg	Δ Calculated Weights[b] (kg)					
						D	D(C)	WFCA	A	B	B'
I	157.8	43.0	81	3.1	4.8	5.0	4.1	3.9	5.3	5.1	4.6
II	157.3	46.7	88	3.1	5.0	5.5	3.5	3.3	5.9	5.8	5.6
III	159.6	48.6	89	2.7	1.9	2.7	3.8	2.2	2.7	2.5	2.7
VII	163.5	55.2	98	2.1	2.3	2.6	3.2	2.3	2.0	3.1	3.2
XI	168.0	61.3	103	2.0	0.4	1.1	2.0	0.5	1.1	1.1	1.2
XII	165.5	63.3	110	1.9	2.5	3.0	2.6	2.4	2.1	2.7	3.8
XIII	167.9	70.1	118	2.4	3.7	5.9	3.7	3.8	3.8	4.0	4.6

[a]*Height and weight at age 14.6 years.*
[b]*Calculated weights from D(11 girths), D(C), 6 Diameters.*

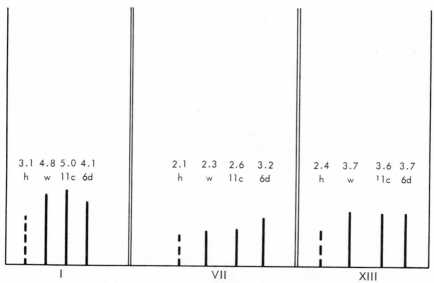

| 3.1 | 4.8 | 5.0 | 4.1 | | 2.1 | 2.3 | 2.6 | 3.2 | | 2.4 | 3.7 | 3.6 | 3.7 |
| h | w | 11c | 6d | | h | w | 11c | 6d | | h | w | 11c | 6d |

| I | VII | XIII |

Fig. 5.8 Growth of adolescent females, 14.4 to 17.2 yrs, over a period of 2.5 yrs is represented as gain in stature (*h*), weight (*w*), and in relative weights computed from circumferences (11*c*) and diameters (6*d*). Data represent the average of Groups I, VII, and XIII of 130 girls aligned in order of ascending weight (*N* = 10 girls per group). Group I—age: 14.6 yrs; weight: 43.0 kg; stature: 15.78 dm. Group VII—age: 14.6 yrs; weight: 55.2 kg; stature: 16.35 dm. Group XIII—age: 14.6 yrs; weight: 70.1 kg; stature: 16.79 dm.

with $\underline{3}$ as average fatness, 0 as underweight, and 4, 5, and 6 denoting increasing fatness in increments of about 5% above average for each unit increase on the scale. In regard to muscular development, he was given a "star" rating at age 17 but not at 14.2 years.

The examinee's anthropometric measurements have been scaled to the proportions of the lowest weight group (Group I, Table 5.18) in the longitudinal series of Caucasian boys aligned in order of ascending weight in Grade 9, age 14.5 years. The small examinee, however, is about two years behind Group I in development. Nevertheless, the proportions of this cohort group are selected as *k* values, rather than those of the more distant reference man. In Table 5.18, each girth has been divided by the age-specific proportionality constant of Group I (not shown in the table), and the percentage deviation of each *d* quotient is calculated for the examinee from his age-specific *D* axis. Shoulder girth, for example, is 75.7 cm at age 14.2 years; divided by 18.46 (shoulder *k* from Group I at 14.4 years), it gives a *d* quotient of 4.12 which deviates by −0.7% from the examinee's *D* axis (4.15) at 14.2 years.

These percentage deviations are then plotted for the somatogram (Fig.

5.9). The noteworthy physical characteristics of this boy are undersized thighs but better than average (i.e., of Group I) development of biceps and wrists. His absolute growth rate is generally better than that of the cohort group. It is evident that certain dimensions (shoulder, hip, thigh, knee, and calf girths) have not been altered in their growth pattern from 14.5 to 17 years. It is as though the examinee's body were cast into a mold which expanded uniformly during growth at the anatomical sites enumerated.

Except for definitive evaluation of body build in less common types, cohort analysis represents the special rather than the general procedure. In Table 5.19, dimensional components have been computed as ponderal equivalents derived from Group I constants and from those of the reference man. The results transformed into relative weight gains of the various components are interchangeable and serve to establish the appropriateness and simplicity of a single (reference man) standard.

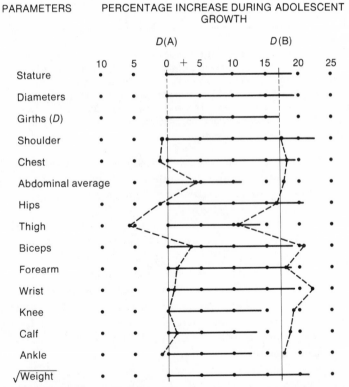

Fig. 5.9 Similarity in shape during growth of diminutive boy from (left) 14.2 yrs; weight: 27.7 kg; stature: 13.62 dm; $D(A) = 4.15$ to (right) age 17 yrs; weight: 43.3 kg; stature: 16.12 dm; $D(B) = 4.86$. The relative percentage increase of the various dimensions from 14.2 to 17.0 yrs is shown by the length of the horizontal lines, left to right (see Table 5.18).

Table 5.18

ANTHROPOMETRIC COMPARISON OF THE GROWTH OF THE SMALLEST BOY (BERKELEY N-A S) WITH THAT OF A COHORT GROUP (I, LONGITUDINAL SERIES)

	Examinee			Group I		
Age	14.2	17.0	% Increase	14.4	17.0	% Increase
h cm	136.2	161.2	18.4	155.1	172.9	11.5
W kg	27.7	43.3	21.1^a	42.2	55.5	20.2^a
D	4.15	4.86	17.1	4.86	5.56	14.4
1.95 $F–h^{0.7}$	4.11	4.85	18.0	4.85	5.55	14.4
6 Diam	109.3	129.9	18.9	131.7	149.5	13.1

Girths	cm	% dev.	cm	% dev.	% Increase	% Increase
Shoulder	75.7	−0.7	92.3	0.8	22.2	17.3
Chest	62.4	−1.4	74.7	1.3	19.7	16.5
Abdominal average	55.1	4.8	60.9	1.3	10.5	11.1
Hips	63.8	−0.7	75.0	−0.8	20.3	14.9
Thigh	35.2	−5.8	40.6	−6.8	13.9	13.8
Biceps	20.6	3.4	25.6	3.7	17.9	21.0
Forearm	18.8	1.9	22.1	0.8	17.4	16.2
Wrist	12.6	0.7	15.1	5.0	18.1	11.2
Knee	26.8	0.0	30.7	2.5	14.5	9.4
Calf	26.4	1.7	29.9	1.7	13.3	10.4
Ankle	17.0	−1.0	19.2	0.8	11.9	8.2

^{a}% Increase $\sqrt{W}$

Table 5.19

GROWTH OF THE SMALLEST BOY (BERKELEY N-A S) ASSESSED FROM PONDERAL EQUIVALENTS AND OTHER PARAMETERS

Age	14.2	17.0	Age	14.2	17.0
h cm	136.2	161.2	1.95 $F–h^{0.7}$	4.11	4.85
W kg	27.7	43.3	D	4.15	4.86
LBW kg	24.9	39.6	$\sqrt{uS–W^a}$	77.5	84.3
6 Diam	109.3	129.9	$uS–D^b$	78.1	84.4
6 Diam/D	26.34	26.73	$uS–D(C)^c$	76.0	83.9

	K Values					
	A	A'	B	B'	WFCA	C
Group I (14.4 yrs)	43.51	28.24	20.10	29.15	17.90	27.10
(17.0 yrs)	43.50	27.95	20.36	28.80	17.45	26.91
Reference Man	43.94	28.64	20.35	28.46	17.07	26.18

	Conversions to Ponderal Equivalents (kg)						
Cohort Analysis	D	A	A'	B	B'	WFCA	C
Age 14.2	28.2	28.5	29.0	30.4	28.9	28.7	26.6
Age 17.0	43.5	43.1	43.5	44.9	45.1	45.1	43.0
Diff.	15.3	14.6	14.5	14.5	16.2	16.4	16.4

Ref Man Analysis

Age 14.2	28.2	27.9	28.2	28.3	30.3	31.5	28.5
Age 17.0^d	+15.3	14.3	13.2	16.8	15.9	15.8	16.8

$^a\sqrt{183.6 \ W/h^{1.7}}$, W in kg, h in dm.
$^b 69.5 \ D/h^{0.5}$
$^c 69.5 \ D(C)/h^{0.5}$, D(C) from 6 Diam/Cohort K(C) constants.
^{d}+ age 14.2 ponderal equivalents.

Is this body underweight? The answer is "No," if the criterion of underweight is disproportionately reduced soft tissue mass relative to skeletal size. Body density at age 14.8 years was 1.0996 (Siri's helium chamber technique), essentially the constant for fat-free mass. Overall, ponderal, perimetric, and bi-metric (frame size) components are well balanced in this male. Thus, at age 14.2 years, $uS–W$ is 77.5, $uS–D$ (78.1), and $uS–D(C)$, 76.0; at age 17.0 years, $uS–W$ is 84.3, $uS–D$ (84.4), and $uS–D(C)$, 83.9. In this small boy there is consonance between the derivatives from weight/stature $(uS–W)$, from perimetric size $(uS–D)$, and from the diameters $(uS–D, C)$.

2. *Growth of an underweight boy.* In Table 5.20, the dimensions of an under-

Table 5.20

GROWTH OF AN UNDERWEIGHT BOY, 14.2–16.7 YEARS

Rating	1	1	% Increase
h cm	156.3	177.6	13.6
W kg	34.8	53.0	22.9[a]
D	4.43	5.18	16.9
6 Diam	127.1	147.7	16.2
6 Diam/D	28.69	28.51	
$uS–W$	59.7	73.2	22.6
$\sqrt{uS–W}$	77.3	85.5	10.6
$uS–D$	77.9	85.4	9.6
$uS–D(C)$	85.1	92.8	9.3

Girths	% dev. from D	% dev. from D	% Increase
Age	14.2	16.7	14.2–16.7 yrs
Shoulder	1.6	4.4	20.1
Chest	−3.6	−2.5	18.1
Abdominal 1	−2.2	−7.3	11.1
Abdominal 2	0.2	−7.7	7.4
Hip	4.5	4.2	16.6
Thigh	−7.0	−8.9	14.6
Biceps	−10.8	0.0	31.2
Forearm	−3.4	0.6	20.6
Wrist	8.8	10.8	19.1
Knee	9.3	6.8	14.2
Calf	1.8	0.2	15.0
Ankle	0.7	−0.8	15.3

Components	D	A'	A	B	B'	WFCA	C	LBW
Gain kg	17.5	14.6	15.5	20.8	19.8	19.0	20.5	17.6

[a]*Square root of the percentage increase.*

weight boy have been converted to d quotients and the deviations of these quotients from the respective D axes at 14.2 and 16.7 years form the pattern outlines in the somatogram (Fig. 5.10). The reference k values are the mean proportions for 17-year-old Caucasian boys. The examinee is, by definition,

PARAMETERS

PERCENTAGE INCREASE DURING GROWTH
OF AN UNDERWEIGHT ADOLESCENT

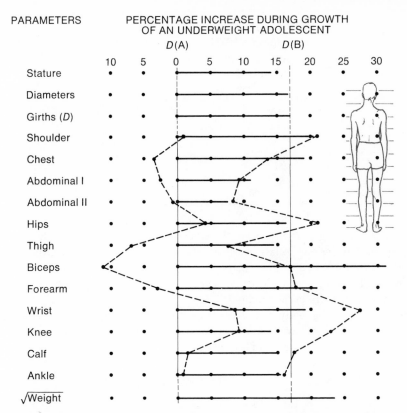

Fig. 5.10 Change in shape during growth of an underweight boy from (left) 14.2 yrs; weight: 34.8 kg; stature: 15.63 dm; D(A) = 4.43; to (right) age 16.7 yrs; weight: 53.0 kg; stature: 17.77 dm; D(B) = 5.18 (see Table 5.20).

underweight, in that lean body weight calculated from six diam and stature is greater than body weight. This follows from the high Bi-metric/Perimetric (B/P) ratio of 28.69 for this examinee compared with the *LBW* conversion constant of 28.0 employed in the Berkeley N-A Survey. For the reference man, $K(LBW)$ is 27.8, which would render lean body weight for the examinee even higher. At age 16.7 years, lean body weight (54.8) is still somewhat higher than body weight (53.0 kg).

The effect of weight-lifting exercise to develop arms and shoulders is observed in the somatogram and in the accelerated percentage increase of biceps girth.

3. *Largest boy in the ninth grade.* Compared with the smallest boy, the largest boy (age 14.5 years) weighs more than 100 kg (220 pounds) and is 48.4 cm (19.1 inches) taller. His ponderal unit size ($uS\!-\!W$) is 167, which is 67% greater than $uS\!-\!W$ (reference man) scaled to 100 for all statures. The square root of $uS\!-\!W$ is 129.2, which is nearly identical with 128.6 for $uS\!-\!D$

(unit perimetric size). On the other hand, $uS–D(C)$, which is unit bi-metric or frame size, is much lower (107.4), in support of predominance of soft tissue over skeletal mass. The following data give a comparison of size modules of the three adolescents.

Size Modules		Small Male Type	Underweight Male Type	Overweight Male Type
$uS–W$		60.0	59.7	167.0
$\sqrt{uS–W}$		77.5	77.3	129.2
$uS–D$		78.1	77.9	128.2
$uS–D(C)$		78.4	85.1	107.4
Reference Man	100			

The somatogram (Fig. 5.11) depicts the shape of the overweight boy as he appears to be, i.e., relatively small shoulders and wrists, and large thigh and abdominal girths. The reference proportions (Table 5.21) are the k values of Berkeley N-A Caucasians (age 17.2 years) and are closely identified with those of the reference man.

How does the body pattern of this large boy compare with a cohort group, that is, the heaviest group (Group X) in the weight-ordered series of decile groups? Another set of d quotients were calculated from the k values

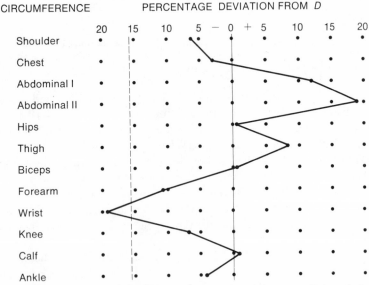

Fig. 5.11 Shape of the largest boy in Berkeley N-A Survey (9th-12th grades). Age: 17.4 yrs; weight: 141.8 kg; stature: 18.97 dm; $D = 8.30$; D(Diam.) = 7.05 (– – – vertical).

Table 5.21

GROWTH OF THE LARGEST BOY IN THE NINTH TO TWELFTH GRADES
(BERKELEY N-A SURVEY)

	9th Grade	12th Grade	Group X^a
Age	14.5	17.4	17.1
Rating	6	6	6
h cm	184.6	189.7	181.5
W kg	129.2	141.8	96.5
1.95 F–$h^{0.7}$	7.99	8.29	6.95
D	7.95	8.30	6.83
6 Diam	174.2	185.0	164.4
6 Diam/D	21.92	22.29	24.07
$\sqrt{uS}$–W	129.2	132.2	113.3
uS–D	128.6	132.4	111.4
uS–$D(C)$	107.4	112.8	102.4
Girths	% *dev.*[b]	% *dev.*[b]	% *dev.*[c]
Shoulder	−8.4	−6.5	−2.6
Chest	−1.6	−3.5	−1.0
Abdominal 1	7.4	12.3	5.9
Abdominal 2	14.9	19.1	8.4
Hip	0.5	0.5	−1.6
Thigh	10.6	8.7	4.5
Biceps	−4.3	0.5	−1.6
Forearm	−10.6	−10.6	−6.0
Wrist	−17.0	−19.3	−11.7
Knee	−4.1	−7.0	−3.8
Calf	3.4	1.0	2.9
Ankle	−0.2	−4.8	0.5
6 Diam/D	−16.5	−15.1	−7.4

[a]*The heaviest group in the longitudinal (Caucasian) series.*
[b]*% deviation from proportions of Caucasian boys, 17.2 years.*
[c]*% deviation from the proportions of Group X.*

of the cohort group, and the percentage deviation of the d derivatives is represented by the horizontal lines in the somatogram. The shape of this large boy deviates appreciably from the mean proportions of his closest cohorts (Table 5.21).

Relative weights (Table 5.22) were calculated for components A, A' B, B', $WFCA$, and C from six diameters. An alignment of these relative weights forms a high to low obesity gradient from A' to C(Ref W). The gain in relative weights from age 14.5 to 17.4 years suggests increasing fatness, but frame size weight has increased as well. This gain may, however, be discounted in part by the overlay of fat on skeletal sites of measurement—notably, chest and pelvis.

What should this obese-muscular boy weigh? The reference (C) weight permits a first approximation but does not allow for better than average muscularity. Since fat accumulation around forearm, wrist, calf, and ankle

Table 5.22

COMPONENT ANALYSIS OF GROWTH DATA PERTAINING TO
THE LARGEST MALE IN THE BERKELEY N-A SURVEY

Age						*Component Weights* (kg)				
Age	*h*	*W*	*D*	*A'*	*A*	*B*	*B'*	*WFCA*	*C*	*LBW*
14.5	184.6	129.2	128	144	137	116	118	113	89.1	78.3
17.4	189.7	141.8	142	163	157	131	124	119	102.5	90.1

			Anthropometric Score[a]				
Age	*D*	*A'*	*A*	*B*	*B'*	*WFCA*	*C*
14.5	—	12.5	7.0	−7.2	−7.8	−11.7	−30.4
17.4	—	14.8	10.6	−7.7	−12.7	−16.2	−27.8

[a]*% deviation of component weights from D weight.*

(*WFCA*) is minimal relative to other girths, we may select as monitor weight $W(WFCA)$, which is 113 kg (age 14.5 years) and 119 kg (age 17.4 years). Another guideline is equivalence of A' and B or B' components. In regulated weight reduction (to be discussed in Chapter 10), relative loss of weight from the trunk (A components) is about twice that from the extremities (B', *WFCA* components). An objective in weight reduction is to normalize A' weight which, in the case of the large boy, is 22 kg greater than $W(D)$ or body weight. If we subtract this excess from $W(D)$, the reduced weight (120 kg) is approximately *WFCA* "monitor" weight. Following loss of 22 kg, a second anthropometric examination and underwater weighing and radiogrammetry provide the definitive data for a statement of "optimal" weight.

Table 5.23

COMPONENT ANALYSIS OF AN ATHLETE (BERKELEY N-A S)

Age	17.7 yrs							
Rating	2.5		*Muscular Scale: Lean to Fat*					
		0	1	2	3	4	5	6
h cm	185.0	Weight kg		88.2		uS–W		113.6
D	6.56	6 Diam		168.4		uS–W		106.6
1.95 F–$h^{0.7}$	6.60	8 Diam		201.4		uS–D		106.0

			Ponderal Equivalents (kg)	*Component Analysis*				
Age	*W*	*D*	*A'*	*B*	*B'*	*WFCA*	*B–B*	*C*
16.7	88.0	87.5	86.0	93.0	90.1	87.9	86.3	80.6
17.7	88.2	87.3	77.7	96.8	90.7	88.1	92.3	82.5
Anthro. Score[a] (age 17.7 yrs)	−		−11	10.9	3.9	0.9	5.7	−5.5

[a]*% deviation of the ponderal equivalents from D weight.*

4. *Adolescent Athlete.* On inspection, the examinee was rated 2.5 (lean-fat scale), and accorded a "star" for muscularity. However, the tabular data (Table 5.23) and somatogram (Fig. 5.12) are pallid compared with the

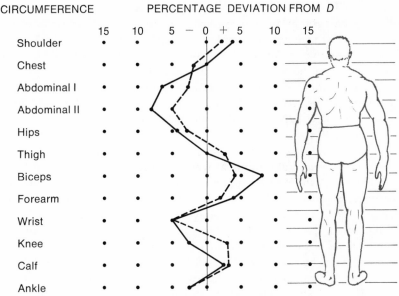

CIRCUMFERENCE   PERCENTAGE DEVIATION FROM *D*

Fig. 5.12 Somatogram of outstanding muscular development in an adolescent male from age 16.7 yrs (broken line) to age 17.7 yrs; weight: 88.2 kg; stature: 18.50 dm; *D* = 6.56

photograph as representation of exceptional muscularity. Measurements made one year apart at ages 16.7 and 17.7 have been converted to ponderal equivalents which can be related to age, stature, scale weight, and *uS–W*.

Age	h	W	uS–W	A'	B	B'	B–B	C
16.7	183.1	88.0	115	87.5	93.0	90.1	86.3	80.6
17.7	185.0	88.2	114	77.7	96.8	90.7	92.3	82.5
				−8.3	3.8		6.0	1.9

After a year-long physical development program, there was loss of fat from *A'*, gain in muscle (presumably in the enlargement of *B* and *B–B* components), a slight increase in stature, and no increase in body weight. A presumptive estimate of "excess" muscle is 9.5 kg (age 17.7)—the difference between *B* and the average of *B* and *A'* (= 87.3 kg). Lean body weight (from eight diameters and *h*) is 73.3 kg; corrected lean body weight is 73.3 plus excess muscle, which is 82.8 kilograms.

Body Composition

Berkeley N-A Survey

The body has been described in terms of size and shape. In the following paragraphs another approach is outlined in the effort to quantify muscle and fat content and to relate the anthropometric "surface" findings to more definitive results obtained from body density and potassium determinations. Total body potassium was assessed from gamma emission of the minute amount of ^{40}K (the only naturally present radioisotope in the body) measured by Dr. Robert Martin in the 2 pi heavily shielded "human counter" at the U.S. Naval Radiological Defense Laboratory, San Francisco (see Chapter 2, page 33).

The results bring together three independent parameters for assessment of lean body weight and minimal weight (females) of 89 boys and 93 girls (age 16 years) who participated in the Berkeley survey. It was this multi-parameter approach in 1963 which bolstered the validity of the densitometric technique for estimation of lean body weight in the female, as well as the significance of the entity, *Minimal weight*. In the female, as previously mentioned, values higher than 1.080 are seldom encountered. Four of Wilmore's leanest females had less than 7% fat ($\cong 1.083$ density). To the following densitometric data obtained on the leanest subject, we have added anthropometric lean body weight, minimal weight, and reference weight.

h	W	$Density$	$\% Fat$	LBW	LBW^a	$Min\ W^a$	$Ref\ W^a$
166.8	43.2	1.086	5.7	40.8	38.0	46.1	53.5

^{a}*Anthropometric from eight diameters and h; K(LBW), 36.0; K(Min W), 33.5; and K(Ref W), 31.1. The constant 33.5 (K, Min W) in the female, converts the eight diameters to LBW (anthro.) in the male.*

Table 5.24

BODY COMPOSITION DATA PERTAINING TO BERKELEY ADOLESCENTS
(N-A S), AGE 16 YEARS

	N	h	v^a	W	v^a	Lean Body Weight			Coefficients Variation^a		
						Anthro.	^{40}K	Sp. Gr.	Anthro.	^{40}K	Sp. Gr.
Males											
Caucasian	54	174.1	3.6	64.6	19.1	55.7	54.7	55.5	13.5	13.1	14.8
Negro	24	175.4	4.7	71.2	19.2	56.1	59.6	59.2	10.6	13.5	15.3
Oriental	11	166.1	4.2	56.0	15.9	50.0	51.0	50.9	13.8	13.9	12.4
Females											
Caucasian	59	164.7	3.9	57.0	15.1	41.6	41.3	41.2	11.3	14.0	14.4
Negro	25	162.8	2.8	59.7	21.0	42.0	42.2	42.7	11.9	11.8	15.8
Oriental	9	158.1	3.8	48.5	9.9	37.7	35.0	37.0	6.5	4.9	9.2

^{a}*Coefficients of variation: $\sigma/mean \times 100$.*

TABULAR DATA AND COMMENTS. In Table 5.24, are mean values for lean body weight computed from six diameters and stature, from ^{40}K, and from specific gravity. The anthropometric conversion constants were 27.8 (male, lean body weight), 29.84 (Caucasian and Oriental females, lean body weight), and 29.48 (Negro females), for six diameters (4 TD, wrists, ankles) and stature. Lean body weight (^{40}K) was computed from total potassium gm/2.46 (males) and total potassium gm/2.28 (females).

Lean body weight (specific gravity) was calculated from the abridged Rathbun-Pace formula,

$$\% \text{ Fat} = \frac{1.100 - \text{Sp. Gr.}}{0.002}$$

The percentage of body fat calculated from density (specific gravity—0.005) water temperature, 31°–32° C., by substitution in Siri's equation is interchangeable with that calculated from the above-stated formulation.

Table 5.25

COMPARISON OF SCALE WEIGHTS WITH MINIMAL AND
LEAN BODY WEIGHTS OF LEAN GIRLS, AGE 16 YEARS[a]

				Lean Body Weights *kg*		
	h	*W*	*Minimal W*	*Anthro.*	^{40}K	*Density*
	Caucasian					
	158.6	57.6	47.0	40.8	34.7	36.0
	167.7	56.6	50.1	43.5	45.0	44.8
	173.4	56.2	56.4	48.9	43.7	42.4
	174.0	54.1	51.4	44.6	40.8	41.7
	169.8	52.7	49.7	43.1	34.4	39.5
	174.9	51.7	49.7	43.1	41.4	39.0
	167.9	46.7	46.3	40.2	38.5	39.0
	159.0	41.8	42.1	36.5	34.9	32.0
	153.9	40.5	36.5	31.7	29.2	28.6
average	169.9	49.1	47.4	41.2	36.1	37.4
	Negro					
	162.8	51.9	50.1	44.5	41.4	44.4
	166.2	43.6	43.8	38.9	36.8	34.6
	160.3	43.7	40.9	36.3	39.3	34.1
	160.1	41.1	37.5	33.3	37.1	35.7
	161.2	47.2	40.7	36.2	36.5	38.2
average	162.1	45.5	42.6	37.8	38.2	37.4
	Japanese (Nisei)					
	163.3	50.3	43.4	37.7	43.6	40.7
	158.3	39.1	39.9	34.6	32.3	34.9
	161.9	50.1	47.3	41.1	39.1	34.4
	156.3	51.2	42.0	36.4	36.2	38.8
	150.7	50.9	42.4	36.8	38.4	42.3
	149.0	57.0	42.4	36.8	29.3	39.1
	158.1	48.5	43.4	37.7	35.0	37.0
average	156.7	49.6	43.0	37.3	36.3	37.7

[a]*Berkeley N–A Survey.*

The coefficients of variation (σ/mean $\times$ 100) for lean body weight calculated for the several parameters are in the usual range of 10 to 14%, if we exclude the small sample of Oriental girls. There is good agreement for the three racial groups in mean values for lean body weight (male) with the exception of the lower value of 56.1 lean body weight (anthro.) for the Negro, accounted for, in part, by the conversion constant (27.8, reference man). The racial difference in bi-iliac width requires a somewhat lower constant for Negroes compared with that for Caucasians and Orientals. The female anthropometric data were corrected for the racial difference.

In Table 5.25, minimal and lean body weights were calculated for Caucasian, Japanese (Nisei), and Negro girls (age 16). The same conversion constant (27.8) which was employed for the calculation of male lean body weight for the three races was used in the calculation of all female minimal weights. Scale weights may approach equality with minimal weights, but there are generally wide differences (in contrast to male weights), between

Table 5.26
COMPARISON OF SCALE WEIGHTS WITH LEAN BODY WEIGHTS OF BERKELEY MALE ADOLESCENTS

		Lean Body Weights kg			
h	*W*	*Anthro.*	^{40}K	*Density*	*Density*
Caucasian (Age 14–15 yrs)[a]					
167.5	53.5	51.5	—	53.5	1.110
167.6	57.4	50.8	—	57.4	1.110
171.7	58.3	58.3	—	53.2	1.109
[b]184.1	65.5	67.3	—	65.5	1.102
[b]189.5	70.0	68.8	—	70.0	1.101
Caucasian (Age 16 yrs)[c]					
176.8	60.9	59.9	55.1	59.4	1.090
185.7	60.8	63.8	53.3	60.8	1.096
169.0	64.0	55.1	62.2	64.0	1.095
Negro (Age 16 yrs)[c]					
151.2	42.3	39.2	38.1	40.6	1.087
184.5	67.5	57.7	64.4	67.2	1.094
174.1	65.0	54.1	61.6	62.7	1.088
186.5	75.3	67.3	70.5	71.5	1.085
170.1	55.3	51.4	52.3	51.2	1.080
Japanese (Age 16 yrs)[c]					
159.4	44.1	43.0	45.3	41.5	1.083
158.5	52.1	53.1	46.9	48.9	1.083
158.8	55.7	49.6	52.0	49.9	1.073
Chinese (Age 16 yrs)[c]					
166.2	56.7	50.3	49.9	52.9	1.081
165.0	53.0	47.7	44.9	49.3	1.080

[a]*Siri determinations in the helium-dilution chamber*
[b]*Brothers.*
[c]*Berkeley N-A Survey. % Fat = (1.100 − Sp. Gr.)/0.002*

scale weight and lean body weight determined from density, ^{40}K, and frame (diameter) size. The data are to be viewed as good approximations obtained in routine examination without repeated trials, and are of value chiefly because of the correctness of the conversion constants.

MALE *LBW* RELATIVE TO SCALE WEIGHT. In contrast to females, the weights of the leanest males (Table 5.26) are not consistently different from lean body weight estimated from specific gravity, ^{40}K, or the anthropometric diameters. Occasionally density will be higher than 1.100 in young males. Thus, at age 16, eight out of 19 examinees had body densities in the range of 1.100 to 1.110 as ascertained by Dr. Siri in rigidly controlled helium chamber technique.

CORRELATIVE RESULTS. The correlation between lean body weight ascertained from several parameters applies to a subsample (30 boys, 30 girls) on whom plethysmographic studies were made of residual air and other fractions of lung volume.

LBW			*30 Males*		*30 Females*	
Specific gravity	^{40}K	r	.938	r	.745	
			89 Males		*93 Females*	*S.E. of est.* ($\pm kg$)
Specific gravity	^{40}K	r	.88		.89	M 3.8 F 2.7
Specific gravity	Anthro.	r	.86		.86	M 3.9 F 2.8
^{40}K	Anthro.	r	.80		.83	M 4.7 F 3.3

Although muscle mass may be a highly variable fraction of *LBW* in the female, it was not possible to separate technical error from morphologic variation in this analysis. The primary purpose has been served in the establishment of near identity of mean values of lean body weight assessed by three independent techniques. The same constant (density: 1.100) for the lean body mass appears to be applicable both to males as well as females.

CORROBORATIVE DATA: ^{40}K AND DENSITY. In a fundamental investigation by Myhre and Kessler (92), body fat of 100 males in the age range of 15 to 87 years was estimated from body density (underwater weighing) and ^{40}K counting in a 4-pi liquid scintillation chamber. The correlation in estimate of body fat by the two methods was 0.87, comparable to that of the Berkeley study. However, the ^{40}K method produced absolute values of lean body weight higher than those obtained densitometrically in 82 out of 100 subjects. The conversion constant, total potassium in mEq to *LBW*, 68.1 mEq (2.663 gm) per kg of lean body weight, was deduced by Forbes et al. (56) from data on three cadavers. This constant is substantially higher than 62.9 mEq (2.46 gm) per kg of lean body weight in the Berkeley study and an earlier consummate investigation in man and the rodent by Talso et al. (128). In an analysis of protocol data kindly made available by Drs. Myhre and Kessler, it appears that the use of a lower constant (e.g., 2.46 gm potassium per kg of *LBW*) brings about rather good agreement in densitometric and ^{40}K estimates of lean body weight (Table 5.27). A rounded value of 2.5 gm

Table 5.27

CALCULATIONS OF LEAN BODY WEIGHT FROM DENSITOMETRIC
AND ^{40}K DATA, MALES[a]

Number	Age Range	h	W	LBW[b]	LBW[c]	LBW[d]	LBW[e]
					Lean Body Weights		
17	15–17	177.4	68.0	60.8	60.7	59.8	59.2
23	18–23	180.1	75.7	69.3	69.2	66.6	66.1
24	24–34	179.0	77.2	64.5	64.4	63:3	63.4
16	40–48	177.0	81.0	65.5	65.3	62.4	62.9
12	50–58	172.2	84.3	62.4	62.2	60.7	62.3
8	60–87	168.6	66.5	45.7	45.6	49.9	50.9

[a]*Protocol data from Myhre and Kessler (92) as analyzed in this chapter.*
[b]*LBW (kg) = Total potassium gm/2.46.*
[c]*LBW (kg) = 2 × muscle mass, muscle mass is 69% K/3.4*
[d]*LBW (kg) from % Fat = (1.100 − Sp. Gr.)/0.002*
[e]*LBW (kg) from % Fat = 457.0/d_{body} − 414.2 (Brŏzek et al., 37).*

of potassium per kg of lean body weight would have brought the lean body weight (^{40}K) data in even better accord with lean body weight (males) computed from densitometric formulas.

In addition, lean body weight was approximated as twice muscle mass (i.e., $LBW = 2 \times$ muscle mass) where muscle mass is estimated from total body potassium in the manner described in the next paragraph. Prominent in Table 5.27 is the relative loss of potassium in the oldest age group. This loss is evident in the much lower LBW (^{40}K) than in lean body weight determined by densitometry.

RETROSPECTIVE VIEW OF BODY POTASSIUM. Potassium is chiefly intracellular (about 98%) and opens a pathway to an estimate of "active protoplasmic mass." Moore and his co-workers (89) have outlined the premises of this patently rewarding field, and the reference constant of 150 mEq of potassium per liter of intracellular water is a highly useful deduction from their analyses. Thus, if the cell mass is two-thirds water, then, as a general approximation, 100 mEq (3.91 gm) of potassium may be allotted to each kg of cell mass. If to this mass is added extracellular fluid (ECF), and if the cell mass plus ECF consists of about 79% water (supported by the studies of Allen et al., 3) there will be about 3.24 gms of potassium per kg in the combined entity.

If, as a rounded number, 70% of the body's store of potassium is in muscle, then

Muscle Mass (kg) = 0.70 Total Body K/3.4

A concentration of 3.4 gm (87 mEq) of potassium per kg of muscle is tantamount to 116 mEq of potassium per liter of muscle water on the analytical basis of about 75% as the water content of muscle.

Lean body weight can be estimated correctly only if the cell mass is a biologically constant percentage of lean body weight, as is true for any extrapolation of lean body mass constituents. In those males with highly developed (hypertrophied) musculature, the single constant (2.46 or 2.5 gm potassium/kg lean body mass) cannot be used since excess muscle with its relatively high potassium content (3.4 gm/kg lean body mass) would lead to an everestimate of lean weight. A tri- or multi-dimensional concept of the lean body mass as proposed by Anderson (5) and von Döbeln (136) properly allocates total body potassium to muscle, viscera, and other tissues. Compartmentation of the body, however, is a matter of quantitative assessment and not calculated projection of components.

Nevertheless, we can make an estimate of muscle mass in the following manner without recourse to measurement of creatinine in muscle and viscera.

For this computation, we estimate lean body weight from frame size (i.e., eight diameters and h) and then allocate 2.46 gms of potassium to each kilogram of calculated lean body weight. Then,

$$\text{Excess Muscle} = \frac{\text{Total K} - LBW(\text{anthro.})\text{K}}{3.4}$$

Examples of this elementary calculation follow.

1. *Professional Football Player*
Lean body weight (anthro.) from eight diameters and h = 79.2 kg
Total potassium lean body weight (anthro) = 2.46 × 79.2 = 194.8 gm
Total potassium measured as ^{40}K   274.4 gm
Excess potassium (274.4 − 194.8) = 79.6 gm
Excess muscle (79.6/3.4) = 23.4 kg)
Corrected $LBW = LBW$(anthro) + 23.4 = 102.6 kg
2. *Weightlifter*
Lean body weight (anthro.) = 71.7 kg and potassium in lean body weight
    (anthro.) = 176.4 gm
Total potassium measured as ^{40}K was 213.5 gm
Excess potassium (213.5 − 176.4) = 37.1 gm
Excess muscle (37.1/3.4) = 11 kg
Corrected $LBW = LBW$(anthro.) + 11 kg = 82.7 kg

ESTIMATE OF MUSCULAR MASS IN THE FEMALE. Assessment of mean muscle mass in the young adult female is restricted because of meager data. The following compilation is from the Berkeley N-A Survey and from Los Alamos as reported by Allen, Anderson, and Langham (2) for females whose total body potassium was determined in a 4-pi liquid scintillation counter which has served well as a standard of reference.

Berkeley N-A S	*h*	*W*	*Total K*	*Muscle*	*LBW(^{40}K)*
			gm	kg	kg
59 females (age 16.2 years)	164.7	57	94.2	19.4	41.3[a]
80 females (16–27 years)	—	56.6	99.7	20.5	43.7

[a]*LBW (Sp. Gr.) 41.2 kg, LBW (anthro.) 41.6 kg*

In this tabulation, the constant employed to convert total K_{gm} to LBW_{kg} was 2.28 (i.e., total $K/2.28 = LBW$). This value from the Berkeley survey pertains to a concentration of 81 mEq (comparable to 87.3 mEq in the male) per liter of total body water from data of McMurrey et al. (88). If the lean body mass consists of 72% water ($\cong$ 73% in the fat-free body), then potassium per kg of lean body mass is 58.3 mEq, or 2.28 grams. Certainly the derivation is circuitous, but mean estimates of lean body weight so derived in the Berkeley survey agree closely with densitometric and anthropometric estimates of lean body weight.

Summary

The detailed presentation serves to document relationships heretofore not utilized, and to provide standards for anthropometric reference. Essential in the quantification of body build is dichotomy of body weight into ponderal equivalent girths and stature. Weight therefore has been resolved into a perimetric and a linear component. Comparison of perimetric size of the trunk of the body with that of the extremities evaluates fatness and muscularity.

With reference to diameters, there is remarkable proportionality between frame size and mean weights relative to stature during the growth period from age four years upward. Further, the conversion constants for transformation of diameters into estimates of mean weight are not only altered slightly but are nearly identical for males and females.

Body composition data obtained on University of California (Berkeley) students which Wilmore has analyzed, and similar data pertaining to Berkeley adolescents lend additional support to the feasibility and accuracy of underwater weighing for routine estimate of body fat. The multi-parameter evaluation (anthropometric, densitometric, and kaliometric) of Berkeley adolescents provides assurance that lean body weight in the female can be calculated without alteration of constants (d_{lean} 1.100, d_{fat} 0.90) by substitution in the same hyperbolic formulation applicable to the male.

A substantial contribution in this chapter are data supporting the complementary relationship between lean body weight in the male and minimal weight (certainly not lean body weight) in the female. This relationship, as shown in Fig. 5.13, indicates that various parameters are interchangeable or directly comparable between lean body weight (male) and minimal weight (female). If the seemingly high estimate of essential fat in the female is 14% of minimal weight, it follows that excess of storage fat is the same in terms of percentage in the reference man and woman, despite the wide difference in total content of body fat.

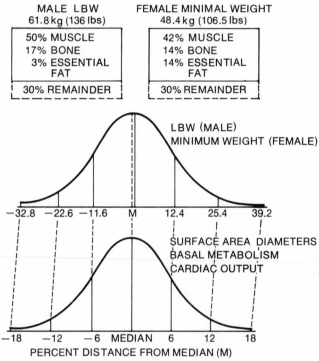

Fig. 5.13 Upper diagrams outline the gross composition of the lean body mass in males and the structural counterpart, minimal weight mass, in the female. The lower curves indicate that for comparable statures, values of *LBW* (male) and minimal weight (female) at the same relative position on the Gaussian curve are related by identical conversion constants to such parameters as frame size, basal metabolism, and cardiac output (Fig. 4, p. 30, in *Obesity*, edited by Nancy Wilson, courtesy of F.A. Davis Co., Philadelphia, Ref. 21).

Chapter 6 / Overweight and Underweight

Orientation

OVERWEIGHT AND DISEASE. Obesity acquired in adult life is a major clinical problem in industrialized countries with a high standard of living. In childhood the proclivity toward obesity may be determined largely by genetic traits and augmented by improper diet and lack of exercise. Insurance companies report greater mortality ratios for overweight than for underweight individuals. The mortality, for example, after the age of 35 may be 30 to 40% higher for obese persons than for individuals in the minimal weight category. The overweight are more prone to die from diabetes, cardiovascular–renal disease, and cirrhosis of the liver. However, in the insurance data a separation has not been made between overweight as an expression of frank obesity and overweight due to large bone structure and heavy muscle mass. Chapter 1 pointed out that the lean individual of small size has a greater surface area, a higher basal metabolism, and larger caliber blood vessels per unit of lean body mass than the large-sized person. This superior morphologic endowment raises the question whether or not any undesirable attributes attach to underweight in the healthy person.

We will consider two primary subdivisions often confluent, namely, hypertrophy of muscular tissue (and probably increase in bone mass), and the far more common condition of overweight due to fatness. The third category, which is less amenable to facile evaluation, relates to the muscular athlete or workman (as the longshoreman) who acquires progressive fat layering with age. The advantages of muscular hypertrophy relative to strength, as demonstrated notably in increased world shotput records, and to storage protein available in illness, are obvious. But there is a vexing and unanswered question: Is the weight-lifter or football player who acquires 10 to 15 kg of hypertrophied muscular tissue (augmented at times with anabolic adjuvants) subject to the same physical impairments which attend accumulation of equal quantities of fat tissue? One major difference between excess fat and excess muscle (which will be considered in Chapter 10) is the heavy insulin drain imposed by fat.

To analyze overweight we need to consider standard height–weight tables, which can be greatly simplified if restricted to weights of young adults. Such mean weights contain about 12% body fat in the male and approximately 25% in the female.

Height-Weight Tables

MALE WEIGHTS. In Table 6.1, mean weights relative to stature are in three columns. Weights in column 1 have been calculated from our

Table 6.1

STANDARD WEIGHTS FOR YOUNG ADULT MALES

Stature (inches)	Calc. Mean Weights (lbs) $(1)^a$	$(1a)^b$	Age	Military Mean Weights $(2)^c$	$(3)^d$	Military $\pm$ Dev. from Mean Weights -1.645σ $(4)^e$	$+1.645\sigma$ $(5)^e$
78	192	—	—	193	153	244
76	184	22	—	184	146	233
75	180	22	179	180	143	227
74	176	22	175	176	139	222
73	172	22	171	172	136	217
72	168	23	167	168	133	211
71	164	24	164	164	130	207
70	160	25	160	160	127	202
69	156	25	156	156	124	197
68.5^a	154^a					
68	152	25	152	153	121	192
67	148	25	148	149	118	188
66	144	26	144	145	115	183
65	141	26	141	142	113	179
64	137	25	137	139	110	175
63	134	25	133	136	107	171
62	130	—	129	132	105	167

^{a}Mean W (lbs) = $0.1166h^{1.7}$ (inches); mW (kg) = $0.545h^{1.7}$ (dm).
^{b}Age relative to mean W from Equitable Assurance Tables, 1940.
^{c}From Newman (cited in 65), Army Separatees (1946), age 20 years.
^{d}From Karpinos (72), Army Registrants (1943), age 25–29 years.
^{e}Range of weights from 10th to 90th percentile (Karpinos, 72).

derivation,

Mean weight $= 0.1166\ h^{1.7}$, W in pounds, h in inches.

In column 1a tabulates the ages which apply to the stature-specific mean weights in the Equitable Life Assurance Tables (1940). In column 2 are weights from Newman (93) for Army Separatees (age 20) in 1946. In column 3 are weights from Karpinos (72) for Caucasian registrants for the draft ($\cong$ 96,000) in 1943–1944. These weights derived for the age group (25–29) may be regarded as representative of all white registrants in this age group,

Log $W = a + b\ h$, a is Log 1.48355, b is 0.01029, and h is height in inches.

In columns 4 and 5 are values from Karpinos of ± 1.6449 standard error of estimate which embraces the range of 10 to 90%, respectively, of the population around the mean.

In Table 6.2 are weights for the 5 (-2σ), 10(-1.65σ), 90 $(+1.65\sigma)$,

Table 6.2

PROJECTED DISTRIBUTION OF STANDARD WEIGHTS
FOR YOUNG ADULT MALES

2.0	1.65	1.65	1.0	(−) S.D. (+)	1.0	1.65	1.65	2.0
2.3	5	5	16	*Percentile*	84	95	95	97.7
				% Dev. from				
25	21	—	(6.7ᵃ)	*Mean Weight*	(7.5ᵃ)	—	26	32

			h	*m Weight*				
Calc.	*Calc.*	*Kᵇ*	*(inches)*	*(lbs)*	*Kᵇ*	*Calc.*	*Calc.*	
144	152	153	78	192	244	242	253	
138	145	146	76	184	233	232	243	
132	139	139	74	176	222	222	232	
126	133	133	72	168	211	212	222	
120	126	127	70	160	202	202	211	
			68.5ᶜ	154ᶜ				
114	120	121	68	152	192	192	201	
109	115	115	66	145	183	183	192	
103	108	110	64	137	175	173	181	
98	103	105	62	130	167	164	172	

ᵃ*% deviation of F at ±1σ(F = $\sqrt{W/h}$), refer to text.*
ᵇ*From Karpinos (72), Caucasian registrants (1943), age 25–29 years.*
ᶜ*Mean weights calculated from: W(lbs) = 0.1166h¹·⁷, h in inches. The constant (0.1166) was derived from the single pair of underlined values. Metric weights: W (kg) = 0.545h¹·⁷, h in dm.*

and 95 $(+2.0\sigma)$ percentiles. These weights were computed on the assumption that the coefficient of variation for the factor F (i.e., $\sqrt{W/h}$) is 7.5% for $(+)$ deviations and 6.7% for for $(-)$ deviations. Then for $(+)\sigma$, % dev. from $mW = mW[(1 + c.v.\ \sigma)^2 - 1]$ and for $(-)\sigma$, % dev. from $mW = mW[(1 - c.v.\ \sigma)^2 - 1]$. It is observed in Table 6.2 that at the 95th percentile $(+2\sigma)$ the weights are 32% greater than middle values, and at the

5th percentile, 25% less than mean weights. At the 10th (-1.65σ) and 90th $(+1.65\sigma)$ the calculated weights are in close agreement with weights recorded by Karpinos for military registrants.

DISTRIBUTION OF PONDERAL EQUIVALENTS. Since $3F$ and D are interchangeable for adults, the weights in Table 6.2 at ± 1.65 and 2.0σ can be replaced by weights calculated from $WFCA$ girths and from diameters. The following estimates are derived from coefficients of variation for $WFCA$ and six diameters (Table 1.2).

2	1	$(-) \sigma (+)$	1	2
% dev.[a]	c.v.		c.v.	% dev.[a]
10.6	5.3	WFCA	7	14
8.8	4.4	6 Diam	5	10
20	10.3	W (WFCA)	14.5	30
16.8	8.6	W (6 Diam)	10.3	21

[a]*% deviation from mean weights*

These data show that the range of the ponderal equivalents, especially W(Diam), is restricted compared with standard weights in Tables 6.1 and 6.2, and the following example is cited.

	-2σ	Mean	$+2\sigma$
W (WFCA)	125	156	203
W (Diam)	130	156	189
Standard	117	156	206

Thus, for a given stature, W(Diam) would tend to be an underestimate of the weight of large men and an overestimate of the weight of small men.

Mean weights (Tables 6.1, 6.2) relative to stature alone, are designated "standard" weights, in contrast to *reference weights* derived from frame size and stature. The central values in the tables incorporate about 12% fat, or slightly higher than the estimate of excess fat in the reference man. The weights in the percentile columns to the right of the mean may likewise comprise the same percentage of fat to merit the designation "normal" weight for young male adults. Thus, an athlete 72 inches tall may be relatively lean at 222 pounds. By contrast, a sedentary person of similar weight may carry a 30% fat burden. This points to the need to separate fat from lean in the overweight, and we have recourse to densitometry and anthropometry for this separation.

MALE LEAN BODY WEIGHTS. In Table 6.3, mean lean body weights relative to increments of stature have been projected from densitometric

Table 6.3

PROJECTED DISTRIBUTION OF LEAN BODY WEIGHTS
FOR ADULT MALES

2.0	1.65	1.0	(−) S.D. (+)		1.0	1.65	2.0	2.58
2.3	5	16	Percentile		84	95	97.7	99
23	19	11.4	% Dev. from Mean LBW[a]		12.4	21	25	33.4
			h (inches)	*m LBW* (lbs)				
131	138	150	78	170	191	206	212	227
125	131	143	76	162	182	195	202	216
119	126	137	74	155	174	187	194	207
114	120	132	72	148	166	178	185	197
109	114	126	70	141	159	170	176	188
106	112	123	69	138	155	166	173	184
			68.5[b]	136[b]				
103	109	118	68	134	151	162	168	179
99	104	113	66	128	144	155	160	171
93	98	107	64	121	136	146	151	161
89	93	102	62	115	129	139	144	153

[a]*Coefficient of variation for F(LBW) was postulated as 6%:*

$$\% \text{ dev. from } m\,LBW = (+) \; m\,LBW[(1 + 0.06\sigma)^2 - 1]$$
$$(−) \; m\,LBW[(1 - 0.06\sigma)^2 - 1]$$

[b]*Mean LBW (lbs) = 0.103h^{1.7} (inches); m LBW (kg) = 0.481h^{1.7} (dm). All calculations of m LBW derive from the constant (0.103) calculated from the underlined values.*

data. The formula

$$m\,LBW = 0.204h^2, \quad h \text{ in dm}$$

has been altered to conform with reference to the power of stature, to the standard weight equation, and,

$$LBW(\text{kg}) = 0.481h^{1.7}(\text{dm}); \quad LBW(\text{pounds}) = 0.103h^{1.7}(\text{inches}).$$

These formulas are applicable for the calculation of adult male lean body weight and not lean body weight during the growth period.

The distribution of lean body weight is predicated on a coefficient of variation for $F(LBW)$ of 6%—somewhat higher than a coefficient of variation for frame (diameter) size (i.e., about 5%) and lower than a coefficient of variation for the *WFCA* girths. Percentage deviation from the mean was computed from the formulas in a footnote to Table 6.3, and extrapolation was made to the 99th percentile to embrace lean body weight of present day professional football players (last column in the table). However, lean body weights for those athletes reported by Wilmore in Chapter 7 exceed those in the table in some cases by a considerable margin.

Female Weights. Three categories of mean weights have been calculated for adult females: (1) standard, (2) minimal, and (3) lean body weight. The standard weights are representative of those for young women and reflect actuarial weight–height standards of 1940. These weights can be computed from the same type of formula applicable to the male, with alteration only in the constants.

Standard W(pounds) $= 0.1049h^{1.7}$(inches); W(kg) $= 0.49h^{1.7}$(dm).

Two additional elementary formulations serve as well.

Mean W(pounds) $= 4x - 135$, for stature (x) 65 inches

and above; Mean W(pounds) $= 3x - 70$ for stature (x) less than 65 inches. Minimal weights (pounds) were computed from

$0.893h^{1.7}$(inches); in kg, from $0.417h^{1.7}$(dm).

Minimal weight in the female is tantamount to lean body weight in the male (Chapter 4). For the reference woman, stature 64.5 inches (163.8 cm), minimal W is 106.5 pounds (48.4 kg). This value was calculated from the sum of eight diameters (reference woman) divided by 33.5 which is $K(LBW)$ for the reference man.

Min W(reference woman) in kg $= (173/33.5)^2 \times h_{dm} \times 0.111$.

Table 6.4

MEAN WEIGHTS CALCULATED FOR YOUNG ADULT FEMALES

	1.28	(−) S.D. (+)		1.28	
	10	*Percentile*		90	
		% Dev. from			
	17	*Mean Weight*		20	
Stature (*inches*)		*Standard Weight*[a]		*Minimal Weight*[b]	*LBW*[c]
75	134	162	194	138	122
74	131	158	190	134	120
73	128	154	185	131	117
72	125	151	181	128	114
71	122	147	176	125	111
70	119	144	173	122	109
69	116	140	168	119	106
68	113	137	164	116	104
67	110	133	160	114	101
66	108	130	156	111	98
65	105	127	152	109	96
64.5		125		106.5	94.6
64	102	123	148	105	93
63	100	120	144	102	91
62	97	117	140	100	88
61	95	114	137	97	86
60	92	111	133	94	84

[a]*Standard weight (lbs)* $= 0.1049h^{1.7}$ *(inches), Total fat 27%.*
[b]*Minimal weight (lbs)* $= 0.893h^{1.7}$ *(inches), Total fat 14%.*
[c]*LBW (lbs)* $= 0.794h^{1.7}$ *(inches), Total fat 3%.*

Therefore, for the same frame size and stature, lean body weight in the male is identical with minimal weight in the female.

Lean body weights which females cannot attain in the healthy state, were calculated from LBW (pounds) $= 0.794h^{1.7}$ (inches), LBW (kg) $= 0.417h^{1.7}$ (dm). Lean body weight for the reference woman is 94.6 pounds (43 kg), stature is 64.5 inches (163.8 cm). This mean value, adjusted for stature, is taken from the mean lean body weight of 43.4 kg (h: 164.9 cm) for U.C. Berkeley females (148).

All categories of female weights (Table 6.4) for statures above 70 inches and below 63 inches require confirmation. The distribution of the female standard weights is in accord with the variance projected for the male weights (Table 6.2). Since densitometric data currently are inadequate, no attempt has been made to project minimal or lean body weights for the female. Such weights, however, can be readily approximated from frame size, or from girths of the wrist, forearm, calf, and ankle, in combination with stature.

Overweight Related Primarily to Excess Musculature

BODY BUILD (WEIGHT TRAINING) TYPES. The normal weight of a lean muscular athlete may well exceed 30% of average weight for stature recorded in standard tables. Excess muscle is primarily responsible for the greater lean bulk, but bone also may be ancillary, as revealed by thickened cortex of the long bones in radiography. Weightlifters show some remarkable examples of muscular hypertrophy.

Anthropometric and biochemical–physical data (Table 6.5) describe and quantify this regularly induced alteration of body shape and composition. Composite data are presented for three similar males; for two men who differ markedly in size the data are analyzed individually.

SOMATOGRAM (FIG. 6.1) COMPOSITE DATA. Body enlargement is predominant in the arms and appreciable in shoulder, chest, and knee girths. On the negative side of the vertical axis are the abdominal girths and those of hips, thigh, calf, wrist, and ankle. Since gluteal musculature apparently does not hypertrophy during the course of weight training, we may make a presumptive estimate of body weight prior to training calculated from the ponderal equivalent of hip girth. This perimeter of all the girths has the highest correlation with body weight ($r \cong .93$); the correlation is appreciably higher when hip c, combined with stature h, is converted to a ponderal equivalent. In Table 6.5, W(hips), is 72.3 kg and scale (body) weight minus W(hips) gives a presumptive estimate of excess muscle (i.e., as a result of hypertrophy) of 8.1 kilograms. Total potassium ($K_e = 185$ gms) may be

Table 6.5   ANTHROPOMETRIC AND BIOCHEMICAL–PHYSICAL DATA PERTAINING TO WEIGHT LIFT EXAMINEES

| | Age | h | W | St.W^a | uS–W^b | A' | Biceps | Ponderal Equivalents^c (kg) | | | | | |
								B	B'	WFCA	B–B	C	Hip
Composite^d	26	175.7	80.4	71	113	74	105	94	90	86	90.7	—	72.3
WS	39	179.5	103.6	74	140	98	144	110	97	89	95	83	87
B	30	172.7	86.1	69	125	83	107	92	82	82	84	79	72.1

| | Biochemical-Biophysical Data | | | | Lean Body Weight (kg)^e | | | | |
	Total Body Water kg	Total Potassium K_e (gm)	^{40}K	Density	(1)	(2)	(3)	(4)	(5)
Composite^d	51.4	185	194	1.081	71.4	74.8	73.2	72.9	—
WS	—	—	213.5	1.065	—	88.2	—	83.2	71.7
B	53	185	196	1.078	73.6	72.9	73.3	73.2	69.9

^{a}Standard weight = 0.545h$^{1.7}$ (dm).

^{b}uS–W (Unit size–weight) = 183.6W/h$^{1.7}$, W in kg, h in dm.

^{c}A'(Abdominal average + Hip c). B (shoulder/4, biceps, forearm, calf c), B–B (shoulder/4 or bideltoid, and bitroch. widths), C (eight diameters).

^{d}Composite comprises three weight lift trainees of similar build.

^{e}LBW: (1) TBW, (2) density, (3) combined TBW and density (Siri), (4), K_2 or ^{40}K, (5) Anthro. (eight diameters).

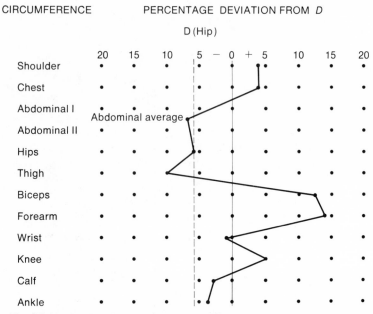

CIRCUMFERENCE   PERCENTAGE DEVIATION FROM *D*

D (Hip)

Fig. 6.1 Somatogram of composite weight lift exercise group. Age: 26 yrs; weight: 80.4 kg; stature: 17.57 dm. $D = 6.50$. D(Hip) is projected as body D prior to muscular training.

allocated to excess muscle and to muscle present prior to exercise hypertrophy.

Excess muscle K = 27.5 gms (from 8.1 kg × 3.4 gms of K per kg of muscle).

Total K − 27.5 = 157.5 gm ("normal" K content) and "normal" lean body weight may be computed in two ways:

(1) 157.5/2.46 = 64.0 kg, on the assumption that average potassium per kg of lean body weight is 2.46 gm, and

(2) 70% (157.5)/3.4 = 32.4 kg of muscle mass; in this allocation about 70% (or somewhat less) potassium is in muscle and the remainder chiefly in viscera. If the lean body mass of the male normally consists of 50% muscle, then, Composite *LBW* = 2 × 32.4 or 64.8 kg and "Normal" *LBW* (64.8 kg) + 8.1 kg (excess muscle) = 72.9 kg, which represents "corrected" lean body weight. Lean body weight from total body weight and density (Siri's technique and combined equation) is 73.2 kg; excess fat amounts to 7.2 kg, or about 9% of body weight.

The biophysical estimates of excess fat may be compared with those obtained from anthropometry as exemplified by individual data.

Individual Data (WS), somatogram (Fig. 6.2 and 7.2). From Chapter 5, *LBW* (anthro.) × 2.46 = 176.4 gm K and total K (213.5 − 176.4) = 37.1

CIRCUMFERENCE   PERCENTAGE DEVIATION FROM *D*

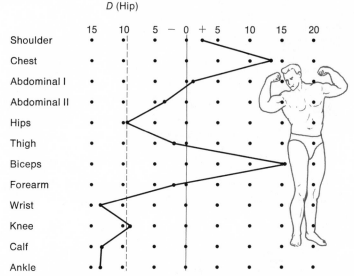

Fig. 6.2 Somatogram of muscular hypertrophy (WS), weight lift exercise. Age: 39 yrs; weight: 103.6 kg; stature: 17.95 dm. *D* = 7.33. *D*(Hip) = 6.62 and is projected as body *D* prior to muscular hypertrophy.

gm. Excess muscle $(37.1/3.4) = 11$ kg, and corrected $LBW = LBW$ (anthro.) $+ 11$ kg $= 82.7$ kg.

A second computation outlined previously follows:

Scale $W(103.6$ kg$) - W$(Hips) $= 16.6$ kg excess muscle and accounts for (16.6×3.4) 56.4 gms of K.

Total K $- 56.4 = 157.1$ gms of normal K and Normal $LBW = (157.1/2.46) = 63.9$ kg.

Corrected $LBW = (63.9 + 16.6) = 80.5$ kg compared with an earlier estimate by Behnke and Royce (26) of 86.8 kg (LBW) in which K was not partitioned between normal LBW and excess muscle.

Individual Data (B), somatogram (Fig. 6.3, 4.2).

Scale W (80.5 kg when Hip girth was measured) and W(Hips), 72.1 kg, then scale $W - W$(Hips) $= 8.4$ kg of excess muscle. K in excess muscle $= 28.6$ gms. Total $K_e(185$ gm$) - 28.6$ gm $= 156.4$ gms.

Normal muscle $= 70\%$ $(156.4)/(3.4) = 32.2$ kg and Normal $LBW = (2 \times 32.2) = 64.4$ kg.

Corrected $LBW = 64.4 + 8.4 = 72.8$ kg

LBW $(TBW$, density, Siri) $= 73.3$ kg.

The close agreement between various estimates of lean body weight for WS and B is undoubtedly fortuitous; further comments regarding these examinees are pertinent. At the age of 27 (prior to "body building") WS weighed 177 pounds (80.5 kg). Subsequently, during the course of weightlift exercises,

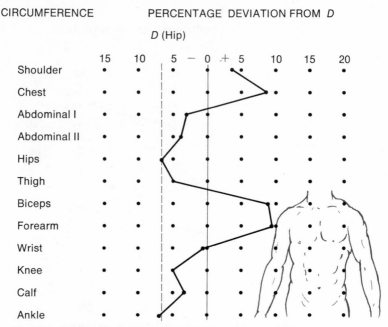

CIRCUMFERENCE   PERCENTAGE DEVIATION FROM *D*

D (Hip)

Fig. 6.3 Somatogram of muscular hypertrophy (B), weight lift exercise. Age: 30 yrs; weight: 79.0 kg; stature: 17.40 dm. *D* = 6.51. *D*(Hip) = 6.11 and is projected as body *D* prior to muscular hypertrophy.

he gained 27 pounds and became a highly rated competitor in Mr. Universe contests. At a weight of 204 pounds (92.7 kg) he felt that he had reduced to minimal fat. Gain in weight from 93 kg to his current weight of 103.6 kg is largely fat as estimated from the reviewed specific gravity and ^{40}K data (i.e., $LBW = 88.2$ kg).

It is evident that in the heavily muscled man, the single conversion constant (e.g., 2.46 gm potassium per kg of lean body weight) will give an overestimate of lean body weight. It is correct in principle, as the examples show, to allocate potassium to normal lean body weight (2.46 gm/kg LBW) and to excess muscle (3.4 gms of potassium per kg of muscle).

Examinee B (age 30) was presumably gaining muscle between the biochemical examination by Boling et al. (31), when his weight was 78.6 kg, the densitometric determination (weight, 80.5 kg), and the anthropometric examination when his scale weight was 86.1 kg. The ponderal equivalent, W(Hips) of 72.1 was calculated from hip girth when body weight was 80.5 kg.

OVERWEIGHT IN MALES OF ATHLETIC BUILD. The military's rejection of the overweight athlete in World War II in part stimulated the densitometric studies of professional football players. Table 6.6 gives examples of athletic

Table 6.6

OVERWEIGHT IN MALES OF ATHLETIC BUILD

| | | | | | | | | | *Ponderal Equivalents (kg)* | | | | |
Age	h	W	St. W	uS–W	A′	Biceps	Hips	B	B′	WFCA	B–B	C
Physical Education Majors												
21	176.1	93.1	72	129	84	110	80	95	79	77	76	80
20	177.8	94.9	73	130	90	104	89	97	90	88	87	79
20	182.7	93.0	76	122	96	94	91	92	86	86	85	83
Athletes (Shot-Put)[a]												
27	188.5	130.0	80	163	133	157	120	146	121	119	117	105
24	194.7	122.8	85	145	125	158	115	134	119	112	114	103

[a]*Second athlete is a former indoor world record holder.*

males whose overweight can be attributed primarily to muscularity and undetermined bone size, but in whom accumulation of fat is apparent. The three physical education majors represent a much larger sample of the primary investigation of Dr. Juno-Ann Clarke at San Francisco State College. These men were generally 20 to 30% over standard weight, as evident in the tabular ($uS-W$) figures, and considerably above frame size (Ref C) weight. Muscular development of the arm is reflected in the high W(Biceps) values for the first two examinees. General muscular development (with the exception of the thigh) is assessed from preponderance of the B component (shoulder/4, biceps, forearm, calf) over A' (Abdominal average, hips), or body weight. Relative fatness is evident in preponderance of A' (trunk) over B' (extremity) girths, which amounts to 10 kg for the third physical education examinee.

In the two exceptional athletes in the shot-put (Table 6.6) who are grossly overweight by standard tables ($uS-W$ 163 and 145; standard $= 100$), W(Biceps) and $W(B)$ are predominant compared with $W(A')$ and scale weight. However, initial fatness appears in the somewhat higher $W(A')$ compared with $W(B')$ relative weights. There are obvious limitations in the attempt to differentiate fat from lean tissue by means of anthropometer and tape measure. These restrictions contrast to the definitive densitometric data from Wilmore and radiography of the arm, as advanced by Carlstein's technology.

		Densitometric		Radiogrammetric	
h	W		LBW		LBW
cm	kg	% Fat	kg	% Fat	kg
188.5	130.0	21.7	101.8	20.4	103.5
194.7	122.8	17.8	101.0	17.1	101.8

The scale weight of the second athlete is about eight to ten kg lower at the peak of training. Without recourse to specialized techniques, it is evident from the modest bulge (Fig. 6.4) that there is an incipient fat overlay on the massive body build. The "Luxus girdle" can be measured readily as the difference between iliac (skeletal) width, and skin contact (flesh) width. Further, if a broad blade anthropometer is pressed against the iliac crests, the fat overlay can be measured directly on a millimeter scale superimposed on the broad blades. This is a project for follow-up.

LONGSHOREMEN—FAT DOMINANCE VS. MUSCULARITY. Chapter 5 presented some data regarding age changes in these men who are endowed physically for heavy-duty work. A high percentage of the longshoremen in the San Francisco Bay Area are men of powerful build, many of whom, in the older age brackets, have accumulated excess fat during the current era of

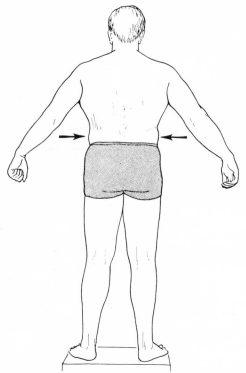

Fig. 6.4 Shot-put athlete. Initial stage of development of a "Luxus Girdle."

automation and curtailed hours of work. Some medical information in connection with a well-documented, ten-year multiphasic follow-up examination (1961) by Borhani et al. (32) is appropriate to interpretation of the anthropometric data. There was no indication of a steady gradient between mortality and degree of overweight in this population. Overweight, however, was deduced from standard height–weight tables, and not from the definitive anthropometric examination for the purpose of assessing fat relative to excess muscularity. The most significant finding in the medical examination was "the positive and sustained association between cigarette smoking and increased risk of mortality from coronary heart disease and all causes, irrespective of other factors such as hypertension and electrocardiographic abnormalities, which are also associated with high mortality" (32).

GROUP DATA—LONGSHOREMEN. Anthropometric data representative of 2300 examinees are aligned in 12 groups in order of descending weight (Table 6.7). The size of the A' (trunk) component measures relative fatness compared with the lean (extremity) components, B', $WFCA$, and the widths $(B–B, C)$. The $B–B$ widths are bideltoid and bitrochanteric; C was limited usually to biacromial, chest, and bitrochanteric widths.

Table 6.7   ANTHROPOMETRIC CHARACTERISTICS OF GROUPS OF LONGSHOREMEN ALIGNED IN WEIGHT ORDER

Group (N = 10 per Group)	Age	h	W	St. W	uS–W	A'	Biceps	Ponderal Equivalents (kg)			
								B'	WFCA	B–B	C
1	55	182.5	131.7	78	175	157	136	109	102	101	99
2	54	177.4	121.9	72	169	128	127	101	97	96	91
3	48	178.6	108.1	73	148	122	110	95	92	93	87
4	47	183.9	106.2	77	138	118	110	96	92	93	90
5	42	182.6	101.3	76	133	108	120	97	91	91	88
6	43	179.2	94.5	74	128	101	109	90	87	88	86
7	42	181.5	86.6	75	115	88	99	85	84	82	75
8	44	177.1	84.6	72	118	89	96	80	78	78	80
9	42	180.7	76.7	75	102	77	85	77	76	76	77
10	73	165.2	60.2	64	94	68	53	55	55	60	61
11	58	173.2	59.9	70	86	63	61	60	60	64	65
12	35	169.2	58.8	67	88	59	62	58	57	61	64

The ponderal equivalent of the single girth (biceps) is a measure of muscularity when corrected for excess fat. Frame size (C) weight is well below scale weight through the sixth group, but in the ninth through twelfth groups, $W(C)$ is equal to or somewhat higher than scale weight. Men in the low weight groups (10, 11, 12) were generally from the clerical force.

INDIVIDUAL DATA—LONGSHOREMEN. The component analysis (Table 6.8) embraces an older, obese–muscular group, and a group of lean–muscular men who are a decade younger. The same anthropometric criteria of fatness and muscularity outlined previously apply to these groups. As individuals become fat, the arm (at least to middle age) enlarges nearly in proportion to the A' trunk girths. If Δ fat (from $W(A')$ — Scale weight) approximates excess fat, then a correction (in the right direction, if not absolute) can be made for arm fat to reveal unemcumbered muscularity. Applied to the data in Table 6.8, this correction reduces W(Biceps) to the size of the relatively lean component, $W(B')$, unless arm musculature is highly developed. Thus, from mean values $(N = 10)$,

$$\Delta \text{ fat } (A' - W) = 25 \text{ kg, and}$$
$$W(\text{Biceps}) - 25 = 111 \text{ kg (mean } W(B') = 109 \text{ kg)}$$

If a "half" correction (i.e., 25/2) is applied to $W(B')$, then $W(B') - 12.5 = 96.5$ kg, which is somewhat less than mean Ref (C) W, which is equal to 99.3 kilograms. This type of correction has some clinical confirmation, as we shall see in connection with dietary-induced weight reduction (Chapter 10) in which relative weight loss from $W(A')$ is about twice that of $W(B')$.

In the lean-muscular longshoremen (Table 6.8), the ponderal equivalents of A', B', and $WFCA$ are on a par with scale weight in contrast with greatly elevated W(Biceps).

TWO UNUSUAL "STRONGMEN." Data in Table 6.9 pertain to an old longshoreman (examinee 10 in Table 6.8) who at the age of 74 (in 1967) may well have been the strongest man in the world at this age in weight lifting events, and to a young weight lifting athlete, age 25. Noteworthy in the older examinee is the exceptional development of the biceps and, by contrast, the much smaller thigh and calf musculature which, together with the hips, shows appreciable decrease from age 70 to 74 years. Presumptive estimates of excess fat are about 10 kg (from W(Hips) $- W(C)$, or $W(A')$ $-$ Scale W), and of excess muscle, 12 to 15 kg from Scale $W - W$(Hips), or $W(B)$ $-$ $W(C)$. The sum of excess fat and muscle (22 to 25 kg) subtracted from scale weight approximates Ref (C) frame size weight.

In the young weight lifter, an estimate of excess fat is 38 kg (from W(Hips) $- W, C$), and excess muscle, 18 kg (from Scale $W - W$, Hips). His large thigh and calf musculature is commensurate with scale weight. Anthropometric comparison of the old and the young strongmen is afforded

Table 6.8   INDIVIDUAL COMPARISON OF OBESE-MUSCULAR AND LEAN-MUSCULAR LONGSHOREMEN

No.	Age	h	W	St. W	uS–W	A'	Biceps	$(R)^a$	B'	WFCA	B–B	C
Obese-Muscular												
1	58	186.7	151	79	191	187	150	114	122	114	126	134
2	48	191.5	137	83	165	157	134	114	114	116	108	100
3	58	181.3	136	75	181	165	134	105	103	97	97	97
4	57	187.6	135	80	169	166	133	102	106	97	94	94
5	47	192.3	128	83	154	143	154	129	121	116	109	103
6	54	184.4	127	77	165	159	132	100	105	96	99	95
7	55	177.1	129	72	179	153	123	99	111	107	89	93
8	54	171.3	129	68	190	155	149	113	106	97	103	90
9	55	180.5	125	74	169	156	116	85	97	90	89	89
10	68	172.5	120	69	174	130	139	129	101	91	97	98
Mean	55	182.5	132	78	175	157	136	111	109	102	101	99
Lean-Muscular												
1	42	181.3	94.3	75	126	97	108	—	96	96	92	87
2	33	186.9	93.2	79	118	93	112	—	96	90	91	93
3	42	181.5	91.4	75	122	95	106	—	95	95	89	85
4	45	180.5	91.4	75	122	90	106	—	88	83	87	82
5	40	176.4	88.0	72	122	89	118	—	88	82	83	81

Ponderal Equivalents (kg)

^{a} Reduced W(Biceps): W(Biceps) − (W(A') − Scale W).

Table 6.9   ANTHROPOMETRIC COMPARISON OF AN OLD AND A YOUNG WEIGHT LIFT STRONGMAN

						Ponderal Equivalents (kg)							
	Age	h	W	A'	Biceps	Hips	Thigh	Calf	B	B'	WFCA	B–B	C
Old	70	172.5	121.4	129	144	112	93	92	114	106	96	104	96
	74	171.5	119.1	127	141	108	83	87	111	105	94	103	99
Young	25	187.0	161.4	162	203	143	175	168	163	135	135	132	105

Percentage Deviation of Dimensions from D Axes

	Head	Neck	Shoulder	Chest	Abdominal 1	Abdominal 2	Hips	Thigh
Old	-18.5	-0.9	-2.6	13.1	15.6	12.3	-4.2	-15.6
Young	-11.2	1.2	-2.8	7.6	14.1	11.5	-4.7	2.8

	Biceps	Forearm	Wrist	Knee	Calf	Ankle	Diameters
Old	10.1	-2.6	-8.7	-2.6	-13.5	-16.6	-7.9
Young	13.5	4.9	-21.5	-19.7	3.1	-19.6	-18.3

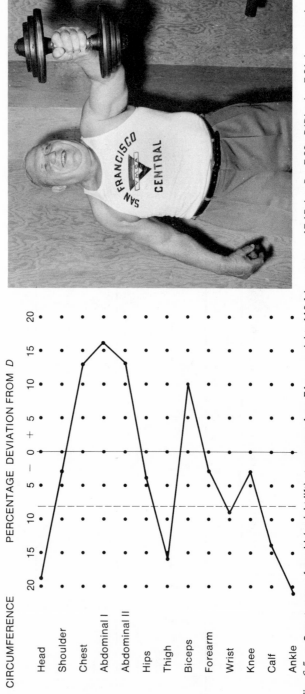

CIRCUMFERENCE   PERCENTAGE DEVIATION FROM D

Fig. 6.5 a. Somatogram of an old (weight lift) strongman. Age: 74 yrs; weight: 119.1 kg; stature: 17.15 dm. $D = 7.83$; D(Diam) = 7.21 (– – – vertical to left of D). b. Karl Norberg, reputedly the strongest old man in the world. At age 50 he began lifting weights, and despite a near-fatal and crippling accident in his 60s he can bench press 405 pounds with his legs elevated, thrust a 100-pound barbell straight forward with the arm fully extended, in standing position. He can hold two 80-pound dumbbells straight out and then elevate them over his head. At his present age (80 yrs) he enjoys excellent health and maintains his ability to bench press 400 pounds. Photograph courtesy and with the permission of the San Francisco Central YMCA.

142

by the percentage deviation of dimensions from respective *D* axes (Table 6.9) and the somatograms (Fig. 6.5, 6.6).

Obesity—The Prime Cause of Overweight

Types of Obesity. The classical experiments of Dr. Jean Mayer (85) have established the multiple etiology of obesity in the small mammal. In regard to man, ". . . while the evidence is neither as complete nor as conclusive as would be desired, indications are that in man, as in experimental animals, genetic traits largely determine, if not obesity, at least potentialities for overeating (or underexercising) and obesity."

Body composition relative to obesity is of special interest in the small mammal. Thus, hereditary obese mice have greater quantities of adipose tissue than weight-matched normal animals, and may have from two to four times more fat than lean siblings maintained on a greater caloric intake. The histologic section of the panniculus adiposus of obese mice contains more numerous and larger fat cells as compared with similar tissue from nonobese littermates (Fig. 6.7).

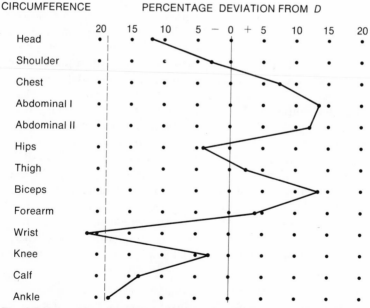

Fig. 6.6 Somatogram of a young (weight lift) strongman. Age: 25 yrs; weight: 161.4 kg; stature: 18.70 dm. *D* = 8.72; *D*(Diam) = 7.12 (– – – vertical to left of *D*).

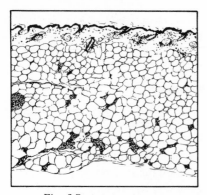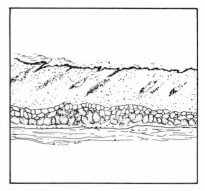

Fig. 6.7 Adipose tissue of panniculus adiposus of obese mice contains more numerous and larger fat cells (left), compared with similar tissue from nonobese littermates (right). (F. Hausberger, *Anat. Rec.,* 135 : 113, Figs. 2A and 23, 1959. Reproduced by permission of author and publisher.)

If certain strains of obese animals are reduced to normal weight by underfeeding, the fat content may still be considerably higher than that of normal animals. However, if certain strains of hereditary obese mice are placed on restricted diets to ensure normal weight, their life span may be normal in contrast to the greatly shortened longevity of animals allowed to become obese.

In man, adolescent (early onset) obesity and maturity onset fattening are well established by images of the "fat boy," on the one hand, and, on the other, the sedentary former athlete at age 40 and older. The difficult problem is the control of obesity in the adolescent without disrupting the normal growth pattern. Unless exercise is combined with judicious dietary regulation, the "reduced" fat boy may look like a somewhat emaciated "Fat Boy." Long-awaited studies by Hirsch and Knittle (69) on the cellularity of obese and nonobese human adipose tissue point to the marked increase in adipose cell number in obesity. Weight loss is achieved by decrease in cell size while cell number remains high. An important consideration in these studies and collateral animal investigation is that early onset obesity may be associated with greater increases in cell number. In the small mammal, underfeeding—but only in early life—can lead to a permanent reduction in the number of adipocytes. The critical importance of dietary regulation in early life will be referred to again in Chapter 10. In the adult during the course of experimental induction of fatness, increase of cell size is adequate to explain fat gain with qualification.

QUANTITY AND COMPOSITION OF ADIPOSE TISSUE. The extensive investigations of Pitts (103, 104) and a subsequent paper by Pitts and his co-workers (105) provide the only substantial data available on the total quantity of adipose tissue in the body. In the guinea pig (normal littermates) fat-free adipose tissue amounts to about 4% of fat-free weight $(F-FW)$ in the male and about 7% of fat-free weight in the female. In a random bred population of guinea pigs, however, there was wide individual dispersion in mass of fat-free adipose tissue relative to fat-free weight in animals reared in the same manner (105).

Adipose tissue free of fat has the gross composition of cellular tissue (i.e., cells plus extracellular fluid) generally in the body, namely, about 79% water and 21% residual solids, chiefly protein. The density of this mass varies with glycogen content and other substances in the approximate range of 1.054–1.060. The ratio of water to residue within the adipocytes tends to be fixed during either fat gain (hypertrophy) or depletion of lipid in fat cells. Random development of new adipocytes (hyperplasia) probably occurs when fat cells normally present attain maximal saturation (about 85%) with triglyceride. The density of human adipose tissue in different sites varies from 0.91 to about 0.96 gm per ml.

MEAN BODY WEIGHTS AND THRESHOLD OF OBESITY. If the assumption (with allowance for wide individual scatter) holds that in man, as in the small mammal, fat-free adipose tissue normally present constitutes about 4 to 4.5% of male lean body weight and 6.5 to 7% of female lean body weight, then estimates can be projected to explain the mean cumulative fat with age in American adults.

INCREASE IN STANDARD WEIGHTS WITH AGE AND FAT GAIN

Reference Male			*Reference Female*
LBW 62 kg 3%		Essential Fat	Minimal *W.* 48.4 kg 14%
	Storage Adipose Tissue (% *saturation*)		
	(*M*)	(*F*)	
Fat-free 2.8 kg +8 kg lipid Standard weight 70 kg (20–24 yrs)	0 74	0 75	Fat-free 2.8 kg +8.4 lipid Standard weight 56.8 kg
+6.4 lipid Standard weight 76.4 kg[a] (over 45 yrs)	84	86	+8.6 lipid Standard weight 65.4 kg[a]

[a]*Weights are from Equitable Life Assurance Tables (1940) for males (69 inches tall), and females (65 inches tall) for ages 45 years and over.*

The tabular data show that when adipose tissue is 75% saturated with lipid, mean body weight is 70 kg (male) and 56.8 (female). When adipose tissue becomes 85% saturated with lipid, mean weight increases to 76.4 kg (male) and 65.4 kg (female). These values approach the anatomic limits for uptake and storage of lipid by adipose tissue normally present in adults. With these considerations in mind, we can postulate that the threshold of obesity is attained when fat storage constitutes about 20% of male weight (lean body weight + 14.4 kg of fat), and 30% of female weight (minimal weight + 17.0 kg of fat). This storage or acquired fat is in addition to "essential" or organ fat (which has never been quantified), approximated as 2 kg in the reference male ($\cong$ 3% lean body weight), and 7 kg in the reference female ($\cong$ 14% minimal weight).

Additional fat gain following saturation of adipose tissue presumably is accompanied by recruitment of new lipocytes (hyperplasia) as in lower animals. This statement is histologically supported by the dissections of Pitts (103, 104) and Pitts et al. (105) which show that with fat gain in obese animals there is a rectilinear increase in water and solids in adipose tissue. We can interpret this increase as consistent with formation of new lipocytes (hyperplasia) and not enlargement (hypertrophy) of existing cells.

EARLY ONSET OBESITY—MALES. The data in Table 6.10 pertain chiefly to obese adolescents in the Berkeley N-A Survey. The following characteristics are typical: abdominal 2 is much larger than abdominal 1, thighs are exceptionally large, and the wrists are proportionately reduced, when the girths are scaled to the proportions of the reference man. Data for single girths are presented for only two examinees—one was the largest adolescent in the Berkeley survey, the other was an older Navy man who was obese from childhood.

The second part of Table 6.10 is a component analysis of data for comparison with similar data in Table 6.8 pertaining to obese–muscular longshoremen. The less well developed biceps, W(Biceps), is evident in the adolescents with the exception of examinees 4, 5, and 7, who have some characteristics of maturity onset fatness. In these three examinees the ponderal equivalent of the lower extremity is not predominant as it is in the other obese youth. W(Hips) and scale weight agree. Excess fat, as previously pointed out, can be approximated from the difference between W(Hips) and $W(C)$, frame size weight.

DATA PERTAINING TO OBESE FEMALES. All of the examinees (Table 6.11) with the exception of number three, are from the Berkeley N-A or Wilmore-Behnke surveys. The fat burden in the first three examinees is undeniably large; in examinee 1, fat(kg) exceeds lean body weight, and weight reduction poses a formidable problem. The second examinee exemplifies the failure to control adolescent fat gain, in her case between ages 14.5 and 16 years.

Examinee 3 acquired excess fat in early adult life. The value for $W(WFCA)$ is of 73 kg, relatively low; the heavy overlay of fat on the shoulders and upper part of the arms (strikingly evident on inspection) contributes substantially to dominance of upper over lower ponderal equivalents.

Table 6.10

ANTHROPOMETRIC CHARACTERISTICS OF EARLY ONSET OBESITY IN MALES

Examinee	Shoulder	Chest	Abdominal 1	Abdominal 2	Hips	Thigh	Biceps	Forearm	Wrist	Knee	Calf	Ankle
					Percentage Deviation of Girths from Their Respective D Axes							
1	-6.1	-3.4	12.1	18.4	-0.5	11.6	-2.6	-11.0	-17.2	-3.0	1.7	-2.0
2	-5.9	1.9	11.2	16.3	-0.7	4.4	-5.3	-9.2	-20.4	2.0	-1.8	-6.2

Examinee	Age	h	W	A'	Biceps	Hips	B'	WFCA	C	LBW^a	Upper Ext.^{b}	Lower Ext.^{c}
				Ponderal Equivalents of Single and Component Girths (kg)								
1	16.4	188.4	135	150	127	133	119	116	97	81.3	111	137
2	33	181.5	121	137	109	120	109	89	—	—	103	121
3	23	177.8	128	151	121	122	95	88	90	69.1	107	98
4	17	184.9	106	119	114	104	87	86	80	69.8	94	95
5	16	178.3	105	111	112	100	94	90	78	74.3	93	100
6	16	167.5	103	113	97	102	86	80	67	62.9	83	107
7	15	175.8	93	104	98	94	82	78	76	62.9	84	84
8	16	166.8	85	97	66	90	74	72	61	55.1	67	85

^{a}LBW(anthro), 1, 4; LBW (^{40}K), 3; LBW (densito.), remaining examinees.
^{b}Weight calculated from shoulder/4, biceps, forearm, wrist girths, and stature.
^{c}Weight calculated from thigh/2, knee, calf, and ankle girths, and stature.

In the remaining examinees, elevation of $W(A')$, the B to C gradient, and the disparity between upper and lower ponderal equivalents are negligible, despite the low densitometric values. However, if allowance is made for essential fat, which amounts to about 14% of reference (C) weight, then the amount of storage fat is not too high. With reference to examinees 4, 5, and 6, for example, relatively lean $W(WFCA)$ is not too divergent from body weight. These university women represent sturdy, well nourished individuals, but for them obesity is a potential rather than actual problem.

Underweight

The designation "underweight" as applied to the healthy person has little meaning. There are many males, particularly during late adolescence, whose body weights are close to lean body weight calculated from skeletal diameters and certainly well below reference (C) or frame size weight. If individuals are undernourished, or if their health is impaired, it is important to ascertain the amount of "fall-off" from frame size weight, as well as the percentages of individuals in the low percentiles of body weight.

Our anthropometric definition of underweight is, for the male, weight which is less than lean body weight calculated from diameters and stature, and, for the female, weight which is less than minimal weight computed in the same manner (i.e., with the same conversion constant) as is lean body weight (anthro.) for the male. A concept reiterated in this monograph is the parallelism between male lean body weight and female minimal weight, as well as the distinction between lean body weight and minimal weight in the female. Minimal weight is greater than lean body weight by reason of sex-specific "essential" fat in mammary glands and other tissues. In contrast to the leanest male, whose body density may be 1.100 or even higher, in the female body density is seldom higher than 1.075, commensurate with little more than 10% fat. A notable exception pertains to Wilmore's densitometric data on champion women distance runners and on a case bordering on anorexia nervosa.

The exceptionally lean female (from Wilmore's survey) weighed 43.2 kg $(h: 166.8 \text{ cm})$ and had only 2.4 kg of body fat (5.7% of weight, density 1.086). Calculated weight from the girths $(D = 4.85)$ and stature was 43.5 kg; minimal weight (from eight diameters and h) was 46.1 kg, and lean body weight (anthro.) was 39.9 kg compared with lean body weight (density) of 40.8 kg. Anthropometric data (examinee 1, Table 6.12) are presented for comparison with similar values pertaining to the leanest females in the Berkeley N-A Survey. The somatogram of examinee 1 (Fig. 6.8) shows the wide deviations from the D axis for the following dimensions:

Table 6.11

ANTHROPOMETRIC CHARACTERISTICS OF OBESE OR LOW DENSITY FEMALES

Examinee	Age	h	W	A'	B^a	WFCA	C	$Upper^b$	$Lower^c$	Fat^d	LBW	Density
						Ponderal Equivalents (kg)						
1	16	160.2	120	138	105	88	78	96	114	66	54	0.975
2	14.5	167.3	92	91	88	81	74	87	89	37	55[e]	—
2	16.0	168.5	101	97	95	85	77	99	100	44	57[e]	1.019
3	36	158.8	101	115	92	73	71	89	82	48	53[e]	—
4	23	177.8	82	83	86	84	80	84	92	25	57	1.031
5	22	178.7	75	83	73	72	69	73	80	25	50	1.025
6	23	164.6	71	75	68	67	59	64	77	24	47	1.023
7	22	167.6	62	71	60	57	62	59	60	25	37	1.018
8	19	172.2	69	72	70	65	63	69	74	23	46	1.024
9	20	155.0	57	61	54	53	52	53	51	21	36	1.017
10	20	157.6	55	57	54	55	49	52	54	18	37	1.024

[a] B component in place of B': comprises shoulder/4, biceps, forearm, calf girths.
[b] Upper: shoulder/4, biceps, forearm, wrist girths.
[c] Lower: thigh/2, knee, calf, ankle girths.
[d] Total fat (kg): includes both storage and essential (organ) lipid.
[e] Anthropometric LBW. Densito. (LBW) for examinee 2 (age 16) is 62 kg.

Table 6.12

ANTHROPOMETRIC DATA PERTAINING TO LEAN FEMALES

Examinee	Age	h	W	Min. W	A'	Ponderal Equivalents (kg) WFCA	Upper[a]	Lower[a]	Lean Body Weight (kg) Anthro.	Density	^{40}K
1	15.9	166.8	43.2	46.1	40.3	52.5	45.9	46.2	39.9	40.8	—
2	15.6	174.9	51.3	49.7	52.3	54.9	51.8	55.9	43.2	39.0	41.3
3	15.9	168.3	47.0	47.3	50.2	50.7	50.3	48.5	41.7	34.9	36.5
4	15.8	163.1	48.9	45.9	49.8	51.7	52.8	50.3	39.8	40.3	—
5	14.4	166.2	44.2	43.9	45.5	46.5	50.5	42.3	38.1	35.8	36.8
6	15.6	171.7	60.5	56.5	66.2	57.3	58.3	59.9	49.0	—	—
6[b]	16.9	173.4	56.1	56.5	62.6	57.1	57.9	59.1	49.0	42.4	43.7
		174.4	54.7	58.1	59.9	56.5	56.4	56.4	50.4	—	—
Ballet											
1	21	163.5	47.3	48.4	47.3	47.8	47.7	46.4	41.9	—	—
2	35	166.4	50.5	50.1	48.2	48.1	49.1	46.9	43.4	—	—
3	22	170.2	50.0	50.6	49.6	48.5	47.2	47.5	43.8	—	—

[a] Defined in Table 6.11.
[b] Dietary restriction to reduce abdominal girths in A' component.

CIRCUMFERENCE   PERCENTAGE DEVIATION FROM *D*

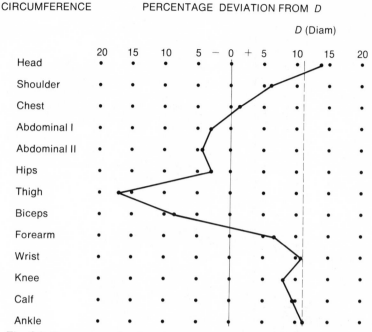

Fig. 6.8 Somatogram of underweight female (Examinee 1, Table 6.12). Age: 16 yrs; weight: 43.2 kg; stature: 16.68 dm. *D* = 4.85; *D*(Diam) is about 11% to the right of *D*.

Head	*Abdominal 1*	*Abdominal 2*	*Hips*	*Thigh*	*Biceps*	*Wrist*	*Calf*	*Ankle*
14.3	−3.8	−4.0	−3.4	−17.8	−7.8	11.0	10.0	12.0

Body weights of the leanest Berkeley adolescents (Table 6.12) are in close agreement with minimal but not lean body weights. Upper and lower component weights approach equality except in examinee 5, who has a marked reduction in relative size of the lower extremities. Examinee 6 merits special comment. Her diet was restricted at age 14.4 years in the effort to reduce abdominal girth which was, in part, successful. Nevertheless, at age 16.9 years, despite the loss of 5.8 kg, the A' component is still higher than *WFCA*, upper and lower component weights, and scale weight is 3.4 kg less than minimal weight. The change in body configuration in response to induced weight loss is observed in the somatogram (Fig. 6.9). The large A' component (chiefly the average abdominal girth) may well be a genetic trait.

Data pertaining to three ballet dancers (Table 6.12) show that minimal weight is not incompatible with extended daily strenuous exercise. The near equality of the several ponderal equivalents with minimal weight and scale weight denotes symmetry of body build. Reference (C) weights commensurate with frame size would be 6 to 8 kg higher, and only through rigorous exercise

Table 6.13   ANTHROPOMETRIC PARAMETERS OF LEAN ADOLESCENT MALES RELATIVE TO BODY DENSITY

Number	Age	h	W	Ponderal Equivalents (kg)				Lean Body Weight (kg)		
				A'	B	WFCA	C	Anthro.	Densito.	Density
1	15	167.3	51.4	51.2	50.9	57.3	59.2	51.9	51.4	1.110[a]
2	16.7	181.1	69.2	61.5	73.2	75.6	68.2	60.5	69.2	1.109[a]
3	14.3	166.0	56.1	54.6	56.8	59.4	55.6	51.7	56.1	1.110[a]
4[b]	14.8	184.1	65.5	63.9	61.5	63.8	74.8	66.5	65.5	1.102[a]
5[b]	16	187.5	66.8	65.9	63.8	66.2	75.6	67.4	66.8	1.102[a]
6	19	197.3	97.4	94.7	97.7	97.5	93.3	86.9	88.9	1.083[c]
7	14.4	151.0	34.3	34.8	34.9	38.2	38.5	35.9	34.3	1.101[a]
										LBW (^{40}K)
8	15.5	170.3	46.5	46.4	46.7	49.1	54.5	48.3	42.5	47.7
9[d]	15.7	181.6	62.8	68.1	60.6	64.7	71.5	63.5	52.1	48.9
10[d]	15.8	176.4	53.0	54.5	52.2	54.9	64.6	57.3	50.7	51.1
11[d]	16.6	173.0	53.9	53.9	52.3	56.4	59.7	53.9	48.5	49.1
12[d]	15.3	168.1	45.5	43.6	42.6	48.6	52.2	46.3	42.8	41.9

[a]Helium dilution chamber technique (Siri).
[b]Brothers.
[c]Underwater weighing (Wilmore).
[d]Inspection rating: Underweight. Density: 9 (1.061), 10 (1.083), 11 (1.075), 12 (1.082).

CIRCUMFERENCE   PERCENTAGE DEVIATION FROM *D* AXES

I + *D* (Diam)   R + *D* (Diam)

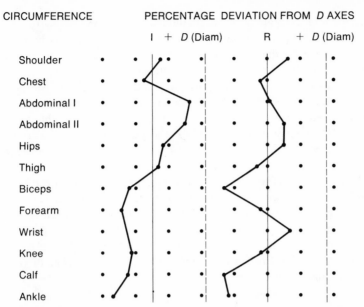

Shoulder

Chest

Abdominal I

Abdominal II

Hips

Thigh

Biceps

Forearm

Wrist

Knee

Calf

Ankle

Fig. 6.9 Change in body shape following dietary-induced weight loss of a lean female (Examinee 6, Table 6.12). Initial (I) prior to weight reduction—age: 14.4 yrs; weight: 60.5 kg; stature: 17.17 dm; *D* = 5.71; *D*(Diam) = 6.03. Minimal weight from frame size = 56.5 kg. Reduced (R) following weight reduction—age: 16.9 yrs; weight: 54.7 kg; stature: 17.44 dm; *D* = 5.48; *D*(Diam) = 5.92. Minimal weight from frame size = 58.0 kg.

and a restricted diet are minimal or near minimal weights achieved by these talented performers.

LEAN ADOLESCENT MALES. In Table 6.13, scale weights of eight out of 13 lean adolescents are less than lean body weight (anthro.) which may be considerably divergent, however, from densitometric and ^{40}K determinations of lean body weight. Examinees 9, 10, 11, and 12 were rated underweight on inspection. In these linear adolescents, body density does not attain the high values ($\cong$ 1.100) recorded by Dr. Siri in his helium chamber determinations. With reference to component weights, A' (trunk) and $WFCA$(extremity) ponderal equivalents, approximate scale weight. In some examinees who are patently underdeveloped, there was relative decrease in the size of the B component.

Summary

The determination of what an individual should weigh, especially if he is both obese and muscular, can be resolved in part by comparison of the ponderal equivalents of trunk and extremity girths. The B, B', $WFCA$ components comprising girths of the shoulders, biceps, forearm, wrist, knee, calf, and ankle, are the relatively lean and muscular regions of the male body. This is also true for the female with the exception of the upper part of the arm, which may be the site of gross fat accumulation in adult life.

The basis of a new concept of weight standards is referrable to comparison of ponderal equivalents. $W(WFCA)$ alone serves as a guide for the estimate of proper weight on an individual basis. Bideltoid and bitrochanteric widths $(B–B)$ are ancillary to $W(WFCA)$ for the purpose of monitoring the occasional person (usually female) who may have exceptionally small forearms and legs.

With regard to frame size, classical measurements have been extended to include four trunk and four extremity diameters. Each set can be converted to ponderal equivalents for the comparison of relative growth rates of trunk and extremities. The eight diameters (together with stature) serve for the calculation of reference, minimal (female), and lean body weights.

Finally, tables can be compiled for ready comparison of trunk with extremity girths relative to stature.

Chapter 7 / Body Build and Composition of the Athlete

The athlete is a member of a unique segment of the total population in terms of the composition and build of his or her body. Knowledge of the build and composition of various types of athletes representing different sports is helpful in gaining a better understanding of the complexity of body composition. In addition, it provides insight into what the physical requirements might be for the various sport activities or for the various positions or events within a given sport. Welham and Behnke (139) in 1942 used a group of 25 professional football players to demonstrate the difference between overweight and obesity. Similarly, in an unpublished study of the body composition of Masters or Seniors track and field athletes (competition limited to age 40 and above), Wilmore, Pollock, and Miller demonstrated that what are considered normal relative fat values for men over 40 years of age are considerably above those which can be attained through proper exercise and nutrition. Thus, the gradual increase in fat or obesity tissue seen with advancing years is not necessarily a consequence of true biological aging.

As in previous chapters, the present chapter represents only the work of the present authors, which represents only a fraction of what has been published over the years. While these data are extremely interesting and provoking, investigations need to be continued and expanded to include more athletes and a better representation of sport activities. Likewise, only a limited amount of data are available for females, and this is an area in which a great deal of research needs to be conducted. The present data will be presented in sections according to the activity.

155

Football

The majority of the 25 professional football players in the Welham and Behnke study (139) had been previously selected as college All-Americans. The primary interest was in determining whether obesity or weight per se was the chief factor tending to produce low values for specific gravity. In a previous study of 99 healthy men in the military service (22), the "high" specific gravity group had an average body weight of 148.7 pounds, while the "low" specific gravity group averaged 176.0 pounds. The degree of obesity was found to be the factor responsible for variations in specific gravity.

Table 7.1

BODY COMPOSITION AND LUNG VOLUMES
OF PROFESSIONAL FOOTBALL PLAYERS, 1940–1941[a]

Subject	Height cm	Weight kg	Density gm/ml	Fat %	LBW kg	Fat kg	RV L	VC L	TLC L
Linemen									
1	184.8	87.3	1.086	5.8	82.2	5.1	1.570	6.010	7.580
2	185.7	83.4	1.086	5.8	78.6	4.8	1.792	6.600	8.392
3	183.7	86.1	1.083	7.1	80.0	6.1	1.341	6.000	7.341
4	184.5	93.5	1.081	7.9	86.1	7.4	1.930	6.300	8.230
5	190.4	100.2	1.076	10.0	90.1	10.1	1.383	6.800	8.183
6	183.1	88.3	1.066	14.4	75.6	12.7	1.284	5.400	6.684
7	183.9	98.7	1.061	16.5	82.4	16.3	1.429	5.620	7.049
8	184.5	95.7	1.059	17.4	79.0	16.7	1.388	4.500	5.888
9	191.2	117.9	1.059	17.4	97.4	20.5	1.665	7.250	8.915
10	188.0	98.7	1.055	19.2	79.8	18.9	1.226	4.660	5.886
11	185.5	101.4	1.046	23.2	77.8	23.6	1.488	5.940	7.428
12	182.5	114.2	1.046	23.2	87.7	26.5	1.500	4.880	6.380
Mean	185.7	97.1	1.067	14.0	83.1	14.1	1.500	5.830	7.330
Backs									
13	183.1	82.3	1.092	3.3	79.6	2.7	1.562	5.650	7.212
14	175.3	84.4	1.090	4.1	80.9	3.5	1.402	6.400	7.802
15	183.9	88.5	1.090	4.1	84.9	3.7	1.500	6.600	8.100
16	175.8	83.3	1.089	4.6	79.5	3.8	1.415	4.625	6.040
17	182.8	86.5	1.089	4.6	82.6	3.9	1.560	6.500	8.060
18	175.7	77.4	1.089	4.6	73.9	3.5	1.438	5.600	7.038
19	184.4	85.5	1.083	7.1	79.5	6.0	1.339	5.320	6.659
20	187.6	85.3	1.080	8.3	78.2	7.1	1.301	5.310	6.601
21	179.2	81.7	1.079	8.8	74.5	7.2	1.483	5.370	6.853
22	174.4	86.3	1.075	10.5	77.3	9.0	1.330	5.700	7.030
23	185.9	89.2	1.075	10.5	79.9	9.3	1.593	6.550	8.143
24	189.8	95.4	1.075	10.5	85.4	10.0	1.563	6.600	8.163
25	175.6	88.4	1.073	11.3	78.4	10.0	1.187	5.600	6.787
Mean	181.0	85.7	1.083	7.1	79.6	6.1	1.436	5.833	7.268
Total Mean									
	183.1	91.2	1.075	10.4	81.3	9.9	1.471	5.831	7.302

[a]*Adapted from Welham and Behnke (139). Appreciation is expressed to Dr. Welham for providing information relative to the positions of these athletes.*

Table 7.2

BODY COMPOSITION AND LUNG VOLUMES
OF PROFESSIONAL FOOTBALL PLAYERS, 1969–1971

Subject	Height cm	Weight kg	Density gm/ml	Fat %	LBW kg	Fat kg	RV L	VC L	TLC L
Defensive Backs									
1	181.6	85.7	1.088	4.9	81.5	4.2	1.165	4.486	5.651
2	189.2	83.9	1.081	7.7	77.4	6.5	1.307	4.689	5.996
3	184.2	89.6	1.079	9.0	81.5	8.0	1.495	5.219	6.714
4	182.9	80.6	1.078	9.3	73.1	7.5	1.191	5.169	6.360
Offensive Backs and Receivers									
5	177.8	85.5	1.090	4.0	82.1	3.5	1.150	5.297	6.447
6	182.9	88.2	1.088	5.1	83.7	4.5	1.148	5.275	6.423
7	184.8	96.5	1.081	8.0	88.9	7.7	1.671	4.800	6.471
8	182.9	85.0	1.076	10.2	76.3	8.7	1.054	5.586	6.640
9	189.9	91.7	1.074	10.9	81.7	10.0	1.614	6.584	8.198
10	189.2	101.4	1.073	11.2	90.1	11.3	1.653	5.033	6.686
11	185.4	98.3	1.072	11.6	86.9	11.4	1.428	6.280	7.708
12	—	84.0	1.085	6.2	78.8	5.2	2.173	6.010	8.183
13	—	94.6	1.081	7.9	87.2	7.4	1.510	4.800	6.310
14	181.0	92.8	1.082	7.5	85.8	6.9	1.239	5.740	6.979
Linebackers									
15	189.2	108.3	1.065	14.9	92.1	16.2	1.909	7.465	9.374
16	193.0	111.3	1.061	16.5	92.9	18.4	1.847	7.230	9.077
17	190.5	107.0	1.061	16.5	89.4	17.6	2.457	5.900	8.357
18	188.0	104.5	1.060	16.8	87.0	17.6	1.273	6.718	7.991
19	188.0	105.5	1.047	22.8	81.5	24.1	1.374	5.314	6.688
20	—	109.0	1.045	23.5	83.4	25.7	1.362	5.250	6.612
Offensive Linemen (including tight ends)									
21	193.0	100.9	1.088	4.8	96.1	4.9	1.347	6.098	7.445
22	195.6	111.5	1.073	11.4	98.8	12.7	1.811	7.551	9.362
23	193.0	103.9	1.066	14.2	89.2	14.7	1.336	5.351	6.687
24	194.3	111.1	1.064	15.1	94.3	16.8	1.990	5.741	7.731
25	194.3	114.7	1.069	12.9	99.9	14.8	1.983	6.181	8.164
26	198.1	120.2	1.059	17.3	99.5	20.8	1.755	7.085	8.840
27	191.8	114.6	1.047	22.7	89.6	26.0	1.177	6.451	7.628
28	190.5	119.5	1.035	28.3	85.8	33.8	1.309	5.951	7.260
29	—	120.0	1.065	15.0	102.0	18.0	1.887	6.680	8.567
30	193.0	112.5	1.065	14.6	96.1	16.5	1.599	6.642	8.241
31	192.4	127.2	1.059	17.6	104.8	22.4	1.966	5.314	7.280
32	—	102.7	1.071	12.3	90.0	12.6	1.713	6.320	8.033
Defensive Linemen									
33	191.8	108.6	1.071	12.8	94.8	13.9	1.832	7.059	8.891
34	191.8	108.4	1.069	12.9	94.4	14.0	1.426	5.991	7.417
35	197.5	126.6	1.053	19.9	102.0	24.6	1.261	5.970	7.231
36	191.8	114.4	1.064	15.2	97.0	17.4	1.673	5.784	7.457
37	191.8	114.9	1.060	16.9	95.4	19.5	2.212	5.895	8.107
38	193.0	122.1	1.055	19.4	98.4	23.7	1.169	5.854	7.023
39	194.3	121.1	1.047	22.6	93.7	27.4	1.735	5.929	7.664
40	185.4	133.3	1.033	29.2	94.3	38.9	1.069	5.033	6.102
41	191.8	115.0	1.046	23.5	88.0	27.0	0.966	4.315	5.281
42	192.4	123.3	1.063	13.6	106.6	16.7	1.402	5.133	6.535
43	201.9	143.4	1.041	25.7	106.5	36.8	1.800	6.337	8.137
44	191.0	116.1	1.069	13.1	100.9	15.2	1.994	6.422	8.406

Table 7.2 Continued

Summary—Mean Values

Defensive Backs								
184.4	85.0	1.081	7.7	78.4	6.6	1.290	4.891	6.180
Offensive Backs and Receivers								
184.2	91.8	1.080	8.3	84.1	7.7	1.464	5.541	7.005
Linebackers								
189.7	107.6	1.057	18.5	87.7	19.9	1.704	6.313	8.017
Offensive Linemen and Tight Ends								
193.5	113.2	1.064	15.5	95.4	17.8	1.656	6.280	7.936
Defensive Linemen								
192.9	120.6	1.056	18.7	97.7	22.9	1.545	5.809	7.354
Backs and Receivers								
184.3	89.8	1.081	8.1	82.5	7.4	1.414	5.355	6.769
Linemen and Linebackers								
192.6	115.1	1.059	17.4	94.8	20.3	1.621	6.098	7.719
Total Group								
190.2	107.0	1.066	14.4	.90.9	16.2	1.555	5.862	7.417

With a mean weight of 200 pounds, the football players had a mean specific gravity value of 1.080.

Of the 25 football players, 17 were physically unqualified for military duty or first class insurance on the basis of their weight. This was determined by allowing 15% above the average values in the standard height–weight tables as the upper limit. Of these 17, 11 had exceptionally high specific gravity values, indicating low levels of body fat. This was the first attempt to show the inadequacy of predicting "ideal" weight from standard height–weight tables. The characteristics of these ball players are presented in Table 7.1.

Wilmore and Haskell, in an unpublished study, assessed the body composition of 44 professional football players between the years 1969 and 1971. Of these 44 players, ten had attained the status of All-Pro or All-League, and all but six were starting members of their respective teams during the 1969, 1970, and 1971 seasons. Body composition and lung volume data are presented in Table 7.2. The players are separated by position into defensive backs, offensive backs and receivers, defensive linemen, offensive linemen, and linebackers. Body density was determined by hydrostatic weighing and the residual volume by the nitrogen dilution technique (145). Relative fat was calculated from body density using Siri's equation (117).

Of these five groups, the defensive backs are the lightest, the shortest, have the highest body density, the lowest relative fat, and the lowest total lung capacity. The defensive linemen are the heaviest, least dense, and have the greatest relative fat. The general characteristics of the backs and receivers are similar regardless of position, as are the linemen and linebackers. A complete anthropometric work-up for an All-Pro linebacker is presented in Table 7.3 and Fig. 7.1.

Table 7.3

ANTHROPOMETRIC AND COMPOSITION DATA FOR AN ALL-PRO FOOTBALL LINEBACKER

Stature: 18.80 dm, 74.0 inches				Weight: 108.32 kg, 238.30 lbs			
D = 7.106	$3F$ = 7.202		$uS-W$ = 135.7	Reference Weight = 101.96 kg			

| *Anthropometric Girths* | | | | | *Anthropometric Diameters* | | |
Site	k^a	c	d	Dev^b	Site	$k(RW)^a$	$k(LBW)^a$	c
Shoulder	18.47	132.4	7.17	0.9	Biacromial	6.77	7.18	46.2
Chest	15.30	107.8	7.05	−0.8	Bideltoid	7.53	7 98	55.2
Abdominal					Chest	5.00	5.31	35.0
Average	13.07	94.6	7.24	1.9	Bi-iliac	4.77	5.06	32.8
Hips	15.57	115.0	7.39	4.0	Bitroch.	5.47	5.79	37.2
Thighs	9.13	62.8	6.88	−3.2	Knee	3.08	3.27	22.0
Biceps	5.29	38.8	7.33	3.1	Ankle	2.32	2.46	17.0
Forearm	4.47	33.3	7.45	4.8	Elbow	2.32	2.46	16.6
Wrist	2.88	19.2	6.67	−6.1	Wrist	1.85	1.96	13.8
Knee	6.10	41.0	6.72	−5.4				
Calf	5.97	40.0	6.70	−5.7				
Ankle	3.75	25.6	6.83	−4.4				

Anthropometric Fractionation of Body Weight

D(A)	7.22	W(A)	106.89 kg
D(A')	7.32	W(A')	109.88 kg
D(B)	7.14	W(B)	104.41 kg
D(B')	6.95	W(B')	99.15 kg
D(WFCA)	6.92	W(WFCA)	98.15 kg
D(B−B)	7.11	W(B−B)	103.59 kg
D(C)	6.99	W(C)	100.19 kg
		W(AB)	= 108.39 kg
		W(ABC)	= 105.14 kg
		LBW	= 90.69 kg

^{a}*k values from reference man.*
^{b}*Percent deviation from D.*

In comparison with the professional football players of the 1940–1941 era, the present ball players are considerably taller, heavier, fatter, and possess more lean body weight. The lung volumes are remarkably similar in spite of the greater size of the present day ball players. For the linemen, the highest lean weight in the present group is 9.6 kg heavier than that found in the 1940–1941 group. For the backs, this difference is 4.7 kg in favor of the present group. Unfortunately, performance data are not available for the 1940–1941 group to determine whether this increase in body size has influenced such factors as speed, agility, and strength.

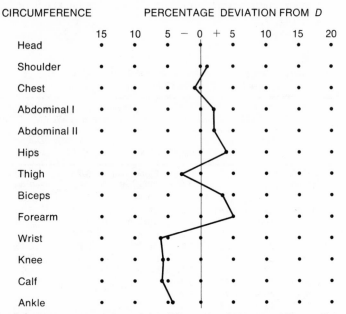

Fig. 7.1 Somatogram of all-pro football linebacker, 1971. Age: 26 yrs; weight: 108.3 kg; stature: 18.92 dm. *D* = 7.106.

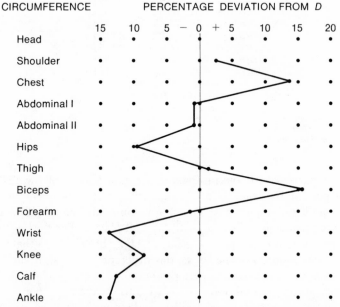

Fig. 7.2 Somatogram of weight lifter (WS). Age: 39.0 yrs; weight: 103.6 kg; stature: 17.95 dm. *D* = 7.330.

Weight Lifting

Behnke and Royce (26) studied the characteristics of a group of four weight lifters. This is a particularly interesting group of athletes to study because of the preponderance of muscle tissue. As can be seen from the data in Table 7.4, the anthropometric determination of both body weight and lean

Table 7.4

ANTHROPOMETRIC DETERMINATION OF BODY COMPOSITION
IN WEIGHT LIFTERS[a]

Subject	EK		RJ		RS		WS	
Age, yrs	22.4		22.1		20.6		39.0	
Stature, dm	18.00		17.44		17.86		17.95	
Weight, kg	105.0		89.3		86.5		103.6	
D	7.35		6.88		6.56		7.33	
Circumference, cm	*d*	*% Dev*	*d*	*% Dev*	*d*	*% Dev*	*d*	*% Dev*
Shoulder	7.28	−1.0	7.06	+2.6	6.79	+3.5	7.51	+2.5
Chest	7.90	+7.5	7.09	+3.1	7.16	+9.2	8.33	+13.6
Abdominal Average	7.43	+1.1	6.67	−3.1	6.02	−8.2	7.28	−0.7
Hips	6.96	−5.3	6.41	−6.8	6.05	−7.8	6.62	−9.9
Thigh	7.65	+4.1	7.32	+6.4	6.76	+3.0	7.45	+1.6
Biceps	8.34	+13.5	8.32	+20.9	8.13	+24.0	8.45	+15.3
Forearm	7.70	+4.8	7.58	+10.2	7.14	+8.8	7.21	−1.6
Wrist	6.51	−11.4	6.35	−4.4	6.04	−7.9	6.35	−13.4
Knee	6.56	−10.7	6.15	−10.6	5.56	−15.2	6.48	−8.8
Calf	7.27	−1.1	6.41	−6.8	6.37	−2.9	6.68	−12.6
Ankle	6.88	−6.4	6.05	−12.1	6.00	−8.5	6.35	−13.4
W(A)	103.1		83.2		72.2		95.9	
W(B)	117.6		103.7		98.6		115.0	
W(C)	81.7		72.0		72.4		80.5	
W(ABC)	107.9		92.8		86.7		104.2	
LBW	72.7		64.1		63.8		71.7[b]	
Excess Muscle (WB) − W(ABC)	13.7		15.9		10.3		15.3	

[a]Adapted from Behnke and Royce (26).
[b]LBW from ^{40}K = 86.8 and from specific gravity = 88.2.

body weight is greatly influenced by the unusual degree of muscularity. $W(B)$, which represents the muscular component, is greatly elevated above the actual weight. $W(ABC)$ subtracted from $W(B)$ gives a fairly good representation of what could be considered as excess muscle, i.e., that above the normal development of the individual.

These four individuals are characterized by small hips, wrists, knees, calfs, and ankles, and exceptionally large biceps. Three of the four lifters have highly developed chests, and two have very large forearms. Subject W.S. was a champion weight lifter at age 27, and prior to his intensive muscular training, he weighed 86 kg. His somatogram is illustrated in Fig. 7.2.

Channel Swimmer

Unpublished data obtained by Behnke and Wilmore is available on a long distance channel swimmer. This particular individual was an Army officer who was in peak conditioning for channel swimming. He had just successfully completed the distance of 26 miles between the Farallon Islands and San Francisco. His anthropometric assessment and body composition data are presented in Table 7.5 and Fig. 7.3. Physique plays an important

Table 7.5

ANTHROPOMETRIC AND COMPOSITION DATA FOR
A CHANNEL SWIMMER

Stature: 18.43 dm, 72.56 inches				Weight: 93.1 kg, 204.82 lbs			
D = 6.830	$3F$ = 6.743		$uS-W$ = 108.9	Reference Weight = 85.90 kg			

Anthropometric Girths				*Anthropometric Diameters*			
Site	k^a	c	d	Dev^b	*Site*	$k(RW)^a$	$k(LBW)^a$	c
Shoulder	18.47	127.3	6.89	0.9	Biacromial	6.77	7.18	42.5
Chest	15.30	107.9	7.05	3.2	Bideltoid	7.53	7.98	50.2
Abdominal					Chest	5.00	5.31	33.6
Average	13.07	94.2	7.22	5.7	Bi-iliac	4.77	5.06	32.5
Hips	5.57	104.6	6.72	−1.6	Bitroch.	5.47	5.79	36.0
Thighs	9.13	62.3	6.82	−0.1	Knee	3.08	3.27	19.3
Biceps	5.29	37.7	7.13	4.2	Ankle	2.32	2.46	14.5
Forearm	4.47	29.6	6.65	−2.6	Elbow	2.32	2.46	14.7
Wrist	2.88	17.5	6.08	−11.0	Wrist	1.85	1.96	11.6
Knee	6.10	38.9	6.39	−6.4				
Calf	5.97	39.4	6.60	−3.4				
Ankle	3.75	23.1	6.19	−9.4				

Anthropometric Fractionation of Body Weight				*Body Composition Through Hydrostatic Weighing*		
D(A)	6.98	W(A)	99.7 kg	Density	1.0391	gm/cc
D(A')	6.94	W(A')	98.5 kg	Relative Fat	26.37	%
D(B)	6.81	W(B)	94.9 kg	Fat Weight	24.55	kg
D(B')	6.55	W(B')	87.9 kg	Lean Body Weight	68.56	kg
D(WFCA)	6.43	W(WFCA)	84.6 kg	Total Body Weight	93.11	kg
D(B–B)	6.63	W(B–B)	88.9 kg			
D(C)	6.48	W(C)	85.7 kg			
		W(AB)	= 97.3 kg			
		W(ABC)	= 96.2 kg			
		LBW	= 76.4 kg			

[a]*k values from reference man.*
[b]*Percent deviation from D.*

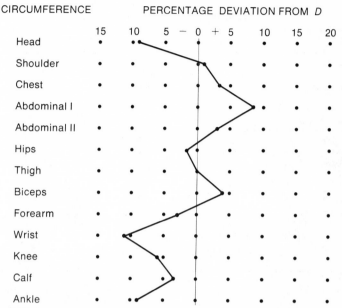

CIRCUMFERENCE   PERCENTAGE DEVIATION FROM *D*

Fig. 7.3 Somatogram of Channel swimmer. Age: 34.0 yrs; weight: 93.1 kg; stature: 18.43 dm. *D* = 6.830.

role in this athletic endeavor, as Behnke illustrated in a previous publication (20). A relatively lean swimmer weighing 80 kg and possessing 10% body fat has a net weight in the water of approximately 6 kg when corrected for the volume of air in the lungs. A corpulant swimmer weighing 100kg with 30% body fat has a net weight of 3.8 kg in fresh water. Thus the athlete weighing 20 kg more in air may weigh 2.2 kg less than a lean swimmer in the water. When corrected for the amount of air normally present in the lungs, the 100 kg swimmer will have neutral or even positive buoyancy. The extra fat helps increase the buoyancy of the swimmer while at the same time providing him with additional protection against cold water. The characteristics of this swimmer fit this pattern perfectly.

Track and Field

Behnke and Royce (26) reported data on three long distance runners. Their characteristics are presented in Table 7.6. These athletes are characterized by excessive leanness, relatively small body size, and a deficiency of arm girth compared to chest size and leg development. Subject RE

Table 7.6

ANTHROPOMETRIC CHARACTERISTICS OF THREE LONG DISTANCE RUNNERS[a]

Subject	*JB*		*RE*		*DL*	
Age, yrs	35		27		34	
Stature, dm	17.52		18.02		18.47	
Weight, kg	66.8		63.4		70.4	
D	5.87		5.58		5.96	
Circumferences	*d*	*% Dev*	*d*	*% Dev*	*d*	*% Dev*
Shoulder	5.46	−5.3	5.57	−0.2	6.00	−0.7
Chest	6.21	+5.8	5.49	−1.6	6.11	+2.5
Abdominal Average	5.75	−2.1	5.74	+2.9	5.84	−2.0
Hips	5.83	−0.7	5.70	+2.2	5.88	−1.3
Thigh	5.74	−2.2	5.55	−0.5	6.17	+3.5
Biceps	5.67	−3.4	4.76	−14.7	5.84	−2.0
Forearm	5.86	−0.2	5.17	−7.3	5.79	−2.9
Wrist	5.69	−3.1	5.55	−0.5	5.69	−4.5
Knee	5.72	−2.6	5.97	+7.0	5.77	−3.2
Calf	5.88	+0.2	5.73	+2.7	6.25	+4.9
Ankle	5.68	−3.4	5.87	+5.2	5.85	−1.8
W(A)	65.5		65.1		69.6	
W(B)	65.7		57.6		73.2	
W(C)	66.6		67.4		72.8	
W(ABC)	65.7		60.0		72.0	
LBW[b]	60.4		59.7		64.5	
% Fat[b]	9.6		5.8		8.4	

[a] *Adapted from Behnke and Royce (26).*
[b] *Calculated from anthropometric diameters.*

demonstrates this most obviously with exceptionally small arms and a $W(B)$ component substantially below $W(A)$ or $W(C)$.

In a separate publication, Behnke (21) reported on the anthropometric and compositional data of a cross-country runner. These data are presented in Table 7.7. This runner is characterized by a relatively large calf and small biceps and abdominal girths. The increase in the relative weights from component A to C is characteristic of lean individuals. His somatogram is presented in Fig. 7.4.

Wilmore, Pollock, and Miller, in an unpublished study, assessed the body composition of champion runners 40 years of age and older. These individuals were all considered to be among the best competitors in the United States for their age, in their particular event(s). The results of this assessment are presented in Table 7.8. The group as a whole is quite lean, although there is an obvious trend for the sprinters to carry considerably more body fat than the distance runners. This could well be a function of the differences in the weekly distances run by these individuals in training for their various events.

Table 7.7

ANTHROPOMETRIC AND COMPOSITION DATA FOR
A CROSS COUNTRY RUNNER

Stature: 19.40 dm, 76.4 inches				Weight: 79.1 kg, 174.0 lbs			
$D = 6.098$	$3F = 6.058$		$uS-W = 93.9$				

	Anthropometric Girths					*Anthropometric Diameters*		
Site	k^a	c	d	Dev^b	*Site*	$k(RW)^a$	$k(LBW)^a$	c
Shoulder	18.47	114.0	6.17	1.2	Biacromial	6.77	—	42.2
Chest	15.30	94.3	6.16	1.0	Bideltoid	7.54	—	46.6
Abdominal					Bitroch.	5.47	—	35.0
Average	13.30	76.6	5.86	−3.9				
Hips	15.57	95.8	6.15	0.8				
Thighs	9.13	53.7	5.88	−3.6				
Biceps	5.29	31.1	5.87	−3.7				
Forearm	4.47	27.1	6.06	−0.6				
Wrist	2.88	17.4	6.04	−1.0				
Knee	6.10	38.0	6.23	2.1				
Calf	5.97	39.1	6.55	7.4				
Ankle	3.75	22.7	6.05	−0.8				

Anthropometric Fractionation of Body Weight

D(A)	6.05	W(A)	76.79 kg
D(A')	5.97	W(A')	74.71 kg
D(B)	6.18	W(B)	80.10 kg
D(B')	6.16	W(B')	79.62 kg
D(WFCA)	6.23	W(WFCA)	81.29 kg
D(B–B)	6.27	W(B–B)	82.46 kg
D(C)	—	W(C)	— kg
		W(AB)	= 78.43 kg
		W(ABC) =	— kg
		LBW =	— kg

[a] *k values from reference man.*
[b] *Percent deviation from D.*
[c] *Adapted from Behnke (21).*

Table 7.8

BODY COMPOSITION ASSESSMENT OF CHAMPION RUNNERS,
AGE 40 YEARS AND ABOVE

Subject	*Speciality*	*Age, yrs*	*Height cm*	*Weight kg*	*Density[a] gm/ml*	*Fat[a] %*	*LBW kg*	*Fat kg*
JK	Walking	41	184.2	71.63	1.087	5.3	67.83	3.80
PW	Distance	41	172.7	53.22	1.083	7.1	49.46	3 76
PM	Distance	43	181.7	61.86	1.108	−3.2	61.86	—
BF	Middle Distance	46	175.5	67.20	1.084	6.6	62.77	4.43
ED	Sprinter	46	176.2	75.30	1.065	14.9	64.09	11.21
AG	Sprinter	53	170.6	70.65	1.061	16.5	58.99	11.66
VM	Middle Distance	60	176.5	70.84	1.100	0.0	70.84	—
KC	Sprinter	63	178.3	69.80	1.063	15.6	58.21	11.59
WF	Distance	63	176.2	73.46	1.077	9.8	66.25	7.21
NJ	Distance	72	169.2	62.78	1.054	19.6	50.46	12.32
DF	Middle Distance	73	179.0	65.22	1.083	7.1	60.59	4.63

[a] *Hydrostatic weighing using Siri's formula (% Fat = 495/D − 450).*

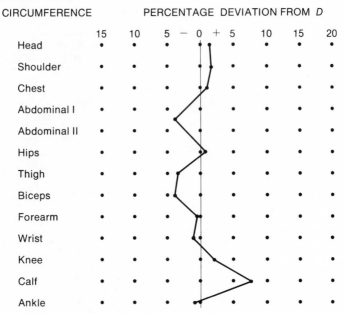

CIRCUMFERENCE   PERCENTAGE DEVIATION FROM *D*

Fig. 7.4 Somatogram of cross-country runner. Age: 26 yrs; weight: 79.1 kg; stature: 19.40 dm. *D* = 6.098.

Most of the distance runners were running between 50 and 100 miles per week, while the sprinters were between 15 and 20 miles per week.

It is interesting to note that two of these individuals had densities of 1.100 or greater. Since this is considered the mean density of the lean tissue, this creates the unreal situation of a deficit body fat. The reason for this must lie in the disproportionate relationship between muscle and bone in these two individuals, in comparison to the average individual. A preponderance of bone over muscle would, in fact, result in such a high body density, since the density of bone exceeds that of muscle. It is felt that the relative high fat percentage for the 72-year-old distance runner also reflects somewhat of an atypical situation. His subcutaneous fat measurements by skin-fold caliper were slightly higher than the other distance runners, but his lean body weight calculated on the basis of the Wilmore-Behnke five variable equation using skin-folds, diameters, and circumferences (refer to Table 4.9) was 55.6, corresponding to a relative fat of only 12.8%. This equation gave relatively accurate estimates of the lean weights of the other runners in this study. The densitometrically determined value for body fat is possibly elevated above the "actual" value. With a loss of bone mineral with aging, the density of the lean tissue would decrease, in which case the predictive equations would overestimate body fat content.

✕ Brown and Wilmore (36) performed a series of physiological and body composition assessments on a group of female distance runners. Two of these runners were considered to be the top female distance runners in the United States, both holding a variety of U.S. and world records. One of these two had won four consecutive U.S. and International cross-country championships. The remaining girls were each considered to be outstanding distance runners. The body composition data for these runners are presented in Table 7.9. It is obvious from these data that female distance runners are also charac-

Table 7.9

BODY COMPOSITION ASSESSMENT
OF OUTSTANDING FEMALE DISTANCE RUNNERS[a]

Subject	Age yrs	Height cm	Weight kg	Density gm/ml	Fat %	LBW kg	Fat kg
LM	21	167.6	49.93	1.081	7.8	46.04	3.89
LF	13	172.7	57.30	1.060	16.9	47.57	9.73
DH	20	170.2	52.53	1.058	17.9	43.12	9.41
SS	18	167.6	58.90	1.077	9.6	53.24	5.66
DB	28	162.8	50.72	1.085	6.4	47.46	3.26
NH	15	163.8	44.25	1.065	14.9	37.66	6.59
KS	13	167.6	44.10	1.059	17.4	36.43	7.67
FL	18	162.8	46.28	1.068	13.5	40.03	6.25
FC	31	171.5	51.97	1.078	9.0	46.28	4.69

[a]*Adapted from Brown and Wilmore (36).*

terized by extreme leanness. For a population of females in approximately this same age range, Wilmore and Behnke (149) found a mean relative fat of 25%. Each of these runners was under 18% fat and four of the nine were under 10%. Undoubtedly, a certain degree of this leanness is accounted for by genetic factors, i.e., you must have a certain body type to be a successful distance runner. However, this excessive leanness is also the result of the tremendous mileage these runners were averaging in their weekly workouts. One of these runners was averaging 80–90 miles/week; the rest were averaging between 50 and 60 miles/week.

In a second study, Brown and Wilmore (35) observed the body composition characteristics of females participating in field events. Each of these girls had been United States National Champion in either the Senior Women's Division, Girls 14–17 Year Old Division, or Junior Olympics, 14–15 Year Old Division. One of these girls represented the United States in the Pan American Games in 1967. The body composition data for these athletes are presented in Table 7.10. The contrast between these field event athletes and the female runners is quite striking, but certainly expected. The athletes participating in the field events have a much greater lean body mass, and,

Table 7.10

BODY COMPOSITION ASSESSMENT
OF FEMALE CHAMPIONS IN FIELD EVENTS[a]

Subject	Event[b]	Age yrs	Height cm	Weight kg	Density gm/ml	Fat %	LBW kg	Fat kg
BP	J	17	175.3	59.05	'1.063	15.8	49.73	9.32
NN	D	22	172.7	87.33	1.022	34.2	57.51	29.82
LL	J, D	18	171.5	61.93	1.062	16.3	51.82	10.11
CK	D	17	171.5	75.72	1.053	21.3	59.60	16.12
LG	S, D	24	181.6	111.05	1.019	35.9	71.17	39.88
CC	S, D	18	163.8	98.42	1.021	34.9	64.06	34.36
TL	D	16	172.7	60.71	1.057	18.5	49.46	11.25
JA	S, J	16	171.5	64.24	1.053	20.1	51.31	12.93

[a]*Adapted from Brown and Wilmore (35).*
[b]*J = Javelin, S = Shot-put, D = Discus.*

particularly in the case of the shot-putters, there is considerably more body fat. Those competing in the javelin were considerably leaner, as a whole, than those competing in either the shot-put or discus. This is more than likely due to the nature of the events; the javelin requires speed through a much longer distance.

It is interesting to note the contrast between NN and CK, both discus throwers. CK has a 2.09 kg greater lean body weight, but is 13.7 kg less in

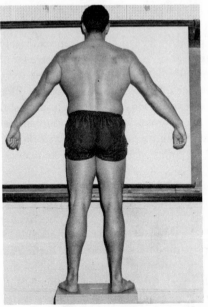

Fig. 7.5 Back view of shot-putters NS (left) and CW (right).

body fat. While both girls were excellent throwers, one can't help but wonder if NN might not have been a better athlete at a much lower body weight, providing the lean weight remained constant.

In 1969, Behnke and Wilmore (unpublished data) had the opportunity to study two outstanding male shot-putters, one of whom, at that time, was the holder of the world indoor record. The anthropometric and body composition data for these men are presented in Table 7.11. Back view photographs of these subjects and their somatograms are illustrated in Figs. 7.5 through 7.7.

Table 7.11
ANTHROPOMETRIC AND BODY COMPOSITION ASSESSMENT OF
OUTSTANDING MALE SHOT-PUTTERS

Subject	NS	CW
Anthropometric Assessment		
Stature, dm	19.47	18.85
Circumferences, cm		
Head	58.4	57.8
Neck	41.7	44.7
Shoulder	142.5	146.9
Chest	123.0	132.7
Abdominal Average	103.5	111.5
Hips	112.5	117.8
Thigh	71.8	73.4
Biceps	44.9	45.8
Forearm	34.0	35.2
Wrist	19.0	19.2
Knee	42.4	41.8
Calf	44.0	48.3
Ankle	24.8	26.2
Diameters, cm		
Biacromial	46.3	47.9
Bideltoid	57.0	59.9
Chest	36.4	37.2
Bi-iliac	31.9	34.7
Bitrochanteric	36.5	38.2
Knee	20.7	22.2
Ankle	15.0	15.5
Elbow	15.9	15.8
Wrist	12.8	12.6
Body Composition		
Weight, kg	121.90	130.50
Density, gm/ml	1.060	1.049
Relative Fat, %	17.1	22.0
LBW, kg	101.11	101.83
Absolute Fat, kg	20.81	28.67

While both of these men were excellent shot-putters and ranked within the top ten in the world at the time they were studied, NS was the better of the two. It is tempting to conclude that at least a part of his superiority was

170 | *Body Build and Composition of the Athlete*

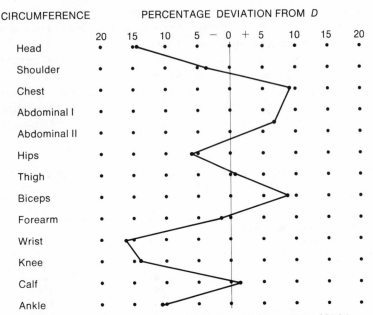

Fig. 7.6 Somatogram of shot-putter (CW). Age: 27 yrs; weight: 130.0 kg; stature 18.85 dm. *D* = 7.990.

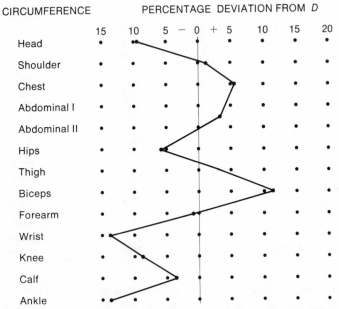

Fig. 7.7 Somatogram of shot-putter (NS). Age: 24 yrs; weight: 122.8 kg; stature: 19.47 dm. *D* = 7.620.

due to his lower fat content, as his lean weight was quite similar to CW. It is now recognized that success in shot-putting is based not only on size and strength, but also on speed. The reduction of nonessential adipose tissue should certainly be of value in increasing one's speed of movement in an event such as this.

Basketball

Behnke and Royce (26) reported in 1966 on their analysis of three collegiate basketball players. These data are presented in Table 7.12. All three players are quite tall and lean, although the relative fat percentage is not much different from the mean value for a college age male (148). There don't appear to be any specific anthropometric measurement sites which differentiate the basketball player from the normal population of college age males other than height.

Table 7.12

ANTHROPOMETRIC ASSESSMENT OF
COLLEGIATE BASKETBALL PLAYERS[a]

Subject	*EV*		*GH*		*RK*	
Age, yrs	18.7		19.0		19.4	
Stature, dm	19.98		20.41		19.24	
Weight, kg	85.4		92.0		80.2	
D	6.25		6.45		6.23	
Circumferences	*d*	*% Dev*	*d*	*% Dev*	*d*	*% Dev*
Shoulder	6.21	−0.6	6.35	−1.5	6.56	+5.3
Chest	6.06	−3.0	6.21	−3.7	6.24	−0.2
Abdominal Average	6.40	+2.4	6.38	−1.1	6.20	−0.5
Hips	6.24	−0.2	6.53	+1.2	6.00	−3.7
Thigh	6.18	−1.1	6.68	+3.6	6.18	−0.8
Biceps	6.18	−1.1	6.71	+4.0	5.92	−5.0
Forearm	6.33	+1.3	6.49	+0.6	6.11	−1.9
Wrist	6.10	−2.4	6.25	−3.1	5.90	−5.3
Knee	6.15	−1.6	6.56	+1.7	6.08	−2.4
Calf	6.53	+4.5	6.58	+2.0	6.65	+6.7
Ankle	6.64	+6.2	6.69	+3.7	6.08	−2.4
W(A)	85.5		91.1		80.5	
W(B)	83.4		91.8		82.2	
W(C)	82.3		86.1		80.9	
W(ABC)	83.9		89.7		81.5	
LBW (anthro.)	73.3		76.6		72.4	
LBW(^{40}K)	76.8		75.6		80.1	

[a]*Adapted from Behnke and Royce (26).*

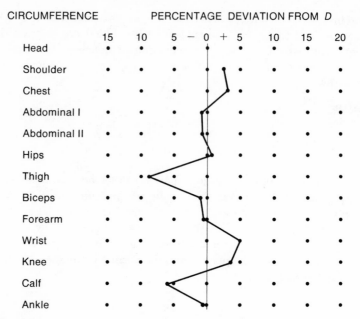

Fig. 7.8 Somatogram of prima ballerina. Age: 30 yrs; weight: 50.5 kg; stature: 16.64 dm. D = 5.280.

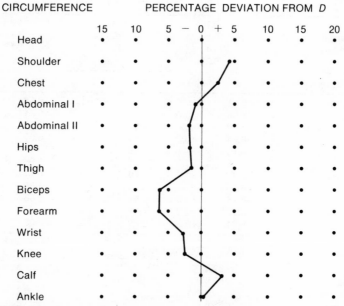

Fig. 7.9 Somatogram of ballet dancers (N = 10). Age: 21.8 yrs; weight: 50.95 kg; stature: 16.64 dm. D = 5.19.

Ballet Dancers

In 1966, Behnke, in an unpublished study, investigated the anthropometric characteristics of ballet dancers. These dancers typically represent exceptionally lean girls accustomed to rigorous exercise and strict dietary control. On the average, these girls were about 9 kg below normal weight for their skeletal size. The somatogram of the prima ballerina is illustrated in Fig. 7.8. Her thigh and calf measurements are over 5% less than would be expected for perfect symmetry. This is undoubtedly due to the excessive use of the lower limbs in the various dancing routines. The somatogram for the ten prime performers in comparison to reference woman is depicted in Fig. 7.9. The musculature of the upper extremities is poorly developed in the dancers when compared to reference woman, while the shoulders and chest are better developed. These results are not surprising when we analyze the requirements of the various dances performed by these girls. They have little if any need to lift with their arms and body as a whole. Additional characteristics of these girls have been presented in Table 4.13.

Summary

Only recently have body composition techniques been effectively utilized to gain a better understanding into the compositional and constitutional requirements of various sports. Success in may sports demands a particular physique, lean body weight, or relative body fat. While it is obvious that the seven-foot center in basketball would not be able to successfully adapt to the physical requirements of a jockey, it is not so obvious that a running back in football should have no more than 10 percent body fat, and the defensive lineman should have at least 90 kg (198.5 lbs) of lean body weight. The application of anthropometric and body compositional analyses to sport has been discussed. It is recognized that this is just the beginning of work in this area, and it is hoped that others will be encouraged to continue these investigations.

Chapter **8** / **Analysis of Radiogrammetric Data**

Radiogrammetry of the Arm (Behnke-Carlstein Survey)

POPULATION SAMPLE. During a period of two years the arms of 50 adult males were x-rayed and trial radiographs were extended to three females. The male group was made up of 33 compressed-air tunnel workers, including supervisors, 11 visiting physicians, several deep sea divers, an Army officer, and two exceptional shot-put athletes. These men, chiefly Caucasians, represented a wide variety of body types. Stature range was 166 to 207 cm, weight range was 58 to 136 kg, and fat (by our methodology) was 6 to 34% of body weight. The majority of the tunnel workers were temporary patients under treatment for decompression sickness, and the purpose of the special examination combined with anthropometry was to ascertain the role of fat relative to incidence of decompression sickness. The time allotted for an individual examination was less than ten minutes for execution of some 35 measurements. There were no reexaminations (radiologic or anthropometric). All of the results obtained on 50 examinees are included in the analysis.

DERIVATION OF CONSTANTS. The conversion of radiographic widths into individual estimates of body fat requires a mean group value for body fat both in absolute units and in percentage. For this purpose diameters are used which can be converted to frame size. Eight diameters (four trunk and four extremity) were measured on a subsample of 30 of the examinees. The following are mean values for the subsample: h (179.1 cm), W (84.9 kg), sum of eight diameters (197.1 cm), sum of three arm girths (97.93 cm), and the sum of 11 girths (654 cm, $D = 6.54$). Radiogrammetric: sum of six fat widths (5.76 cm), bone and muscle $(B + M)$ widths (28.85 cm), bone, muscle, fat (BMF) widths (34.61 cm).

Then, $D(LBW)$ diameters $= 197.1/33.5 = 5.89$, where 33.5 is $K(LBW)$ reference man. Substituting 5.89 in the general formula (7, page 57), mean lean body weight $= 69$ kg, and mean fat $= 15.9$ kg, mean % fat $= 18.7$.

ARM FAT RELATIVE TO S A, 3F, AND B + M. As stated in Chapter 1, Matiegka (84) proposed that the amount of fat in the body could be estimated from the product of surface area, one-half of the thickness of double-layered skin-folds, and a constant. The following formulation embodies this concept modified only in the substitution of six radiographic widths (fat) for skin-folds,

$$W(\text{Fat}) \text{ gm} = S\,A \text{ cm}^2 \text{ (DuBois)} \times \text{Fat cm} \times k$$

With substitution of mean values $(N = 30)$, $k = 0.135$, we can state that the weight of body fat is 13.5% of the product of surface area and radiogrammetric fat widths.

If an alternate surface area formula is employed (i.e., $SA = 3F$ [or D] $\times\, h \times 176.2$), then with appropriate substitution,

$$\% \text{ Fat} = \text{Fat cm}/3F \times k$$

with substitution of mean values $(N = 30)$, $k = 0.0471$.

The percentage of fat may also be approximated as

$$\% \text{ Fat} = \frac{\text{Fat cm} \times k}{B + M \text{ cm}}, k = 94, \text{ and}$$

$$\% \text{ Fat} = \frac{\text{Fat cm} \times k}{BMF \text{ cm}}, k = 112, \text{ where}$$

$B + M$ and BMF are the arm radiogrammetric widths, and the values for k are obtained by substitution of mean data $(N = 30)$ in the formulations.

ANALYSIS OF DATA. Radiogrammetric (arm) and anthropometric data are tabulated for 11 examinees who vary widely in body build and fat content (Table 8.1). The 11 girths, three arm girths, and the radiogrammetric BMF widths were converted to D quotients (Table 8.2), and the divisors (conversion constants) were 100, 15, and 5.29, respectively. The percentage of body fat was then computed from surface area (DuBois), and from $3F$ or from single D conversions substituted in the following formulations,

$$\% \text{ Fat} = \frac{\text{Sum 6 Fat widths cm}}{.0471 \ 3F \text{ or } D \text{ quotients}}, \text{ or } \frac{21.23 \text{ Fat cm}}{3F \text{ or } D \text{ quotients}}.$$

The constants, 15 for arm girths and 5.29 for BMF widths, are derived from the mean values of the respective dimensions $(N = 30)$ divided by 6.54,

Table 8.1

RADIOGRAMMETRIC DATA OF THE ARM
OF 11 MEN WHO VARY WIDELY IN BODY BUILD

Examinee	Age	h	W	3F	*Radiogrammetric mm × 10* Fat	*Radiogrammetric mm × 10* Bone	*Radiogrammetric mm × 10* Muscle	*Bone[a] Cortex (%)*	*Arm Girths (cm)*
1	27	188.5	130.0	7.88	773	798	2840	62	125.7
2	24	194.7	122.8	7.53	612	906	3073	44	122.5
3	65	178.8	91.8	6.79	901	839	2259	43	109.3
4	26	180.3	77.8	6.23	366	730	2075	41	93.9
5	32	167.6	116.0	7.89	1257	684	2575	—	122.1
6	36	186.5	120.0	7.61	1193	736	2554	51	113.6
7	33	179.1	113.1	7.54	1175	849	2180	—	115.4
8	36	185.2	105.0	7.14	1074	762	2199	55	112.6
9	25	178.5	94.6	6.91	870	785	2269	48	106.1
10	32	183.3	82.6	6.37	617	679	2275	62	99.3
11	42	183.0	63.6	5.59	150	733	1680	40	76.5

[a]*Total bone width—medullary space at the three sites of routine measurement.*

Table 8.2

RADIOGRAMMETRIC PERCENTAGE OF BODY FAT COMPUTED
FROM SURFACE AREA AND RELATED PARAMETERS
FOR THE 11 EXAMINEES, TABLE 8.1

	D Conversions[a] 3F	D	Arm g	BMF	*Percentage of Body Fat[b]* SA	*Percentage of Body Fat[b]* 3F	*Percentage of Body Fat[b]* D	*Percentage of Body Fat[b]* Arm g	*Percentage of Body Fat[b]* BMF	*Percentage of Body Fat[b]* B + M
1	7.88	7.99	8.38	8.34	20.4	20.8	20.5	19.6	19.7	20.0
2	7.53	7.62	8.17	8.68	17.1	17.3	17.1	15.9	15.0	14.5
3	6.79	6.82	7.29	7.56	27.9	28.2	28.0	26.2	25.3	27.3
4	6.23	6.22	6.26	5.99	12.5	12.5	12.5	12.4	13.0	12.3
5	7.89	7.96	8.14	8.54	32.2	33.8	33.5	32.8	31.3	36.3
6	7.61	7.61	7.57	8.47	32.4	33.3	33.3	33.5	29.9	34.1
7	7.54	7.68	7.69	7.95	32.4	33.1	32.5	32.4	31.4	36.5
8	7.14	7.32	7.51	7.63	31.4	31.9	31.2	30.4	29.9	34.1
9	6.91	7.01	7.07	7.42	26.2	26.7	26.4	26.1	24.9	26.8
10	6.37	6.48	6.62	6.75	20.5	20.6	20.2	19.8	19.4	19.6
11	5.59	5.69	5.10	4.85	5.8	5.7	5.6	6.2	6.6	5.8

[a]*Dimensions (cm) divided by proportionality constants: D(100), 3 arm girths(15), radiographic bone-muscle-fat widths (5.29).*

[b]*% Fat from SA, see text; % Fat =* $\dfrac{Fat\ cm}{.0471\ 3F\ or\ D\ Conversions}$ *and % Fat =* $\dfrac{94\ Fat\ cm}{B + M\ cm}$

which is the mean value of D. The ratio of BMF widths to arm girths was 35.2% ± 3.6 for the entire group of 50 examinees.

It is apparent from the data (Table 8.2) that the percentage of body fat may be computed from surface area (DuBois), from $3F$ or D, and from arm girths or radiographic widths, with somewhat greater divergence. This follows from the interrelationship between surface area (DuBois) and $3F$ or D conversions. Further, any error arising from disparity of these parameters with surface area computed from DuBois tables, is reduced about twentyfold in the calculation of the fat percentages.

An independent evaluation of arm fat widths as related to estimates of body fat is afforded by lean body weight derived from diameters and from the iliac (Abdominal 2) girth substituted in Wilmore's abridged formula. Table 8.3 compares lean body weights and reduced (R) weights. The former were derived independently of radiogrammetry from eight diameters, the iliac (Abdominal 2) girth, and $WFCA$ (wrist, forearm, calf, ankle) girths, as follows.

Lean Body Weights

$$LBW(8 \text{ Diam}) = 8 \text{ Diam}/33.5 = D(LBW) \text{ Diameters}$$
$$= (D(LBW) \text{ Diam})^2 \times h \times 0.111$$

$$LBW(WFCA) = 0.88\left[W(WFCA) - \frac{W(A') - W(WFCA)}{3}\right]$$

$W(A')$ and $W(WFCA)$ are computed from conversion constants (reference man) and substitution in the general formula (7, page 57). LBW(Iliac) $=$ 44.6 $+$ 1.082 $W -$ 0.74 Abdominal 2 girth

Reduced (R) Weights

Calculations follow from the percentage of body fat assessed from arm radiogrammetry in accord with,

Full Correction: 100 $-$ % fat multiplied by scale weight and the ponderal equivalents of A', arm girths, and girths of the biceps and thigh.
One-Half Correction: 100 $-$ [(% Fat $-$ 12)/2 $+$ 12], applied to the ponderal equivalents of $WFCA$, and the forearm and calf girths.

This somewhat novel correction stems from dietary induced weight loss which in the male is about double (based on girth measurements) in trunk, biceps, and thigh regions compared with relative weight loss in forearm and calf. If body fat derived from radiographic widths is 12% or less, the *full correction* is applied to all of the ponderal equivalents. Essentially, when lean men (i.e., 12% or less body fat) lose weight on a restricted diet, peripheral and trunk girths shrink to about the same degree when converted to ponderal equivalents. Some supporting data will be presented in Chapter 10.

STANDARD ERRORS OF ESTIMATE. It was not feasible to make more than four densitometric determinations of body fat for comparison with radiogrammetric values but the results of this preliminary survey are encouraging. Confirmation of the validity of arm radiogrammetry for estimate of fat percentage and lean body weight is limited to the following data.

Table 8.3

LEAN BODY WEIGHTS AND REDUCED *(R)* WEIGHTS CALCULATED FROM
ANTHROPOMETRIC–RADIOGRAMMETRIC PARAMETERS FOR THE 11 MEN (TABLES 8.1, 8.2)

| | Lean Body Weights[a] kg | | | | | Reduced Weights[b] kg | | | | |
Examinee	Diameters	Iliac g	WFCA	B + M	Scale W	WFCA	A'	Arm g	Biceps Thigh	Forearm Calf
1	93	103	101	115	103	100	106	111	118	120
2	89	100	94	143	102	94	102	126	117	103
3	70	73	73	76	66	69	70	76	70	72
4	70	70	69	66	68	67	67	69	69	69
5	84	75	69	78	77	71	87	82	88	79
6	84	84	81	93	80	81	94	97	83	86
7	75	81	76	76	85	75	79	79	77	78
8	78	81	89	75	72	80	74	79	75	79
9	69	73	83	77	73	73	71	73	71	70
10	70	70	73	74	66	68	69	71	68	70
11	56	56	71	49	61	69	56	50	52	67

[a]LBW calculated from eight diameters, iliac (abdominal 2) girth, WFCA girths, and B + M widths.
[b]Reduced weights: full correction. (100 – % Fat) applied to scale W and the ponderal equivalents of A', arm girths, biceps-thigh girths; half correction applied to WFCA, and forearm-calf girths (see text).

N	Entity	M	Coefficient of Variation	Entity	M	Coefficient of Variation	Standard Errors of Estimate[a]
							kg %
36	(R) Scale W	69.5	15.2	LBW(Diam)	69.0	13.7	4.30 6.2
33	(R) Scale W	67.7	—	LBW(Diam)	67.6	—	2.84 4.2
50	(R) Scale W	69.5	15.2	LBW(iliac)	70.3	15.6	3.96 5.6
50	(R) Scale W	69.5	15.2	LBW(WFCA)	69.8	16.1	3.73 5.4
50	(R) WFCA W	69.6	15.4	LBW(WFCA)	69.8	16.1	2.46 3.6

[a]*Standard error of estimate of (R) Scale W and (R) WFCA weight.*

The standard error of estimate of scale weight reduced in proportion to radiographic fat percentages, from lean body weight (diameters), is satisfactory if several aberrant values are excluded. The $\pm$ error is 4.3 kg (6.2% of the mean) for all 36 examinees on whom frame size was measured. With the elimination of three large men, the standard error is reduced to 2.84 kg (4.2% of mean weight), which is slightly less than one-third of the standard deviation of lean body weight (diameters). The estimate of reduced scale weight from Wilmore's regression equation embodies an error of $\pm$ 3.96 kg (5.6% of the mean weight). This finding is of special interest because the

Table 8.4

MEAN VALUES FOR FIVE SUBGROUPS OF MALES IN
THE RADIOGRAMMETRIC SURVEY (N = 50) ARRANGED
IN ORDER OF DESCENDING WEIGHT

Group	I	II	III	IV	V	Mean	Coefficient of Variation %
Age[a]	35	32	35	35	25	35[a]	—
Stature cm	183.3	184.1	176.6	176.9	177.3	179.6	4.0
Weight kg	105.7	101.1	78.3	76.6	70.8	86.5	20.0
% Fat[b]	25.8	23.2	18.2	15.8	10.9	18.8[b]	—
3F	7.19	7.03	6.31	6.23	5.99	6.55	8.4
D	7.26	7.06	6.33	6.24	6.02	6.58	8.6
Radiogrammetric (mm × 10)							
Fat (F)	875	770	541	472	312	594	47.0
Muscle (M)	2418	2226	2037	2030	2000	2142	11.8
Bone (B)	765	789	723	729	708	743	8.8
Bone/Muscle %	31.7	35.5	35.5	35.9	35.4	34.8	10.8
$\frac{B.\ Cortex}{B.\ Width}$ %	54.5	43.0	49.7	46.9	45.3	47.9	14.8
$\frac{BMF\ Widths}{Arm\ Girths}$ %	35.8	34.6	34.9	34.7	36.2	35.2	3.6

[a]*Range: 21–65 years.*
[b]*Range: 5.7–33.8%; % Fat =* $\dfrac{Arm\ Fat\ Widths\ (cm)}{0.0471\ 3F}$

regression formula was derived from densitometric data on 133 University of California males whose physical characteristics differ widely from those of our heterogeneous sample. Lean body weight (WFCA) calculated from girth measurements alone is in good agreement with reduced lean body weight in accord with the "one-half" correction derived from radiogrammetric fat percentages.

In Tables 8.4 and 8.5 are summaries of anthropometric and radiogrammetric data ($N = 50$) divided into five categories aligned in order of de-

Table 8.5

REDUCED WEIGHTS AND LEAN BODY WEIGHTS CALCULATED
FROM RADIOGRAPHIC–ANTHROPOMETRIC PARAMETERS
FOR THE FIVE SUBGROUPS OF MALES (TABLE 8.4)

Group	I	II	III	IV	V	Mean	Coefficient of Variation %
Reduced Weights[a] kg							
Scale weight	78.5	77.7	63.9	64.5	63.1	69.5	15.2
W(WFCA)	78.7	76.5	65.2	64.2	63.2	69.6	15.4
W(A')	84.1	83.4	65.3	65.2	61.4	71.9	17.9
W(Forearm-Calf)	84.1	77.8	67.5	65.1	65.7	72.0	15.4
Lean Body Weights[b]							
LBW(Diam)	79.2	—	65.3	—	62.4	69.0	13.7
LBW(Iliac girth)[c]	81.3	77.9	66.3	65.1	62.6	70.3	15.6
LBW(WFCA)	80.3	76.4	65.5	64.4	62.2	69.8	16.1
LBW(B + M widths)	86.5	77.5	61.9	63.4	60.4	70.3	17.3

[a]*Full correction: (100–% Fat) applied to Scale W and W(A'), half correction: (see text) applied to W(WFCA) and W(forearm-calf).*
[b]*Computed independently of reduced weights (see text).*
[c]*LBW calculated from Wilmore's regression equation.*

scending weight. The largest error in the estimate of lean body weight accrues to Group I, which also is highest in fat content. This group (containing the two shot-put athletes) showed the heaviest bone cortical thickness (54.5%) as well as the largest amount of muscle. Total bone width, however, was greater in Group II. The mean ratios of bone/muscle radiogrammetric widths are remarkably uniform for all groups except the first, despite the wide individual variation (coefficient of variation 10.8%). The variation of the ratio, *BMF* widths/arm girths, is $\pm 3.6\%$, which, although small is sufficient to account for the large individual divergence between ponderal equivalents calculated from the widths compared with the girth estimates of weight. There is good agreement (Table 8.5) between the calculated means of all parameters and their coefficients of variation.

In concluding this particular survey which is not adequately supported by densitometric data, it is important to utilize collateral information supplied by radiogrammetry. Aging of bone, for example, apart from thinning of the cortex, is observed in eroded and fenestrated medullary cortex of older males—changes which are similar to those in bones of animals exposed to ionizing radiation. By contrast, the well-defined, compact cortex is remarkably uniform in width in the young worker between levels of *AA* and *CC* (Fig. 8.1).

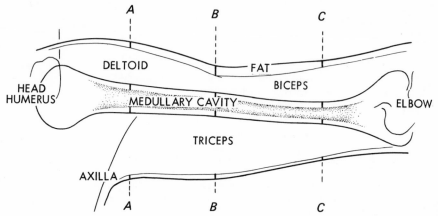

Fig. 8.1 Diagrammatic reproduction from xray film of the arm of a young, lean tunnel worker.

The technique of arm radiography can be improved in the effort to obtain more uniform positioning by support of the forearm. With a fixed, standard position there will be, nevertheless, variation in the ratio of radiographic widths to girths due to differences in shape of arms. It is possible to compensate for these changes by correction of widths to mean arm girth size, e.g., widths = 35.2% of arm girths. This correction is not essential for the estimate of percentage of body fat, but it becomes appreciable when diameters are squared for conversion to ponderal equivalents. Radiography of both arms would improve reliability of measurements and provide better representation of development of the upper extremities, than would radiographs limited to one arm. Lastly, a better assessment of muscular development is evident in the technique employed by H. Harrison Clarke et al. (41) with the arm in 90° flexion and the forearm and muscles rigidly flexed.

Radiogrammetry of the Arm (Three Females)

The triceps skin-fold appears to be the best simple predictor of the percentage of body fat in obese adolescent girls, as established by Seltzer et al. (112). It is pertinent to ascertain, therefore, whether or not body fat of females can be approximated from six radiogrammetric fat widths of the arm, substituted in the formula for males, namely, % Fat = 6 Fat widths/ 0.0471 ($3F$). A comparison of derivations for the reference man and reference woman clarifies this relationship. Thus,

REFERENCE MAN: Body fat is 8.2 kg (70 − 61.8), which amounts to 12% of median weight (69.5 kg), and $3F = 6.00$ from $\sqrt{\text{median } W/h}$, h is 17.40 decimeters. Then, mean fat widths (Arm) = 3.39 cm by substitution of 6.00 ($3F$) and 12 for % Fat in the above cited formulation.

REFERENCE WOMAN: Body fat is approximately 14 kg (56.8 − 42.8 kg), which is 25% of median weight (56.2 kg). $3F$ from median W and stature (16.38 dm) = 5.56, and substitution of 5.56 for $3F$ and 25 for % Fat in the cited formula,

$$\text{Mean fat widths (Arm)} = 6.55 \text{ cm}$$

DERIVATION OF CONVERSION CONSTANTS (FEMALES).

$K(LBW) B + M$(bone + muscle widths)
$3F(LBW) = 4.804$ (reference woman) and 5.655 (reference man)
$K(LBW) B + M = 4.90$ (males), and
$\dfrac{4.804}{5.655} \times 4.90 = 4.16$, $K(LBW) B + M$ (females).
Then *mean B + M widths* $= 4.16 \times 4.804 = 20.0$ cm
$B + M + Fat$ (BMF) *widths* $= (20.0 + 6.55) = 26.55$ cm
Estimate of Mean Arm Girths
$\dfrac{26.55}{0.352} = 75.43$ cm, where 0.352 is the mean ratio, $\dfrac{BMF \text{ widths}}{\text{Arm girths}}$, male
($N = 50$) survey.
$K(Arm\,girths) = \dfrac{75.43}{5.56} = 13.6$, 5.56 is $3F$ (reference woman).
$K(WFCA)$ reference woman $= 16.71$
Independent Estimate of LBW from WFCA, arm girths
$LBW = 0.75\ W(WFCA) - \left[\dfrac{W(\text{arm g}) - W(WFCA)}{3}\right]$, where $W(\text{arm g})$
is substituted for $W(A')$ in the male derivation, and $W(WFCA)$ is reference weight (25% fat) 0.75 $W(WFCA)$ is an estimate of lean body weight.

TABULAR DATA. In Table 8.6 the first two examinees are daughter and mother, respectively, whose anthropometric comparison is presented in Table 5.7. The third examinee has been muscular-obese since childhood (Fig. 8.2).

The unique feature of the analysis (Table 8.6) is the conversion of the radiographic widths of the three examinees to 35.2% of their respective girth size. This correction serves to compensate for discrepancies between width and perimetric size due to variation in arm shape, and possibly deviation from standard positioning of the arm for radiography. The percentage (35.2)

183

Table 8.6 ANALYSIS OF RADIOGRAMMETRIC-ANTHROPOMETRIC DATA PERTAINING TO THREE FEMALES

Exam.	Age	*Anthropometric*						*Radiogrammetric cm*			*Corrected[a] cm*	
		h	*W*	*3F*	*WFCA*	*Arm g*	*Diam*	*Fat*	*Bone*	*Muscle*	*Fat*	*B + M*
1	11.6	164.5	61.4	5.80	98.9	84.1	172.8	9.39	5.87	14.04	9.48	20.10
2	46	186.7	81.8	6.28	107.1	95.7	194.3	11.57	5.89	17.05	11.34	22.49
3	37	172.5	120.5	7.93	125.0	117.5	—	17.75	6.80	19.96	16.61	25.05

	Conversions: D(W)			*D(LBW)*			*Calculated Weights*				
	K: 16.71	*13.6*	*4.79*	*36.0*	*4.16*		*Reduced (R) Weight[c]*		*Lean Body Weights*		
	WFCA	*Arm g*	*BMF*	*Diam*	*B + M*	*% Fat[b]*	*Scale*	*WFCA*	*Diam*	*B + M*	*WFCA*
1	5.92	6.18	6.12	4.80	4.83	34.7	40.1	44.4	41.7	42.3	46.0
2	6.41	7.04	7.18	5.40	5.41	38.4	50.4	57.0	60.4	60.6	57.7
3	7.48	8.64	9.23	—	6.02	44.5	66.9	70.1	—	69.4	68.0

[a] Scaled to arm girth size: $\dfrac{D(Arm\ g)}{D(BMF)} \times$ radiogrammetric widths.

[b] % Fat = 6 fat widths/0.0471 (3F)

[c] (R) Scale weight = 100− % fat × body weight; (R) WFCA, half correction (see text).

[d] LBW computed from D conversions substituted in adolescent or adult general formulas.

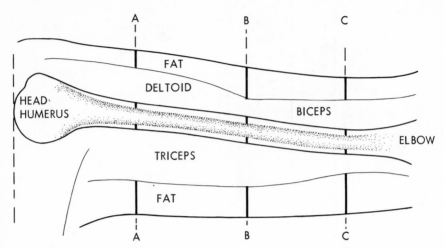

Fig. 8.2 Diagrammatic reproduction from xray film of the arm of an obese female (Examinee 3, Table 8.6).

is the mean ratio of *BMF* widths to arm girths derived from the previously reported survey on 50 males. The correction is negligible for the first two examinees but it is large (2.76 cm) for the muscular-obese woman.

Fig. 8.3 is a diagrammatic representation of the radiograph of the first examinee. At age 11.6 years, epiphyseal nonclosure of the head with the

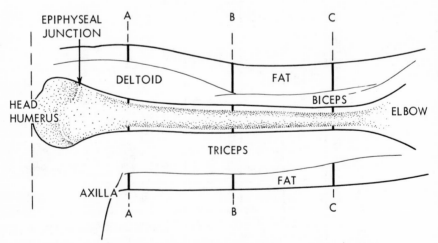

Fig. 8.3 Diagrammatic reproduction from xray film of the arm of a girl age 11.6 yrs (Examinee 1, Table 8.6). Epiphyseal nonunion (arrow) is clearly evident in the xray film.

shaft of the humerus is sharply defined. In Table 8.6, (R) and lean body weights are in close agreement with the exception of $W(WFCA)$ weights. In this preadolescent girl, the extremity girths are relatively larger than those of the trunk, and the conversion constant (16.71) from the reference woman is too low for these $(WFCA)$ girths. Calculated weights were computed from,

$$(D \text{ conversions})^2 \times h^{0.7} \times 0.255$$

The computation of the $WFCA$ weights has been outlined in a previous paragraph.

With the exception of a low (R) scale weight of 50.4 kg, the (R) weights and independently computed lean body weights are within the range of technical error for the technique employed. The matter of scaling to arm girth size (arm girths are measured in mm, and radiogrammetric widths in 0.1 mm) is open to further consideration when more data become available. In the case of examinee 3, the radiographic widths were reduced by the fraction 8.64/9.24 (i.e., $D(\text{Arm g})/D$ (BMF)). Without this reduction, body fat would have been higher than 50% and out of line with other parameters. These preliminary data offer some support to the correctness of the analysis as applied to females.

Analysis of Data on Other Groups

Tanner's Survey of Olympic Athletes, Rome, 1960

Anthropometric as well as radiographic measurements have had limited interpopulation application (apart from graphic representation of mean data) because of restriction of regression analysis generally to populations with similar physical characteristics. In this section, analytical principles previously developed will be applied to data obtained on Olympic athletes by Tanner's proficient investigative team (129). In addition to the usual impediments encountered in field studies was the problem of improvising certain essential facilities. With reference, for example, to radiography of arm, thigh, and calf, "The supply of electric current was scarcely up to the job of penetrating the thigh muscle of our larger athletes . . . the amperage of our sets was so low that we needed a very long exposure. . ." etc. (129).

The characteristics of the athletes are diversity in body build, general leanness, and wide variation in muscular development and frame size. In his analysis of x-ray widths of fat, bone, and muscle in the arm, thigh, and calf, Tanner found virtual independence between regional bone, muscle, and certainly fat widths in this survey as he had in previous studies (130). Estimates were not made of the percentage of body fat of the athletes, and relative amounts of bone and muscle were not assessed quantitatively on an individual basis. Effort will be directed, therefore, to obtain this information from the systematic and consummate data reported (129).

The following tabular data comprise mean values and conversion constants, $K(\text{Ref } W)$, $K(LBW)$, referable to 11 track and field events participated in by 110 athletes.

h cm	178.6		Calc. *LBW* (Diam) 65.8 kg		
W kg	73.8		3*F*(*LBW*)	5.76	
3*F*	6.07	*k*(Ref *W*)^a			$K(LBW)^b$
Girths cm	123.9	20.41	Diameters	104.7	18.17
BMF cm	42.85	7.06	*B* + *M*	40.61	7.05

^{a}*Sum of Dimensions/6.07.*
^{b}*Sum of Dimensions/5.76.*

The factor $(3F)$ is the average of the sum of $3F$ values from each of the 11 events. The girths comprise: arm (extended), thigh, and calf. The radiogrammetric widths $(BMF, B + M)$ represent bone, muscle, and fat measurements of the arm, thigh, and calf. The diameters are biacromial, bi-iliac, knee $(\times 2)$, elbow $(\times 2)$ widths. The essential value is mean lean body weight, which permits an estimate to be made of the weight and percentage of body fat. Pertinent to this estimate derived from frame size are the following constants $(K, \text{Ref } W)$ from the reference man: biacromial (6.77), bi-iliac (4.77), and elbows (2.32). Since Tanner measured femoral knee width (in contrast to tibial knee width, reference man), it was necessary to employ $K(3.26)$ for the knee width which was derived previously from Tanner's data (20). The sum of these $K(\text{Ref } W)$ values is 17.12; $K(LBW)$ equal to 18.17 can be computed from the product $17.12 \times 6.00/5.655$, where 6.00 and 5.655 are $3F$ and $3F(LBW)$ respectively from the reference man.

The value of $3F(LBW)$ of 5.76 for the athletes is obtained from the quotient, *mean Diam*(104.7 cm)/18.17, and mean LBW (kg) $= (5.76)^2 \times h \times 0.111 = 65.8$. The estimate of the mean weight of fat is 8.1 kg (scale weight $-$ 65.8), which is a rounded 11% of body weight.

TABULAR DATA. Group and individual estimate of the percentage of body fat and of lean body weight for selected athletic events are in Tables 8.7 and 8.8.

$$\% \text{ Body Fat} = \frac{\text{Fat widths cm}}{0.0335 \ (3F)}, \text{ or } \frac{200 \text{ Fat widths}}{B + M \text{ cm}}.$$

The constants (0.0335 and 200) were derived from mean values of $3F(6.07)$, $B + M(40.61 \text{ cm})$, and % fat(11) referrable to a mean value of 2.24 cm for the fat widths. The three radiographic sites (arm, thigh, and calf) enhance the validity of the $B + M$ widths as a reference parameter related to surface

Table 8.7

ANALYSIS OF REPRESENTATIVE DATA FROM TANNER'S SURVEY OF OLYMPIC ATHLETES (1960)

Mean Values (10 Athletes per Event)

Event	h	W	X-ray cm			% Fat		(R) Weights		LBW	
			3F	B + M	Fat	3F	B + M	Scale	Girths	Diam	B + M
100–200 m	177.2	70.8	6.00	40.73	1.72	8.6	8.4	64.7	65.4	63.6	65.6
400 m	185.0	75.9	6.07	41.34	1.80	8.9	8.7	69.1	69.2	68.4	70.6
800–1500 m	182.0	70.6	5.91	39.26	1.75	8.9	8.9	64.3	63.2	67.5	62.7
Marathon	171.1	60.4	5.64	36.34	1.78	9.4	9.8	54.7	50.1	58.5	50.1
Hurdles	182.0	73.4	6.02	40.48	2.07	10.3	10.2	65.8	66.0	66.6	66.0
High Jump	189.2	78.4	6.11	40.90	2.14	10.5	10.5	70.2	69.9	73.3	70.7
Wrestling	181.1	85.4	6.40	43.18	3.10	14.5	14.4	73.0	77.5	74.2	77.2
Weight Lift	172.2	85.7	6.40	45.35	3.29	14.7	14.5	73.1	75.8	66.7	79.6
Shot-put	189.7	103.9	7.00	47.18	3.77	16.1	16.0	86.8	94.0	86.0	94.3
Mean 11 Events											
	178.6	73.9	6.07	40.61	2.24	11.0	11.1	65.5	65.5	66.4[a]	65.4

[a] From K(LBW) diameter, reference man (= 18.17); K(LBW) diameter from sample data is 18.30, m LBW = 65.5 kg.

Table 8.8   QUANTITATIVE ASSESSMENT OF INDIVIDUAL DATA FROM TANNER'S SURVEY OF OLYMPIC ATHLETES (1960)

Event	h	W	3F	X Ray cm		% Fat		(R) Weights		LBW	
				B + M	Fat	3F	B + M	Scale	Girths	Diam	B + M
400 m	183.4	77.7	6.17	44.53	1.47	7.1	6.6	72.2	69.0	67.8	72.5
	188.9	77.8	6.09	41.67	1.54	7.6	7.4	71.9	72.1	72.7	73.3
800 m	182.1	81.6	6.35	41.69	2.76	13.0	13.2	71.0	69.9	68.6	72.5
	179.2	77.7	5.97	42.99	1.60	8.0	7.4	71.5	70.8	68.2	74.1
	186.5	80.5	6.09	41.16	2.59	12.7	12.6	70.3	72.9	76.1	70.8
	181.0	62.2	5.56	36.23	1.57	8.4	8.7	57.0	54.1	67.5	55.6
Marathon	173.8	63.1	5.72	36.03	2.16	11.3	12.0	56.0	53.7	60.3	50.3
	173.9	64.0	5.76	36.55	1.54	9.0	8.4	58.2	51.7	65.0	51.7
	165.3	61.0	5.76	38.24	2.17	12.3	11.4	53.5	51.7	53.5	52.4
High Jump	197.1	88.0	6.34	43.96	2.01	9.5	9.1	79.6	84.3	77.1	85.1
	185.8	82.2	6.31	43.95	1.48	7.0	6.7	76.5	78.3	72.8	80.2
	189.0	79.3	6.61	42.05	1.41	6.1	6.7	74.5	73.0	75.4	74.5
Shot-put	192.7	114.5	7.08	47.71	4.62	19.5	19.4	91.8	97.8	88.8	98.0
	189.7	108.2	7.17	48.19	2.89	12.0	12.0	95.2	99.5	91.2	98.4
	190.3	106.7	7.11	48.34	3.95	16.7	16.3	88.9	96.1	87.0	99.3
	195.5	106.4	7.00	45.73	4.90	20.9	21.4	84.2	89.0	93.0	91.3

area, and as a better composite of the size of bone-muscle mass than that afforded by the arm site alone.

The estimates of body fat either from the $3F$ or $B + M$ formulations are interchangeable. The reduced (R) weights (i.e., $100 - \%$ Fat $\times$ Scale W and W, girths) are comparable to the independently calculated lean body weights from diameters and from radiographic bone and muscle widths. The excess $B + M$ development of the shot-put athletes is apparent in the tables as the difference between $LBW(B + M)$ and LBW(diameters), or (R) scale weight.

The preliminary results of this analysis are encouraging in regard to quantitative assessment and individual comparison of fat, bone, and muscle in athletes. The radiographic data (arm, thigh, calf) despite procurement difficulty, are enhanced in value by the small variance in the ratio, $B + M$ widths/girths, i.e., 34.5% ± 0.25, in contrast with ± 1.27 (mean, 35.2%) for $B + M$(arm)/arm girths in our survey ($N = 50$) of males.

The Growth Period—Maresh Data from McCammon (86)

Over a period of years Behnke has had access to the most complete compilation of radiogrammetric–anthropometric data extant. These data made available by Dr. Marion Maresh amplify one of her papers (83), and a summary of mean values are incorporated in the text by McCammon (86). These values will be used to test the general applicability of the conversion formulations previously outlined, to the growth period of male and female children and adolescents.

MEASUREMENTS AND CONVERSION CONSTANTS. Radiographic bone, muscle, and fat widths were measured at the following sites: forearm, calf, and the lateral half of the thigh at mid-femur level. In addition, fat widths were measured over the insertion of the deltoid muscle on the shaft of the humerus, and over the iliac ("hip bulge") crest. The essential estimate of mean lean body weight (and derived percentage of fat) is from biacromial-bi-iliac widths for males age 18 years, and for females age 17 years. Thus,

Males, age 18: Sum biacromial, bi-iliac diameter $= 68.5$ cm
$K(LBW)$ reference man for these widths is 12.24, and
$D(LBW) = 68.5/12.24 = 5.60$
Mean $LBW = (5.60)^2 \times h^{0.7} \times 0.263 = 62$ kg
Median Weight (age 18) is 66.2 kg, and
median W(fat) $= 4.2$ kg or 6.3% median weight
$K(LBW)B + M = B + M/5.60 = 4.71$, and for the conversion
of 5 fat widths to % Fat,
$\quad$ % Fat (med W) $=$ Fat cm$/0.0852(3F)$. Likewise,

Females, age 17: Sum biacromial, bi-iliac diameter $= 64.4$ cm
$K(LBW)$ reference woman for these widths is 13.24
$D(LBW)$ Diam $= 64.4/13.24 = 4.864$
Mean $LBW = (4.864)^2 \times h^{0.7} \times 0.255 = 43.1$ kg

Median weight (age 17) is 56.7 kg, and median W (fat) = 13.6 kg or 24% of median weight.

With appropriate substitution,

% Fat (median W) = Fat cm/0.0713 $(3F)$, and
$K(LBW)B + M = 4.80$

COMMENTS ON DATA IN TABLE 8.9. The mean values for lean body weight (Diam and $B + M$) derived independently are in good agreement with reduced scale weights both for males and females. That is, the same constants $(K(LBW)$ values) serve to convert diameters and $B + M$ radiographic widths during the growth period from ages five years and upward, to estimates of lean body weights which agree with scale weights reduced by the percentage of calculated fat. Any percentage deviation, however, of the percentage of fat in adipose tissue below 60%, as in infants, or above 70% will impair the accuracy of estimates of body fat.

Total Adipose Tissue (AT) appears to be the correct derivation from radiographic fat widths which reflect the adipose tissue layer as a whole and not the fraction that is lipid. This distinction is important at ages less than five years when adipose tissue has much less than 70% lipid. From analyses of Foman (54) and Baker (7), adipose tissue in infants during the fourth month may contain only about 42% fat, and at one year somewhat less than 50% fat. Hence, at ages less than five years the projected amount of fat based on the percentage of fat in adipose tissue of the young adult ($\cong$ 60 to 70%), is too high. The correct values are derived from the product of total $AT \times$ % fat in adipose tissue. It is now feasible to assess fat routinely in biopsies of adipose tissue, and this matter will be given consideration in Chapter 10. In infants, the remarkable fact as pointed out by Baker and by Foman is that body weight may be allocated to 50% as adipose tissue.

Comparative data on height–weight matched samples of Berkeley and Colorado adolescents afford an independent assessment of the accuracy of estimates of lean body weight in Table 8.9, at least for age 16 years. The following densitometric, kaliometric (^{40}K), and anthropometric data are those reported by Hampton et al. (63) for Berkeley adolescents, and the Colorado data are those from Maresh reported in McCammon's text.

MEAN VALUES OF *LBW* FOR ADOLESCENTS (Age 16 yrs)

	N	h	W	Lean Body Weight[a] kg		
Males						
Berkeley	54	174.1	64.6	(1) 55.7	(2) 55.5	(4) 54.7
Colorado	50	173.3	61.8	(1) 56.3	(3) 56.2	(5) 56.9
Females						
Berkeley	59	164.7	57.0	(1) 41.5	(2) 41.2	(4) 41.3
Colorado	57	165.7	55.5	(1) 42.3	(3) 41.5	(5) 43.3

[a]*LBW calculated from: (1) diameters, (2) densitometry, (3) arm fat, (4) ^{40}K, and (5) radiographic bone plus muscle widths.*

Table 8.9

CONSISTENCY OF ANTHROPOMETRIC–RADIOGRAMMETRIC DATA PERTAINING TO THE GROWTH PERIOD OF COLORADO MALES AND FEMALES[a]

| | | | X-ray cm | | | | Fat^b | | (R) Weight | LBW | |
Age	h	med. W	Fat	B + M	3F	Diam	%	kg	Scale	Diam	B + M
Males											
5	109.5	18.6	5.53	15.31	3.91	42.0	17.9	3.3	15.3	16.5	14.8
8	128.8	26.3	5.18	17.75	4.31	48.1	14.1	3.7	22.6	24.3	22.4
10	139.0	32.8	5.75	19.38	4.61	51.7	14.6	4.8	28.0	29.6	28.1
14	163.2	51.0	4.79	23.24	5.30	60.4	10.6	5.4	45.6	45.2	45.2
16	174.3	61.2	4.13	25.47	5.62	65.3	9.0	5.6	56.2	56.3	56.9
17	176.7	64.4	3.77	25.93	5.73	67.2	7.7	5.0	59.4	59.2	59.5
18	178.6	66.2	3.12	26.38	5.78	68.5	6.3	4.2	(62.0)	(62.0)	(62.0)
Females											
5	108.9	18.5	6.23	15.27	3.91	41.7	22.3	4.1	14.4	14.3	14.3
8	127.7	25.6	6.38	17.62	4.25	47.9	21.1	5.4	20.2	19.8	20.4
10	138.6	32.0	6.93	18.84	4.56	51.8	21.3	6.8	25.2	24.0	24.8
14	162.3	50.9	7.99	22.30	5.31	61.6	21.1	10.7	40.2	38.8	38.7
16	165.7	55.0	9.57	23.42	5.47	63.8	24.5	13.5	41.5	42.3	43.3
17	166.0	56.7	9.49	23.34	5.55	64.4	24.0	13.6	(43.1)	(43.1)	(43.1)

[a] Analysis of data from Maresh (83) and McCammon (86).
[b] % Fat calculated from median weights; percentages for the older males would be considerably higher if fat were calculated from mean weights.

Summary

The applications of a simple, radiographic technique limited to fractional–second arm exposure, have been outlined for routine assessment of body fat and the estimate of lean body weight. A practical and novel contribution is the conversion of fat and bone-muscle widths to individual estimates of percentage fatness and of lean body weight. The principles stemming from arm radiography appear to have broad application, as shown by analysis of data on Olympic athletes and on children and adolescents.

Chapter 9 / Alterations in Body Composition with Physical Activity

The work of a number of investigators over the past 15 years has demonstrated unequivocally that exercise is an effective agent in either the control or alteration of body composition or both. The actual mechanisms involved in precipitating these alterations appear to be considerably more complex than the simple imbalance between calorie intake and calorie expenditure. Because this chapter is again limited in scope to the presentation of experimental evidence gathered by the present authors, only a very small percentage of the total research conducted in this area will be reviewed.

Experimental Studies

In 1969, Moody, Wilmore, Girandola, and Royce (unpublished data), conducted a study on the influence of walking and jogging on the body composition of overweight girls. Forty normal and obese school-aged girls volunteered to participate in an 18 or 36 week program of walking, jogging, or running. The activity was conducted four days a week. Each girl started the program by covering a distance of one mile a day, jogging 50% of this distance. The program was increased gradually until the distance required was between 3 and $3\frac{1}{2}$ miles a day, jogging 75% of this distance.

Hydrostatic determination of body density was conducted at the beginning, midpoint, and termination of the exercise program. Residual volumes were determined only at the beginning and termination of the program using the oxygen dilution method (145). Body weight was measured weekly to the nearest quarter of a pound. Skin-folds were measured at 12 sites every four weeks using the Lange skin-fold caliper. In addition to the skin-fold sites cited in Chapter 3, measurements were taken at the cheek and hip (midaxillary line, three inches below the crest of the ilium). Girths were measured every four weeks at the following sites: chest, bust, abdomen, hips, thigh, calf, and biceps.

The obese group ($N = 28$) exhibited a substantial increase in body density ($\Delta = +0.005$ gm/cc) and a decrease in relative body fat ($\Delta = -2.53\%$) as a result of the exercise program. Lean body weight increased by 1.13 kg while body weight decreased 1.08 kg, resulting in a 2.21 kg loss in absolute fat. The normal group ($N = 12$), while on the same exercise program, showed no significant changes. Neither group demonstrated changes in the sum of the girth measurements, but both groups had substantial decreases in the sum of the 12 skin-folds amounting to 20.9% and 16.0% for the obese and normal groups, respectively. In the normal group, four of the leaner girls actually gained fat weight during the course of the study. The significance of this will be discussed in a later section of this chapter.

In 1970, Wilmore et al. (152) reported on body composition changes in adult men resulting from a ten-week program of jogging. Fifty-five men between the ages of 17 and 59 years participated in a three-day a week, ten-week program of jogging. During this program, the men averaged a jogging speed of 200 m/min., or 7.5 mph, covering a mean distance of 51.75 miles in 413 minutes. The subjects underwent a series of anthropometric measurements, including skin-folds and circumferences, and a hydrostatic determination of body density, both at the beginning and at the conclusion of the program. The results from these tests are presented in Table 9.1.

Small but significant alterations in body composition resulted from this moderate exercise program. No subject exercised more than 24 minutes a day and no more than three days a week. The resulting loss of 1.08 kg of fat is not a spectacular loss, but it is substantial considering the low intensity and short duration of the exercise program. In addition, it is proposed that this is strictly an exercise-induced weight loss; anyone who altered his dietary habits during the study period was excluded from this analysis. The average loss was one-quarter of a pound of fat per week, which would amount to a 13-pound fat loss per year.

The changes noted in subcutaneous fat, as measured by the thickness of the skin-folds, were consistent with previous investigations. The reason for significant decreases in some areas and no change in others is probably related to a combination of the duration and intensity of the training program, and the selective biological patterning of fat. The data on the abdominal circumference changes tend to support this conclusion. The abdominal 1 measure-

Table 9.1

BODY COMPOSITION CHANGES WITH TRAINING, $N = 55^a$

	Pre-Training		Post-Training				
Variable	Mean	S.D.	Mean	S.D.	Mean	S.E.	t
Weight, kg	79.59	10.06	78.58	9.09	−1.01	.331	−3.05^b
Body Density, gm/ml	1.056	0.013	1.059	0.013	0.003	.001	3.73^b
Fat, %	18.88	5.93	17.77	5.71	−1.11	.296	−3.76^b
Lean Body Mass, kg	64.21	6.26	64.35	6.18	0.14	.172	0.84
Skinfolds, mm							
Scapula	16.3	5.7	15.1	5.4	−1.2	.473	−2.56^b
Triceps	11.5	3.8	11.1	3.4	−0.4	.319	−1.36
Chest	12.7	4.5	11.5	4.1	−1.2	.350	−3.50^b
Midaxillary	17.3	7.1	14.3	5.7	−3.0	.569	−5.29^b
Suprailiac	24.9	9.1	24.4	8.7	−0.5	.803	−0.70
Abdominal	24.4	8.8	23.5	8.4	−0.9	.766	−1.16
Thigh	16.9	4.8	16.0	4.6	−0.9	.413	−2.17^b
Circumferences, cm							
Abdominal 1	84.8	7.2	84.0	6.5	−0.8	.335	−2.34^b
Abdominal 2	88.2	8.1	87.7	7.7	−0.6	.403	−1.46

^{a}Adapted from Wilmore et al. (152).
^{b}Significant at the 0.05 level.

ment, or the natural waist, decreased significantly as did its related skinfold site (midaxillary), while the abdominal 2 measurement did not change, which is in agreement with its related skin-fold site (suprailiac).

A similar study of a somewhat older group of male subjects was reported in 1971 (151). Forty-four subjects, with a mean age of 48.1 years, participated in individualized exercise programs (nongroup programs) for a period of 12–15 weeks. The exercise program was only one part of a total program of health enhancement which included nutritional counseling and suggested diets, smoking and alcohol control, and anxiety and tension reduction. The results are therefore confounded by a multivariable approach to bettered health, and the specific effects of exercise alone cannot be isolated. This does not negate the importance of the study, however, as it is necessary to ascertain the influence of the interaction of these variables in this overall approach to health enhancement.

The exercise program was individually prescribed on the basis of the individual's endurance capacity ($\dot{V}O_2$ max). The program consisted of walking, jogging, running, bicycling, or swimming for 15–25 minutes a day, three days a week at 75% of their endurance capacity, as monitored by their training heart rate. A hydrostatic determination of body density was conducted prior to the start and at the conclusion of the exercise program.

The results from this study are presented in Table 9.2. There was a 3.54 kg loss in absolute body fat, representing a 17.5% reduction. This, of course, was mediated by both diet and exercise, although the dietary counsel-

Table 9.2

CHANGES RESULTING FROM THE HEALTH ENHANCEMENT PROGRAM[a]

N = 44	Initial	3 Month	Difference	% Change
Age, years	48.1			
Weight, kg	81.4	78.5	2.9[b]	3.5
Lean Body Weight, kg	61.1	61.8	0.7	1.1
Absolute Fat, kg	20.3	16.8	3.5[b]	17.5
Relative Fat, %	24.5	20.9	3.6[b]	14.7

[a]*Adapted from Wilmore and Haskell (151).*
[b]*Significant differences at the .01 level.*

ing was oriented more towards proper food selection than toward major caloric reductions in the daily food intake.

Brown and Wilmore (35) observed the influence of weight training on five female athletes who were national women's or age group champions in either the shot-put, discus, or javelin. These girls were lifting on the average of three days a week for a period of seven months. Hydrostatic weighings to determine body density were conducted at the beginning and at the conclusion of the training program.

Table 9.3

CHANGES IN THE BODY COMPOSITION OF FEMALE ATHLETES RESULTING FROM A PROGRAM OF PROGRESSIVE RESISTANCE WEIGHT TRAINING[a]

	Weight, kg		Density, gm/ml		Fat, %		LBW, kg		Fat, kg	
Subject	pre	post	pre	post	pre	post	pre	post	pre	post
BP	59.0	61.1	1.063	1.056	15.8	18.7	49.7	49.7	9.3	11.4
LL	61.9	63.6	1.062	1.056	16.3	18.7	51.8	51.7	10.1	11.9
NN[b]	87.3	81.2	1.022	1.033	34.2	29.4	57.5	57.3	29.8	23.9
CK	75.7	75.3	1.050	1.053	21.3	20.0	59.6	60.2	16.1	15.1
LG	111.1	111.9	1.019	1.025	35.9	32.9	71.2	75.1	39.9	36.8
Mean	79.0	78.6	1.043	1.045	24.7	23.9	58.0	58.8	21.0	19.8

[a]*Adapted from Brown and Wilmore (35).*
[b]*Attempted a 1500–1800 calorie diet during the seven-month study period.*

The results from this study are presented in Table 9.3. Three of these girls increased their body weight during the seven-month program, but only two demonstrated an increase in their fat weight, and both of these girls were more than two standard deviations below the mean for girls of this age (149). Two of the girls had a substantial increase in their lean body weight, while the other three remained essentially unchanged.

A companion study was conducted by Wilmore (unpublished data) to determine what changes occur in normal, nonathletic females as a result of a similar weight training program. Nine girls between the ages of 20 and 23 years participated in a ten-week program of progressive resistance weight training, on an average of 2.5 days per week, 40 minutes a day. Hydrostatic weighings and an extensive series of anthropometric measurements were taken at the beginning and at the conclusion of the study. The results from this study are presented in Table 9.4. With the exception of one girl, body

Table 9.4

BODY COMPOSITION CHANGES IN NONATHLETIC FEMALES
AS A RESULT OF A TEN-WEEK PROGRAM OF WEIGHT TRAINING

| Subject | Weight, kg | | Density, gm/ml | | Fat, % | | LBW, kg | | Fat, kg | |
	pre	*post*	*pre*	*post*	*pre*	*post*	*pre*	*post*	*pre*	*post*
AJ	61.5	64.7	1.047	1.046	22.9	23.2	47.4	49.7	14.1	15.0
SS	60.8	61.1	1.045	1.045	23.5	23.7	46.5	46.6	14.3	14.5
AL	58.9	60.3	1.045	1.042	23.8	25.0	44.9	45.3	14.0	15.0
LW	50.9	49.7	1.050	1.053	21.2	20.2	40.1	39.6	10.8	10.1
SP	64.9	65.5	1.046	1.045	23.0	23.5	49.9	50.1	14.9	15.4
MF	49.6	50.5	1.046	1.049	23.0	22.0	38.1	39.4	11.4	11.1
PC	60.0	59.0	1.042	1.042	25.0	24.9	45.0	44.3	15.0	14.7
CR	49.6	49.9	1.063	1.064	15.5	15.4	41.9	42.2	7.7	7.7
JJ	71.7	70.7	1.019	1.022	36.0	34.3	45.9	46.4	25.8	24.2
Mean	58.7	59.0	1.045	1.046	23.8	23.6	44.4	44.8	14.3	14.2

weight remained fairly constant. Lean body weight increased in all but two of the girls, and four of the girls exhibited slight increases in fat weight of one kilogram or less.

In looking at both of these studies, it appears that weight training per se has a marginal influence on changes in the body composition of females. There appears to be a slight increase in lean body weight and a slight decrease in body fat. The increase in lean weight is probably a result of muscular hypertrophy, although significant changes in muscle girths were not noted in either study.

In the study reported earlier by Moody et al., in which body composition changes were observed in obese girls as a result of a walking and jogging program, a group of normal and underweight girls were included in this study for comparative purposes. Four of these girls actually gained both fat and lean weight during the course of the exercise program. Individuals who are chronically underweight find it nearly impossible to gain weight, particularly fat weight. With this in mind, Wilmore, in 1970 (unpublished data), took seven chronically underweight females and put them on a 15-week program of controlled treadmill exercise, five days a week, 30 minutes a day, in an attempt to assist them in gaining weight. Each subject had a previous history of being unable to gain weight. They felt uncomfortable at their present weight and had often attempted to gain weight over several years without success. During the first five weeks, each subject walked at 3.5 mph, starting at 0% slope, with the slope being increased by 1% increments every five minutes. Subsequent work loads were geared to the condition of the subjects. Body weight was recorded each day to within 25 grams.

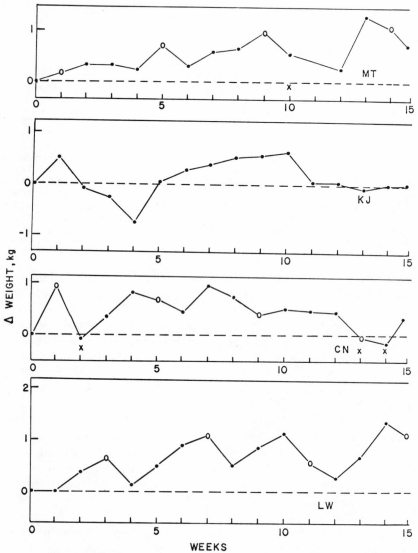

Fig. 9.1 Weight changes in chronically underweight females during a 15-week program of controlled exercise. The open circles indicate menstruation and the x's indicate periods of illness.

Each girl underwent an extensive anthropometric evaluation and a hydrostatic weighing at the beginning, midpoint, and conclusion of the study. Two of the subjects were unable to perform the hydrostatic weighings due to a tremendous fear of the water.

The changes in body weight for each of these girls is illustrated in Figure

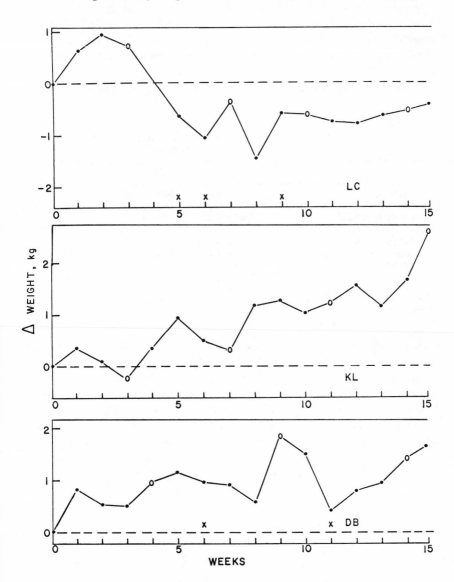

Fig. 9.1 continued

9.1. With the exception of two subjects (LC and KJ) and during periods of illness, there appears to be a slow but steady trend of weight gain. By the seventh week, four of the girls had achieved greater than a one kilogram increase in weight. Of the two girls who showed no weight gain, one (KJ) was more than likely a case of anorexia nervousa in which weight changes were more closely related to the emotional state. The second girl (LC), was the most uncooperative of all seven subjects and missed about 50% of the training sessions for various reasons. Unfortunately, several of the girls developed upper respiratory infections during the study, which severely handicapped their exercise program and contributed to significant losses in weight. Table 9.5 illustrates the changes in body composition with the exercise program.

Table 9.5

MEANS AND STANDARD DEVIATIONS FOR THE BODY
COMPOSITION PARAMETERS

	N^a	*Initial*	*Midpoint*	*Final*
Weight, kg	7	50.12 ± 5.95^b	50.45 ± 5.96	50.74 ± 5.96
	5	48.72 ± 6.58	49.15 ± 6.77	49.51 ± 6.80
Lean Body Weight, kg	5	41.63 ± 4.04	42.61 ± 4.15	42.74 ± 3.85
Absolute Fat, kg	5	7.09 ± 3.29	6.55 ± 3.30	6.77 ± 3.50
Relative Fat, %	5	14.1 ± 5.32	12.8 ± 5.52	13.2 ± 5.44
Density, gm/cc	5	$1.067 \pm .012$	$1.070 \pm .013$	$1.069 \pm .013$
Total Skin-folds, mm	7	123.9 ± 29.4	124.4 ± 29.9	141.8 ± 33.4
	5	115.6 ± 31.1	120.6 ± 35.7	135.7 ± 38.5

^{a}*Two of the subjects failed to complete the hydrostatic weighing.*
^{b}*Mean ± Standard Deviation*

It was anticipated that any weight gain would be distributed between both the lean and fat compartments of the body. The results indicate that the weight gains were solely in lean tissue, with an actual decrease being observed in both absolute and relative fat. It is of interest to note, however, that there was a significant increase in subcutaneous fat as measured by the sum of 12 skin-fold thicknesses. It is unlikely that this was due to measurement error, as each site was assessed a minimum of three times each time measurements were taken to insure reliable data. It appears that there was actually a selective increase in external, subcutaneous fat, but a decrease in internal fat.

Interpretations and Summary

It appears from the limited data presented in this chapter that exercise does mediate a basic change in body composition. There is an increase in the lean body weight which is probably a result of muscular hypertrophy. The muscular hypertrophy is possibly the consequence of an increase in the level of serum–human–growth–hormone (HGH) which has been shown to rise during exercise (70, 109, 127). HGH is considered a protein anabolic hormone, and, in animals receiving growth hormone, the increased deposition of protein is accompanied by a loss of carcass fat (135). This latter finding could be related to the loss of fat which has been a consistent finding in the studies reviewed in this chapter.

The loss of body fat is associated with an increased expenditure of calories. However, the caloric equivalent of the amount of exercise actually performed is under that necessary to account for the fat loss in some studies. It is possible that there is a concomitant decrease in caloric intake with exercise, which results in a caloric imbalance of the magnitude necessary to explain the fat loss. The work of Mayer and his colleagues at Harvard (85) would support this latter concept. They have shown that exercise up to one hour in duration per day tends to suppress the appetite. There is also the possibility that exercise stimulates lipolytic action (44, 101). No definite conclusions can be drawn at this time relative to the causal mechanism(s). It is probable, however, that fat loss with exercise results from a complex series of biochemical reactions which will be totally understood only after many years of research.

Chapter 10 / Dietary Regulation of Body Composition

Populations Subjected to Restricted Diets

During and following World War II, despite the severe hardships and stresses conducive to cardiac disabilities, there was an unexpected sharp reduction in the incidence of and mortality from diabetes and cardiovascular disease in the war-damaged countries. In Norway, for example, although caloric intake per capita was not reduced more than about 300 Calories, there was drastic reduction in fat intake. Coincident with these alterations in diet, there was a substantial decline in mortality, notably in death from circulatory diseases and equally evident for both sexes and all ages (126). No doubt, several factors can be postulated to account for the reduced mortality which subsequently returned (with resumption of the usual diet) to the higher pre-war level. Nevertheless, pathologists for many years have been aware of the advanced atherosclerotic changes in population groups subsisting on diets high in animal fat in contrast to the comparative integrity of vascular tissues of the poorer segment of population subsisting on cereals and deriving their fat chiefly from vegetable oils. This segment of the population also performed the manual labor.

Germany

The German nutritional experience following World War II, which Behnke reviewed firsthand, is unique in history in that some 43 million persons who had subsisted prior to the war on a diet similar to that of Americans had their caloric intake reduced generally (with the exception of farmers and selected groups) to a semistarvation level. Food consisted essentially of bread, potatoes, and meager amounts of animal protein and fat. These strictures contributed to greatly increased infant mortality, inhibition of growth, and arrest of work output except in coal mining and some minor industries where supplemental rations were issued.

Average body weight for males in the 20–45 year age group was 131 pounds in September, 1947. This represents a loss of some 25 pounds from American standard weight for this age group. In the older age groups, limited in their ability to forage for food, weight loss in contrast to the usual maturity weight gain when food is plentiful was greater, as shown by the following data.

DATA FROM THE STREET-WEIGHING PROGRAM IN CITIES (1947)

	Males			*Females*		
Group	20–29	40–49	Over 60	20–29	40–59	Over 60
Weight (lbs)	131.3	128.9	124.5	119.3	117.6	112.2

The average daily deficit in calories projected for a three-year period was about 700 for normal consumers. Adjustment to the reduced caloric level was seen as adaptation (in absence of forced labor), chiefly by decreased activity and fall in basal metabolism. Weight loss accounted for less than 25% of the projected caloric deficit.

Authoritative statements by German work physiologists regarding the effect of caloric restriction on normal work output are pertinent. On an adequate diet a heavy worker will utilize the food equivalent of 3600 Calories per day. Of these some 2000 Calories are necessary for maintenance of basal and "obligate" activity outside of job requirement. There remain 1600 Calories for work proper. If he receives only 2500 Calories, as in the autumn of 1946, he can reduce basal and obligate Calories to about 1800, but the chief reduction is in work output which is now equivalent to 700 Calories.

In this Chapter, we shall enumerate results of tests related to voluntary restriction of diet and the compositional nature of the attendant weight loss. A principal concern is adipose tissue, about which little is known in the human (in contrast to the small mammal).

Quantity and Type of Nutrients

It is consensus that acquired obesity can be corrected by restriction of caloric intake to less than metabolic (basal and activity) requirements.

However, dietary control of obesity alone has been singularly ineffective. There is substantial evidence that in the early stages of growth of the small mammal the number of adipocytes can be controlled by dietary restriction (69). In addition, the type of diet is important. During the weanling period, for example, piglets that were fed a commercial infant food high in fat and low in protein had about double the amount of body fat of piglets fed a standard animal diet low in fat (53). The amount of protein was not the controlling variable in these tests.

In the growing mammal fat gain may be primarily due to an increase in number (hyperplasia) of adipocytes. In the mature animal, fat gain, at least to 25–30% body fat (i.e., to onset of what in man is frank obesity), appears to due to an enlargement (hypertrophy) of existing lipocytes. It is characteristic of the growing mammal that excessive fatness is much more under dietary control than it is under the influence of genotype (111).

An incredible finding in animal nutrition is that lifespan of rodents and some larger species can be extended, not by optimal or overfeeding, but by underfeeding if initiated at the end of the weaning period. In the pioneer report of McCay and Crowell (87), drastic underfeeding of the rats produced stunting and retarded sexual development. In advancing these studies, Berg and Simms (30) maintained rats on a restricted but balanced diet which was 54% of the usual *ad libitum* intake. This modified diet prevented the rats from becoming fat but did not appreciably retard growth as measured by skeletal length. Weight was reduced to a level 40% below that of control rats and life span was prolonged 25%.

Substances Which Accompany Fat Gain or Loss

The distinction is important between fat (F) as extracted from adipose tissue by ether and other solvents, and substances (s) lost or gained in response to dietary manipulation. The existence of the $F + s$ entity (density $\cong$ .92 to .96) has been referred to previously as "tissue gained or lost," excess fat, adipose tissue, and simply fat. Brožek et al. (37) have designated the components gained or lost in response to dietary regulation as "obesity tissue," the reality of which depended upon the uncertainties in determination of an extracellular (thiocyanate) space. Currently, the determination of the ratio of exchangeable sodium and potassium and the constancy of this cation-anion relationship to total body water (tritiated water space) would assure the validity of essential biochemical analysis to assess hydration in obesity.

More substantial is the histologic approach. The painstaking dissections of Pitts (103, 104) have clarified the nature of fat-free substances which accompany fat deposition. Both adipose tissue and nonadipose substance are involved in fat accretion in the small mammal. Within adipose tissue as a discrete entity, Pitts et al. (105) found that the ratio of fat (i.e., extracted lipid) to fat-free residue consisting of solids and water (designated the "fatness ratio") increased from a low of 0.5 to 3.2 during fat gain in normal littermates. *During fat gain there was no change in the mass of fat-free residue* which is indicative of enlargement (hypertrophy) of existing fat cells. In obese mice not only was the fatness-weight ratio higher ($\cong$ 5.2), but there was also a rectilinear increase of residue (water-solids) concurrent with lipid accretion which is indicative of increased cellularity (hyperplasia).

Within adipose tissue, the classical investigation of Allen, Krzywicki, and Roberts (3) revealed a remarkable constancy of water content in human adipose tissue (79.2% $\pm$1.3) free of lipid over the range of 60 to 90% tissue fatness. This diluent effect of lipid on the fat-free moiety of adipose tissue is tabulated in Table 10.1, and it is inferred that fat gain or loss does not alter

Table 10.1

INVERSE RELATIONSHIP OF FAT AND WATER-RESIDUE IN ADIPOSE TISSUE[a]

Fat	Percentage Water	Percentage Residue	Density[b]	Cal/kg[c]
100	0	0	0.900	9400
90	8	2	0.913	8540
85[d]	12	3	0.920	8110
80	16	4	0.928	7680
75	20	5	0.934	7250
65	26	9	0.954	6470
60[d]	32	8	0.956	5960
50	40	10	0.971	5100
25	60	15	1.011	2950
0	80	20	1.054[e]	800

[a]*A projection based on assumption of constancy of fat-free adipose tissue mass.*
[b]*Density: fat (0.90), water (0.993), residue (1.40).*
[c]*Caloric equivalent of adipose or adipose-mimetic "tissue."*
[d]*Usual range of fat percentage in mature adipose tissue.*
[e]*Adipose tissue as a whole, i.e., not cells; density is variable depending on solids present, e.g., glycogen.*

the structure of the lipocyte. It would appear that in the absence of hyperplasia the s fraction of the $F + s$ entity is nonadipose substance—a surmise supported by Pitt's investigations. It is coincidental that the density of tissue weight gain is within the range of density of adipose tissue.

In man, Stern (124) found that the lipid content of the fat cell was highly correlated with the percentage of fat in the body. In his obese patients the amount of lipid per cell was about five-fold greater than in lean subjects.

In application of information in the preceding paragraphs to weight reduction, it would appear that the optimal dietary regimen is one in which the ratio of fat to lean substances is highest. In any case, the density of the tissue lost should not exceed the upper range of density of adipose tissue ($\cong 0.96$).

Dietary Regulated Weight Loss in Man

Principles

The usual nutritional laboratory study is only a few weeks in duration during the course of which healthy men on severely restricted diets lose about 10% body weight. In such tests the substances lost may be chiefly "labile" water and protein stores which together with some loss of fat account for about 2500 Calories per kg of weight loss.

In the treatment of frank obesity, a drastic reduction in food (to 400 Cal/daily) and salt intake as well may be accompanied by the loss of 2 to 4 liters of water, usually during the first week. The reduction of salt intake from eight or more grams daily to about 1.5 grams or less decreases appreciably the size of the extracellular chloride space. Some obese ward patients, in order not to gain weight, must restrict their caloric intake to 800–1000 Calories daily to counter the type of adaptation previously referred to in connection with populations subsisting on restricted diets.

The dietary phase of a regimen for weight reduction embodies not only restriction of calories and alteration of type of food ingested, but regulation of salt and potassium intake as well. The failure of individuals to maintain their reduced weights may be related to the crash methods employed in weight reduction. An ideal program may be projected as a reversal of the manner in which excess fat was acquired. This would entail increase in physical activity and some limitation amounting to several hundred calories in carbohydrates and fats. The enforced war-time restriction in Norway points the way to proper control with due attention to the requirement for animal protein and accessory substances such as vitamins and minerals.

The physiologic cost of weight reduction must be assessed not only in terms of loss of lean tissue, but also in reduction of metabolic activity and capacity for work. Such easily monitored parameters as pulse rate (basal) and blood pressure must be under continual surveillance.

Emphasis is placed on an *idem-diem* regimen in which the same food items are eaten for two meals daily together with a third meal consisting of a limited number of free-choice items. Such diets, properly prepared, coupled with some adaptation and individual motivation, can become standard for metabolic wards and long-term ambulatory therapy.

Experimental Protocol and Test Data, Subject Z

OBJECTIVE. In order to ascertain the effect of several reducing diets on body composition, tests were carried out on Subject Z (age 52 years) who was moderately obese (30% of body weight as fat) when weight reduction was initiated. Earlier weight reduction on the same subject was carried out in 1939 in connection with Navy underwater weighing procedure, and another weight-reducing regimen was completed in 1970. Observations in 1955–1956 will be presented in some datail.

WEIGHT LOSS AND BODY COMPOSITION (TABLE 10.2). In 1940, ingestion of a free-choice but quantity restricted diet by Subject Z was accompanied by weight loss of 8.7 kg (19.1 pounds) over a period of seven months. The spe-

Table 10.2

EFFECT OF DIETARY ALTERATION AND AGING ON BODY COMPOSITION OF SUBJECT Z

		Age	Weight	Density	Volume	TBW	LBW	Remarks
Period I								
3/12	1940	37	92.05	1.051[a]	87.53	—	71.8[b]	Hydro. Weighing
10/9	1940	38	83.18	1.066[a]	78.14	—	71.1	Hydro. Weighing
	1949	46	91.6	1.049	87.32	49.9	69.6	TBW(antipyrine)
Period II								
12/20	1955	52	101.5	1.035	98.06	49.6	69.9	Siri Techniques
3/30	1956	52	86.3	1.047	82.43	48.9	66.6	Siri Techniques
6/29	1956	52	84.4	1.053	80.15	47.5	66.0	Siri Techniques
10/16	1956	53	86.5	1.058	81.76	47.6	67.6	Siri Techniques
11/12	1956	53	83.0	1.058	78.45	45.3	64.6	Siri Techniques
	1959	56	93.6	—	—	48.5	67.4	TBW, [42]K (Boling)
	1960	57	94.6	1.040	90.96	50.2	69.1	Hydro. Weighing
	1963	59	96.8	1.027	94.25	50.1	67.4	Siri Techniques
	1964[c]	61	96.3	1.023	94.13	50.7	66.9	Siri Techniques
Period III								
	1967	64	95.6	1.032	94.79	—	67.3	Hydro. Weighing[d]
	1970	67	87.9	1.043	84.28	—	66.2	Hydro. Weighing[d]
	1971	68	84.3	1.049	80.20	—	65.9	Hydro. Weighing[d]
	1971	68	81.8	1.047	78.13	49.9	66.8	Siri Techniques

[a]Density = specific gravity − 0.005.
[b]%Fat = 1.100 − Sp.Gr./0.002 (Rathbun-Pace abridged formula).
[c]Examinee is diabetic.
[d]Wilmore's technique.

cific gravity tests on Subject Z in 1940 are of some historic interest; they were among the first in which the net volume of the body (i.e., corrected for residual air) was determined. Residual air determinations in the Osserman studies (97, 98) were performed by Dr. Grover Pitts, whose classical contributions have been referred to in connection with dissections of adipose tissue.

At the time Willmon and Behnke (142) introduced nitrogen and helium washout techniques for quantification of residual volume as well as the somewhat abbreviated procedure of pressure drop (within 15 seconds) from 4 to 1 atmospheres.

In Dr. Siri's tests beginning in 1955, body volume was measured in his helium dilution chamber; total body water (*TBW*) was assessed by isotopic dilution with tritiated (HTO) water. In 1949, antipyrine was employed by Osserman et al. (97) as the water-diffusible substance. In tests other than those performed by Dr. Siri, density was ascertained by underwater weighing. The data in Table 10.2 are representative of all total body water and density values. Except for decrement in total body water as a result of the pemmican (high fat-protein) tests, the results are remarkably consistent. The decrease in lean body weight of Subject Z from 1940 (and with assurance from 1949 when total body water was measured) to 1971 is a geriatric alteration.

In the detailed series covering the course of weight reduction from December, 1955, to October, 1956, the overall weight loss was 15 kg (33 pounds). Although the reduced weight in October, 1956, was the same as in October, 1950, body density (1.058) was well below the value (1.066) of the earlier period. The density of the tissue lost during this period of weight reduction may be computed as 0.92, from which the estimate is made of loss of fat amounting to 12.75 kg, and of lean tissue, 2.25 kg. It is evident from the data (Table 10.2) that the reducing regimen could have been terminated at the end of 100 days (30 March 1956).

RESTRICTED DIETS AND LIPOPROTEIN PATTERNS. Lipoprotein patterns were followed in response to the following diets: (1) restricted free-choice items, (2) corn oil-milk powder, (3) butter fat-milk powder, (4) fat-free carbohydrate (CHO) diet, and (5) a pemmican diet, essentially fat and protein (Table 10.3).

Daily exercise superimposed on a sedentary base was augmented by 30 minutes of heavy manual labor for warm-up followed by 15 to 45 minutes of ocean swimming (depending upon the temperature of the cold water).

The lipoprotein patterns in response to dietary alteration are in accord with previous findings of Gofman, Jones, Lindgren, and co-workers (61, 62) who conducted the ultracentrifugal analyses in the Donner Laboratory of Medical Physics, University of California at Berkeley.

A. Caloric restriction was accompanied by an immediate decrease in Svedberg (S_f) lipoprotein levels. The atherogenic index $(A.I.)$ was reduced from 122 (conducive to coronary heart disease) to 73 (well below the borderline level of 89 which separates coronary-prone from those individuals less likely to develop coronary occlusion). This index relative to S_f fractions of beta lipoproteins was initially formulated as,

$$A.I. = 0.1(S_f\,0 - 12) + 0.175(S_f\,12 - 400)$$

Table 10.3   EFFECT OF ALTERATION AND RESTRICTION OF DIET ON LIPOPROTEIN PATTERNS (SUBJECT Z)

Date (1955–1956)	*Diet*	*Cals.*	*Lipoproteins*[a]		*A.I.*[b]	*Weight*	*TBW*	*LBW*
			0–12	12–400				
12/20	Free Choice	2800	414	460	122	101.5	49.6	69.9
12/23–6/7	Restricted	1400	501	178	81	86.4	47.2	66.0
6/21–6/29	Corn Oil (120 gm) Milk powder	3200	262	155	53	84.4	47.5	66.0
6/30–7/6	Butter (120 gm) Milk powder	3200	350	288	85	84.1	47.6	67.6
10/16–10/24	High CHO (fat-free)	3000	316	412	104	86.5	47.6	67.6
11/5–11/12	Pemmican 45% Fat 45% Prot.	1000	673	231	108	83.0	45.3	64.6

[a]Svedberg ultracentrifugal fractions in mg/percent.
[b]Atherogenic index, see text.

Subsequently the formulation was revised to shift the relatively small, but cholesterol-rich S_f 12 — 20 fraction from the second to the first class.

B. Ingestion of vegetable fat (corn oil, 120 gm/daily) was associated with a further reduction of the atherogenic index to 53.

C. Replacement of vegetable fat with animal fat (120 gms of butter/daily) was accompanied by an elevation of the atherogenic index from 53 to 85, but not into the coronary-prone zone.

D. A high CHO diet (limited to 3.3 gms of fat daily) was complicated by return of the atherogenic index to a level of 104—well into the coronary-prone zone.

E. A low calorie (100 cal/daily) pemmican ration (45% animal fat — 45% protein by weight) was associated with an elevation of the S_f 0–12 class of lipoproteins sufficient to raise the atherogenic index to 108 units.

COMMENTS ON THE LIPOPROTEIN DATA. The influence both of a high animal fat, and notably of a high CHO (fat-free) diet on the Svedberg lipoprotein classes is essentially that reported by Nichols et al. (94) from the Donner Laboratory. Of special interest is the high atherogenic index of 104 associated with ingestion of a low fat–high CHO diet. The pioneer finding is the CHO-associated hyperlipidemia in the 12–400 S_f class which is conducive to coronary heart disease and a reflection of sugar intolerance as well. By oversight, blood glucose levels were not ascertained at the time and the pre-diabetic condition of Subject Z was not established.

In follow-up of Subject Z seven years later, serum glucose levels were markedly elevated and his response to glucose challenge established the diagnosis of maturity-onset diabetes. Subject Z had participated in numerous stress tests and had enjoyed seemingly excellent health for over 40 years. Subsequent to the epoch findings of the Donner Laboratory, the triad of overweight, glucose intolerance, and elevated serum triglycerides is now recognized as an ominous clinical entity. The association of diminished glucose tolerance with obesity will be mentioned in connection with adipose tissue.

COMMENTS ON THE PEMMICAN TESTS. Some difficulties attending the employment of "off-center" diets are apparent from the weight loss (chiefly water) of 4.6 kg during the course of four days as reflected by fluid balance data in Table 10.4. Following the daily ingestion of two meat bars which supplied 1000 calories daily, ketosis supervened within a period of 72 hours. The following blood serum values (mg %) were recorded.

Date	Ketones	Sugar	Cholesterol	Phospholipids
11/9, 1956	15.5	72	286	287

Table 10.4 FLUID BALANCE OF SUBJECT Z DURING THE COURSE OF A RESTRICTED PEMMICAN DIET (NOV. 1956)

Control[a]			Pemmican Tests							
Day	Urine Vol. (24 hrs)	Urinary N[b] gm	Day (Nov.)	Weight lbs	Water	Coffee	Food[c]	Urine Output	Diff.[a]	
1	1025	14.1	5	194.0	500	1000	112	2011	−399	
2	850	12.6	6	190.5	750	1000	112	1779	83	
3	1150	14.5	7	188.0	720	1030	112	1792	70	
4	995	12.7	8	185.0	750	1000	112	1264	598	
5	1000	12.0	9[e]	184.0	750	1000	140[e]	1120	770	
6	1080	12.5	10[e]	183.8	750	1000	140[e]	1108	782	
7	1000	13.3	11[e]	182.8	750	1000	140[e]	1046	844	
8	850	13.0								
9	1100	13.6								
10	920	12.5								

[a] Caloric intake : 1902 (11.5 gm N daily); Fluid intake + metab. water (1908 ml daily).
[b] Analysis: Courtesy of Dr. Harold Harper's Lab (Univ. Calif., San Francisco Medical Center).
[c] Two meat bars daily (45% fat, 45% protein by weight), 1000 calories, total.
[d] Average daily evaporative loss (control test), 900 ml.
[e] 50 gm of glucose added daily to meat bar ration.

A protein deficit of 18 gm daily was incurred despite the otherwise adequate intake of 76.8 gms of animal protein, as revealed by nitrogen balance data. This type of test, implemented in the interest of providing compact emergency rations, illustrates results which may be anticipated from the imposition of crash diets to expedite weight loss.

CHANGES IN SUBCUTANEOUS FAT. Biopsies of ample tissue samples before and after weight loss revealed a 45% increase in DNA (Desoxyribonucleic acid) per unit weight of tissue following weight reduction. Some tabular data with reference to adipose tissue analysis follow (50, 51).

Date of Biopsy	12/19/55	4/10/56
Body Weight, kg	101.5	86.6
Analysis: Fat %	79.2	62.3
Water %	18.0	32.4
Fat/residue, gm/gm	28.2	11.8
Water/residue, gm/gm	6.4	6.1
DNA/residue, mg/gm	4.14	4.02

Since the quantity of subcutaneous fat is proportional to total body fat (up to perhaps 30% of body weight when internal depots attain saturation), then the 12.5 kg of fat lost during the period of restricted dieting represent about 45% of the estimated total of 27.8 kg of body fat. This DNA-calculated value is a rough approximation of the 30.6 kg of total body fat estimated from densitometric analysis.

The ratio in adipose tissue of Fat %/Water-residue %, before weight reduction of 3.81, and after weight loss of 1.65, may well provide a meaningful index of fatness. We may anticipate that analyses of adipose tissue will provide a reliable guide for weight reduction, and with ratios of fat/lean between 1.5 and 2.0 designated as limiting levels. Investigations of Hirsch and Knittle (69) and of Stern (124) provide innovative techniques for assessment of fat per adipocyte. Further, metabolic studies of adipose tissue by Salans, Knittle, and Hirsch (110) reveal the exciting finding that obese adipocytes require much more insulin for glucose conversion than do lean adipocytes.

FLUID INTAKE-OUTPUT DATA. Surveillance of fluid intake-output is an essential part of controlled dietary regulation. In the pemmican test, the negative fluid balance amounted to 3.5 liters over a seven-day period (Table 10.4). The control data in the table pertain to the monitoring of urinary nitrogen excretion as well as fluid intake-output. It was helpful in these tests to have the subject ingest the same amounts of fluids (in the absence of sweating) at the same time periods daily, as well as to utilize a simple unvarying (*idem-diem*) diet which, if properly prepared, is acceptable.

PULSE RATE AND BLOOD PRESSURE (TABLE 10.5). The level of the pulse rate under basal or standard conditions is a criterion, as we shall see later, of

Table 10.5

PULSE RATES AND BLOOD PRESSURES OF SUBJECT Z IN RELATION TO BODY COMPOSITION AND LIPOPROTEIN PATTERNS

	Dec./55–Mar./56	*4/4–6/7*	*10/8–11/9*
Recordings	58	29	24
Pulse Rate (S.D.)	56.5 (5.8)	59 (5.5)	50.5 (2.6)
Systolic B.P. (S.D.)	128 (5.6)	119 (6.1)	118 (4.1)
Diastolic B.P. (S.D.)	81 (7.4)	74 (5.9)	75 (4.0)
	Dec./55 *Free Choice*	*June/56* *Corn Oil* *Milk Powder*	*Oct./56* *Fat-Free*
Weight kg	101.5	84.4	86.5
LBW kg	69.9	66.4	67.4
TBW kg	49.6	47.5	47.6
Density	1.035	1.053	1.058
Lipoproteins mg %			
S_f 0–12	414	262	316
S_f 12–400	460	155	412
Atherogenic Index	122	53	104

metabolic activity. In the tests involving Subject Z, the standard deviation both of pulse rate and of blood pressure was small for a subject engaged in unremitting administrative routine. A significant decrease in pulse rate occurred during the pemmican tests, in which additional exercise was necessary to counteract the otherwise adaptive drop in activity attendant upon a 1000 Calorie diet.

Group Metabolic Deterioration

From the point of view of preventive medicine, the importance of the longitudinal serum lipid determinations covering a selected military population as reported by Allen, Clark, and Wilson (1) can hardly be over-stated. From the following abstracted mean values it is seen that moderate weight increase in young adult males (18–34 years of age) is associated with an accelerated rise in all three classes of Svedberg flotation fractions, and notably in cholesterol.

These foreboding data are especially pertinent in the light of the deterioration of an older group of aviators monitored in the U.S. Navy Pensacola survey. In this rigidly supervised study of Naval aviators initiated by Captain Ashton Graybiel (MC) USN, 964 Naval cadets and 92 flight instructors were

No. Exam.	Age	Weight[a] (lb)	Cholesterol (mg/100 ml)	Lipoprotein Fractions (mg/100 ml)		
				S_f 0–12	12–20	20–400
106	18	156	176	184	21	—
171	19–21	162	198	187	—	—
236	22	165	219	229	22	50
205	23–26	169	239	296	25	80
193	27–30	173	235	319	30.5	96
155	31–34	175	242	330	30.5	112

[a]*Mean stature, approx. 71.3 inches*

examined at the Harvard Fatigue Laboratory in 1940. Twenty-four years later it was possible to re-examine 385 men whose average age was 48 years. Of this number only 12 had neither complaints nor unusual physical findings. Prominent in actual or potential disability were cardiovascular disease and metabolic derangements manifest by the incidence of diabetes, hyperurecemia, gout, and enlarged liver.

Resumé Comments on Diet and Weight Reduction

Weight reduction of the obese by dietary restriction alone has not been successful. Part of the failure can be attributed to the crash reducing regimens imposed on the overweight. A rational approach entails a reversal of those conditions which led to the excess weight gain, namely modest restriction of caloric intake (200–300 Calories) coupled with increase in systematic exercise. The procedure, complicated by abundance and social pressures, is essentially one of long-term reconditioning. The physiologic cost of weight reduction must be assessed not only as concomitant loss with fat of lean tissue as well, but in reduction of metabolic activity and capacity for work. Weight reduction is a judicious procedure which invites systematic control of physiologic and biochemical parameters. Emphasis has been placed on the highly informative data to be derived from biopsy of adipose tissue.

Weight control during infancy and childhood is a pediatric problem. During adolescence such control, apart from curtailment of dietary excess and restriction of fat, is a matter of augmented physical activity. In early adult life the acquisition of excess weight is associated with a rise in serum cholesterol and lipoprotein levels. Both systematic exercise and dietary regulation which features limitation of alcoholic beverages are required to control the early "marital" weight gain. Perhaps the most important contribution of this section is the consideration that the obese person is one who may be losing his tolerance for carbohydrate. The demand of obese tissue for excess insulin is inexorable. Advantage can be taken of routine surgical operations to make histologic and biochemical assessment of samples of this readily spared tissue. Lastly, to paraphrase a Napoleonic aphorism, every obese person carries the baton of the diabetic in his knapsack.

Effect of Weight Reduction on Body Configuration

Somatographic Representation

Partitional anthropometry does not provide a primary measure but rather a provisional or relative estimate of fat loss from regional parts of the body. Relative loss of weight for Subject Z whose compositional data were analyzed in the preceding section is depicted in Fig. 10.1 as the spatial width between axes. Body weight, for example, decreased 16.4% between September, 1955, and June, 1956. Shoulder girth decreased 4.1%, and the

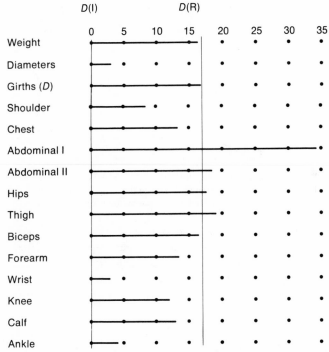

Fig. 10.1 Subject Z, percentage reduction of weight and dimensions. Percentage loss in body weight and in anthropometric dimensions converted to ponderal equivalents from:

$$\frac{(initial)^2 - (reduced)^2}{(initial)^2} \times 100$$

Key: $D(I)$ D axis before and $D(R)$ after weight reduction.

ponderal equivalent of this decrease is 8.0% from,

$$100 \times \frac{(\text{Shoulder g before})^2 - (\text{Shoulder g after})^2}{(\text{Shoulder g before})^2}$$

The somatogram (Fig. 10.2) based on the data in Table 10.6 shows the percentage deviation of each girth from its respective D axis. With the removal of part of the fat blanket, the d quotients following weight reduction

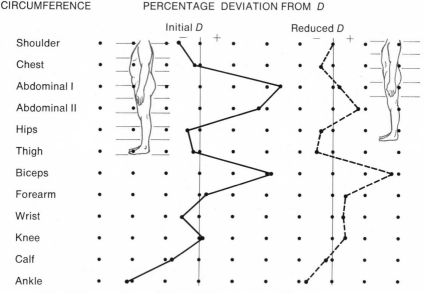

CIRCUMFERENCE   PERCENTAGE DEVIATION FROM D

Initial D Reduced D

Shoulder

Chest

Abdominal I

Abdominal II

Hips

Thigh

Biceps

Forearm

Wrist

Knee

Calf

Ankle

Fig. 10.2 Somatograms of Subject Z before (————) and after (– – –) weight reduction computed from a common D axis. Initial—age: 52 yrs; weight: 100 kg; stature: 17.88 dm; $D = 7.06$. Reduced—weight: 83.6 kg; $D = 6.43$.

tend to be in alignment with the exception of d (abdominal 2), d(biceps), and d(ankle). The last two quotients reflect the genotype or inherited configuration of Subject Z. In the last column of Table 10.6 the effects of aging are apparent from diminished size of thighs and arms, and the increase in the abdominal girths compared with measurements 15 years earlier when the subject was approximately the same weight.

REDUCTION TO BODY WEIGHT AT AGE 25. Initially the objective was to reduce Subject Z to his weight at age 25 years (80 kg). At the end of six months, however, body weight tended to plateau on a level of 85 kg, and the reducing regimen, culminating with the pemmican diet, was attended by rapidly diminishing return with regard to further weight loss and maintenance of body efficiency. At the age of 25, Subject Z should have held to his weight of 80 kg, but having exceeded this optimal limit by 20 kg he was

Table 10.6

CHANGE IN SHAPE OF SUBJECT Z IN RESPONSE TO DIETARY-INDUCED
WEIGHT LOSS AND AGING

		Sept 1955		*June* 1956		*Feb* 1971	
Age		52		52		67	
h		178.8		(178.8)		(178.8)	
Weight		100.0		83.6		84.3	
D		7.07		6.53		6.54	
3*F*		7.09		6.49		6.51	
uS–W[a]		136		114		115	
Sum 8 Diam		203.3		201.1		203.0	

k[b]	*Girths*	*cm*	*% dev.*[c]	*cm*	*% dev.*[c]	*cm*	*% dev.*[c]
18.47	Shoulder	125.7	−3.8	120.6	0	116.6	−3.5
15.30	Chest	108.0	−0.2	97.8	−2.2	102.6	2.5
12.84	Abdominal 1	101.2	11.5	84.7	1.0	86.7	3.2
13.30	Abdominal 2	100.5	9.2	90.8	4.6	93.5	7.5
15.57	Hip	108	−1.9	99.5	−2.1	100.8	−1.0
9.13	Thigh	64.2	−0.6	57.8	−3.1	55.6	−6.9
5.29	Biceps	41.3	10.4	37.7	9.1	36.3	4.9
4.47	Forearm	31.9	1.0	29.8	2.1	29.3	0.2
2.88	Wrist	19.4	−2.7	19.2	2.1	19.1	1.4
6.10	Knee	43.3	0.4	40.7	2.2	41.4	3.8
5.97	Calf	40.4	−4.3	38.8	−0.5	39.5	1.2
3.75	Ankle	23.8	−10.2	23.3	−4.7	23.3	−5.0

[a]*uS–W: unit size-weight = 183.6 $\sqrt{W/h^{1.7}}$, W in kg, h in dm.*
[b]*Proportionality constants from the reference man.*
[c]*Percentage deviation of d conversions from D axis.*

unable to return to the earlier weight. At age 53, he was content to accept
the reduced weight of 83.6 kg, which is actually less than age specific weight
calculated from frame size. Subsequently, there was regain of weight to 96.8
kg (age 59). In 1970–1971 (age 67) a final bout of dietary restriction (plus
not well-tolerated jogging) scaled weight level to 81.8 kg, but the subject now
felt prematurely old.

Contrast Between Hereditary and Acquired Fatness

The somatograms of Subject Z who became moderately fat (31%
body weight as fat) after age 25, and Subject 0 (34.6% fat) who was always
fat, are shown in Fig. 10.3. Both subjects are approximately the same weight,
stature, perimetric (*D*) size, and both have about the same amount of body
water. Frame size (Reference *C* weight), however, is about 5% less for
Subject 0. In July, 1955 (three months preceding the anthropometric measurements) this subject, a Navy man, was sent to a physician for supervised
weight reduction after he had difficulty in fitting into a uniform. At this time
he weighed 111.8 kg; over a period of three months, he was reduced to 98.3
kg (Fig. 10.4). In comparison with Subject Z, 0 has larger thighs and

CIRCUMFERENCE   PERCENTAGE DEVIATION FROM *D*

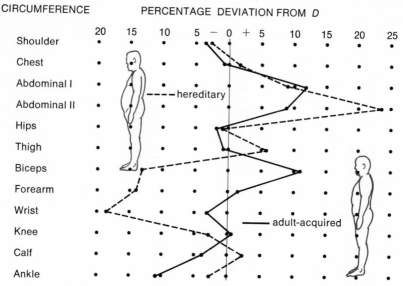

Fig. 10.3 Somatograms comparing adult-acquired (————) and hereditary (– – –) obesity. Hereditary—age: 31 yrs; weight: 98.9 kg; stature: 18.03 dm; *D* = 7.05. Adult-acquired—age: 52 yrs; weight: 100 kg; stature: 17.88 dm; *D* = 7.07.

CIRCUMFERENCE   PERCENTAGE DEVIATION FROM *D* AXES

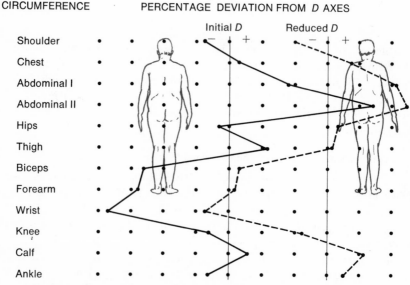

Fig. 10.4 Somatograms of Subject 0 before (————) and after (– – –) weight reduction computed from a common *D* axis. Initial—age: 31 yrs; weight: 98.9 kg; stature: 18.03 dm; *D* = 7.05. Reduced—weight: 85.0 kg; *D* = 6.27.

abdominal girths (notably abdominal 2) but the striking difference is his smaller arm size. Subject 0 was further reduced to about 79 kg (this weight was calculated from perimetric (*D*) size since a reliable scale weight was not obtained).

Somatotype photographs of Subjects Z and 0 were taken before and after weight reduction (Fig. 10.4), and were evaluated by Barbara Heath of Monterey.

Subject Z	Weight: 100 kg	Reduced to 83.6 kg
Somatotype	5 6.5 1.5	2.5 6.5 2
Subject O	Weight: 98.3 kg	Reduced to 85.0 kg
Somatotype	6 4 2	5 4 2

Subject Y is a large obese-muscular adolescent who, between examinations at ages 16.5 and 17.5 years, lost 13.7 kg (Fig. 10.5). The large abdominal and thigh girths are prominent in the somatogram. Loss of this quantity of fat did not alter his "constitutional" configuration.

Subject N, age 23, has been obese since childhood. However, he does not have the relatively large thighs frequently associated with early onset obesity (Fig. 10.6). The extremity girths show more than the usual loss of fat. Body

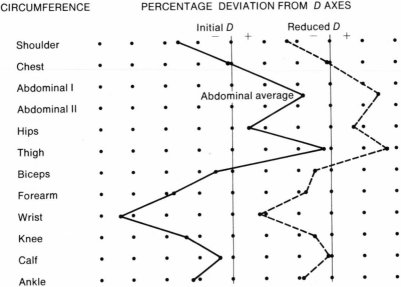

Fig. 10.5 Somatograms of Subject Y before (————) and after (– – –) weight reduction computed from a common *D* axis. Initial—age: 16.5 yrs; weight: 123.9 kg; stature: 19.45 dm; *D* = 7.59. Reduced—age: 17.5 yrs; weight: 110.2 kg; stature: 19.66 dm; *D* = 7.03.

configuration after weight loss (as in Subject Y) is nearly identical to body shape before weight loss, and we can conclude that the initial D (7.01) axis and deviate girths have been shifted, essentially unaltered, to the left. The "Fat Boy" type tends to remain a "Fat Boy" despite appreciable weight loss. These attributes are in contrast to the shape of reduced Subject Z who acquired fatness after the age of 25.

ANALYSIS OF ANTHROPOMETRIC DATA. In Table 10.7, the individual dimensions of Subjects Z, O, N, and Y, have been equated with weight loss scaled for each subject to a common value of 20%. Thus, the ponderal equivalent of each girth is proportional to their squared values as formulated previously. There is a sharp dichotomy between the ponderal equivalents of trunk, thigh, and biceps girths, and the extremity girths. Weight loss in the first grouping is about twice greater than from the extremities.

Table 10.7

THE EFFECT OF DIETARY RESTRICTION ON GIRTH SIZE[a]
OF FOUR MALES (SUBJECTS Z, O, N, AND Y)

	Z	O	N	Y
Age	52	31	23	16
h	178.8	180.3	177.8	194.5
h increase	—	—	—	196.6[b]
W (Initial)	100	98.3	128.2	123.9
W (Reduced)	83.6	78.7	100.9	110.2
% Reduction	16.4	19.9	21.3	11.1

Percentage Loss in Ponderal Equivalents[a]

Adjusted Weight Loss[c] Girths	20	20	20	20
Shoulder	9.8	24.0	20.4	25.6
Chest	21.9	24.5	21.7	26.3
Abdominal 1	36.5	19.3	25.4	44.0
Abdominal 2	22.4	34.7	28.4	32.1
Hip	18.4	24.5	20.0	22.2
Thigh	23.1	23.5	23.6	38.7
Biceps	20.4	22.9	25.5	24.9
Average	21.8	24.8	23.6	30.5
Forearm	15.5	7.4	9.6	9.2
Wrist	2.4	20.5	8.1	5.9
Knee	14.3	19.6	9.0	13.9
Calf	9.5	16.4	15.6	17.3
Ankle	5.0	8.5	7.3	14.8
Average	9.3	14.5	9.9	14.2

[a]Percentage Loss: $\frac{(Girth, before)^2 - (Girth, after)^2}{(Girth, before)^2} \times 100.$

[b]Increase in stature during the period of weight reduction.

[c]Adjusted weight loss = Weight loss $\times \frac{20}{Actual \% Loss}$

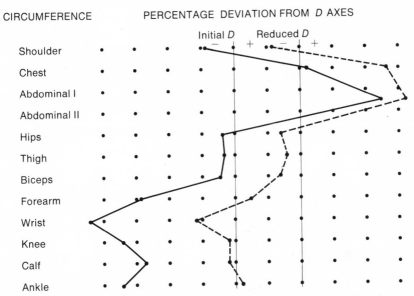

CIRCUMFERENCE   PERCENTAGE DEVIATION FROM *D* AXES

Fig. 10.6 Somatograms of Subject N before (———) and after (– – –) weight reduction computed from a common *D* axis. Initial—age: 23 yrs; weight: 128.4 kg; stature: 17.78 dm; *D* = 8.00. Reduced—weight: 101 kg; *D* = 7.15.

Table 10.8
EFFECT OF RESTRICTED DIETS ON SCALE WEIGHTS AND DIMENSIONAL EQUIVALENT WEIGHTS FOR SUBJECTS Z, O, N, AND Y

	Weight	*Ponderal Equivalent Weights*					
		D	*A′*	*B′*	*B–B*	*WFCA*	*C*
Subject Z							
Initial	100.0	99.1	104.9	98.1	86.9	90.9	82.5
7 mos.	83.6	84.4	84.9	87.3	81.5	84.2	80.5
Loss %	16.4	14.8	19.1	11.0	6.2	7.4	2.4
Subject O							
Initial	98.9	98.3	113.5	85.4	81.5	86.8	80.2
12 mos.	85.0[a]	78.7[a]	88.5	69.5	73.0	72.1	72.7
Loss %	—	19.9	22.0	18.6	10.4	16.9	9.4
Subject N							
Initial	128.2	126.3	151.4	95.0	104.6	90.0	84.1
5 mos.	100.9	98.9	110.9	82.3	96.8	79.1	78.6
Loss %	21.3	21.7	26.8	13.4	7.5	12.1	6.5
Subject Y							
Initial	123.9	121.0	139	106	101.6	103	94.0
12 mos.	110.2	105	116	96.4	94.5	94.7	92.2
Loss %	11.1	14.2	16.6	9.1	7.0	8.1	1.9

[a]*Perimetric measurements were not made at the time scale weight was recorded, and the calc. D(W) is more reliable for this analysis.*

In Table 10.8, weight loss from the A' (hip, average abdominal girths) component is twofold or more greater than relative weight loss from B' (all extremity girths except the thigh), or from *WFCA* and *B–B* (bideltoid-bitrochanteric widths). Ref(C), frame size weight, was not always computed from eight diameters. In obese persons, biacromial and bitrochanteric diameters together with those of the extremities are less subject to error because of overlying fat, than are chest and bi-iliac widths. Loss of subcutaneous fat, for example, in the reduced adolescent (Y) probably tended to mask some growth of frame size commensurate with the gain in stature from 194.5 cm to 196.6 cm.

Comparison of Weight Reduction in Lean and in Fat Males

Two classical experiments, one from Benedict (29) in 1915, the other from Keys and Brožek (75), Taylor and Keys (131), demonstrate the effect of reducing lean men. Benedict's fasting subject received only measured quantities of distilled water over a period of 31 days. In the Minnesota tests, the 32 subjects were lean men in the age range of 20–33 years who subsisted on a cereal-potato diet for a period of 168 days. The projected daily deficit was about 1400 Calories, and combined with *enforced exercise* induced a 25% loss of body weight and marked physical deterioration at the end of the test period. The results of these tests, while of considerable intrinsic importance, are not comparable to conditions in post-war Europe where individuals survived on a lower caloric ration for a period of several years.

ANTHROPOMETRIC DATA—BENEDICT'S FASTING SUBJECT. Although the

Table 10.9

ANTHROPOMETRIC DATA ON BENEDICT'S FASTING SUBJECT

Period	Weight	LBW[a]	Neck	Chest	Abdominal 1	Abdominal 2	Arm	Thigh	Calf
					Girths (cm)				
Initial	60.6	51.0	37.6	87.9	78.0	80.0	25.1	48.8	33.5
31 Days	47.4	45.5	33.5	80.0	62.7	68.1	21.1	38.3	30.0
Loss[b] %	21.8	10.8	20.6	17.2	35.4	27.5	29.3	34.0	19.8

	Initial	5th	12th	19th	25th	31st
			Day of Test			
Weight	60.6	56.4	53.6	51.1	49.3	47.4
W(D)[c]	61.1	58.3	54.6	51.1	47.4	45.2

[a]LBW from Wilmore's (iliac) formula (abridged).

[b]% Loss $= \dfrac{(Girth,\ before)^2 - (Girth,\ after)^2}{(Girth,\ before)^2} \times 100.$

[c]W(D) calculated from the sum of chest, abdominal average, arm, thigh, and calf girths; K(5 girths) reference man = 48.32; stature, 170.7 cm.

number of measurements is limited, it is feasible to compare loss of body weight with girths converted to ponderal equivalents (Table 10.9). Note the high losses from arm, thigh, and abdominal 1 (waist) perimeters. Neck size shrinks proportionally with body weight. Body weights could be calculated accurately from the sum of five girths (chest, abdominal average, arm, thigh, and calf); the sum of the conversion constants were those from the reference man $(K(5) = 48.32)$. The calculation of the initial weight, Calc. $W = (274.3/48.32)^2 \times h \times 0.111 = 61.1$ kg. On the twenty-fifth day of fasting, computed weight fell below scale weight and remained at a lower level until the end of the test. Either there was relatively greater perimetric shrinkage at this time, or change in shape supervened.

Wilmore's equation (LBW from abdominal 2 girth) provides a remarkably good estimate of lean body weight. Calculated lean body weight from his equation was 45.5 kg, or 1.9 kg less than scale weight at the end of 31 days of fasting.

ANTHROPOMETRIC DATA—MINNESOTA TESTS. The striking finding in these tests (Table 10.10) is the large loss of tissue from the arm, thigh, and calf compared with the trunk of young men who were normal in weight (about 12.5% fat) prior to dietary restriction. Densitometric lean body weight is interchangeable with lean body weight calculated from Wilmore's (abdominal 2) formula both initially and at the end of the period of dietary restriction.

In Table 10.11 a comparison is made of body weight and ponderal equivalent (girth) weight losses, of our obese subjects and the Minnesota volunteers. These data emphasize the importance of monitoring the extremity girths for comparison with those of the trunk during the course of dietary restriction.

The lean tissue cost of weight reduction may be assessed quantitatively from the ratio of fat/lean losses. The protein loss, for example, in Benedict's test, was 1.68 kg (estimated from the urinary nitrogen decrement), and from this value tissue loss is assessed as about 8.0 kg. Fat decrease by difference is 5.2 kg, and the fat/lean ratio is in the range of 0.65 to unity. Likewise in the Minnesota tests, the enforced exercise, in conjunction with a diet deficient both in calories and quality, resulted in a protein deficit of 2.68 kg; coupled with densitometric data, fat loss could be projected as about 6.8 kg, and lean tissue loss as 10 kg. Thus, in Benedict's starvation experiment and in the Minnesota restricted regimen (1570 Cal/daily), the fat/lean ratios at the termination of observations were similar (i.e., in the range of 0.6 to unity). By contrast, at the end of about seven months the fat/lean tissue losses (13.9/3.9) for Subject Z were 3.4 to 1.

Table 10.10

EFFECT OF DIETARY RESTRICTION ON ANTHROPOMETRIC PARAMETERS IN THE MINNESOTA EXPERIMENTS

| Period | Weight | Calc. W | Girths (cm) | | | | | d | LBW^a | |
			Chest	Abdominal 2	Arm	Thigh	Calf		Iliac	Diam
Initial	69.4	(69.4)	89.28	78.08	28.49	47.11	37.72	60.7	61.9	61.8
24 weeks	52.6	53.8	82.61	70.70	21.52	37.96	33.01	50.2	49.5	59.8
% Loss^b										
12 weeks	17.4	17.9	14.5	16.8	32.7	27.4	17.1	—	13.7	—
24 weeks	24.2	22.5	18.7	18.0	42.9	35.1	23.4	17.3	20.0	—
12–24 weeks	6.8	4.7	4.2	1.2	10.2	11.7	5.3	—	6.3	—

^{a} LBW: (d) densitometric, (iliac) Wilmore's formula, (Diam) 4 trunk diameters
^{b} % Loss (girths): dimensions squared as in Table 10.9 for comparison with weights.

Table 10.11   PERCENTAGE CHANGE IN BODY WEIGHTS AND ANTHROPOMETRIC PONDERAL EQUIVALENTS OF REDUCED LEAN AND REDUCED FAT MALES

Source	Subj. no.	Age	Weight I^a	Weight R^b	$\%^c$	Chest	% Reduction of Ponderal Equivalents^a Abdominal 1	Abdominal 2	Arm	Thigh	Calf	Scaled W^d
Benedict	1	31	60.6	47.4	21.8	15.8	32.5	25.2	26.9	31.6	18.2	20
Keys et al.	32	25.5	69.4	52.6	24.2	15.5	—	14.9	35.5	29.0	19.3	20
This Study												
Subject Z		52	100	83.6	16.4	21.9	36.5	22.4	20.4	23.1	9.5	20
Subject O		31	98.9	78.7	19.9	24.5	19.3	34.7	22.9	23.5	16.4	20
Subject N		23	128.2	100.9	21.3	21.7	25.4	28.4	25.5	23.6	15.6	20

^{a}Initial weight.
^{b}Reduced weight.
^{c}% Weight reduction.
^{d}Ponderal equivalent weights were adjusted to body weight scaled to 20%.

Further evidence of the "cost" of the Minnesota tests is to be found in the carefully monitored physiologic parameters. Basal metabolism declined 39%, pulse rate 32% (56.1 to 37.8 beats/min) and blood pressure 12% (105.3 to 92.7 mm Hg). The rationale of reducing lean men who subsisted on a nutritionally inadequate diet (apart from caloric restriction) is not clear, but it is certain that loss of lean tissue and physiologic deterioration (if it supervenes) can be quantified for all regimens oriented to weight reduction.

CALORIC DEFICIT AND WEIGHT LOSS. An impressive finding in the Minnesota tests and in the post-war food deprivation in Germany is the relatively small weight loss which can be equated with the caloric deficit. Adaptation in the form of reduced energy expenditure accounts for some two-thirds to three-fourths of the initially projected caloric deficit. In the Minnesota tests, despite an initial caloric deficit projected as some 1900 Calories (Table 10.12),

Table 10.12

DATA FROM THE MINNESOTA AND POST-WAR GERMAN
SEMISTARVATION EXPERIENCE

Dietary Features	*Weight Loss*	*Daily Caloric Deficit* [a]
Minnesota Tests: 32 Young Adults Subjected to Dietary Restriction and Enforced Exercise		
Control: 3492 Cal	69.4 to 52.6 kg	Initial: 1922
Reduced: 1570 Cal.	(168 days)	Avg.[b] 750
Protein: 110 to 49 gm	6.8 kg Fat	Caloric equivalent of
Fat: 120 to 22 gm	10.0 kg Lean	weight loss: 430 Cal/daily
German Experience: 20 Million Normal Consumers		
Caloric level reduced	72 to 59.5 kg	Initial: 1000
from 2400 to 1550 Cal.	(3 Years)	Avg.[b] 177
or less.	8.0 kg Fat	Caloric equivalent of
Food: Chiefly bread,	4.5 kg Lean	weight loss: 82 Cal/daily
potatoes		

[a]*Projected Caloric deficit calculated as the difference between initial and reduced food intake.*
[b]*Calculated as an exponential decline as a result of adaptation (energy expenditure chiefly) of 50% in six months and 98.4% decrease from initial level at the end of 36 months.*

weight loss greatly declined toward the end of the experiment. Expenditure of energy tended to equilibrate with calories ingested so that overall, during the 24 weeks of restriction, loss of fat and lean tissue accounted for only a rounded 400 Calories daily.

A similar projection for the German data indicates that tissue loss of about 12.5 kg over a three-year period (approximately 1000 days) accounts for only 82 Calories daily, despite the initial deficit projected as 1000 Calories daily. Decrease in basal metabolism, in obligate activity, in energy of food assimilation, and what may be termed "a nutritive-induced form of hibernation," accounted for the major portion of the unremitted calories.

Summary

The role of anthropometric and physiologic parameters in monitoring dietary weight reduction is evident from the data presented. The relative loss of fat from the trunk of the body is about twice that from the extremities. The cost of weight reduction must be assessed both in lean tissue loss relative to weight decrement and decreased energy expenditure. The striking adaptation consisting of curtailment of intrinsic (metabolism) and extrinsic (activity) energy expenditure serves to neutralize, exponentially, dietary deprivation. Dietary regulation of body composition chiefly to prevent fat gain, poses long range objectives, in contrast to crash and generally ineffective regimens.

Bibliography

1. Allen, Margaret F., D. A. Clark, and F. H. Wilson, Jr. "Patterns of Change in Serum Lipid and Lipoprotein Levels in a Selected Military Population Over a 14-year Period." *SAM-TR-67-101.* USAF School of Aviation Medicine, Brooks Air Force Base, Texas, October 1967.

2. Allen, T. H., E. C. Anderson, and W. H. Langham. "Total Body Potassium and Gross Composition in Relation to Age." *J. Gerontology* 15 (October 1960), 348–57.

3. Allen, T. H., H. J. Krzywicki, and J. E. Roberts. "Density, Fat, Water, and Solids in Freshly Isolated Tissues." *J. Appl. Physiol.* 14 (1959), 1005–8.

4. Allen, T. H., D. A. Maco, and R. W. Bancroft. "Body Fat, Denitrogenation and Decompression in Men Exercising After Abrupt Exposure to Altitude." *Aerospace Med.* 42 (May 1971), 518–24.

5. Anderson, E. C. "Three-Component Body Composition Analysis Based on Potassium and Water Determinations." *N. Y. Acad. Sci.* 110 (1963), 189–212.

6. Bayley, N., and F. C. Davis. "Growth Changes in Bodily Size and Proportions During the First Three Years: A Developmental Study of Sixty-One Children by Repeated Measurement." *Biometoika* 27, parts I and II (1935), 26.

7. Baker, G. L. "Human Adipose Tissue Composition and Age." *J. Clin. Nutr.* 22 (1969), 829–35.

8. Bayer, L. M., and N. Bayley. *Growth Diagnosis.* Chicago: University of Chicago Press, 1959.

9. Behnke, A. R. "The Absorption and Elimination of Gases of the Body in Relation to Its Fat and Water Content." *Medicine* 24, no. 4 (December 1945), 359–79.

10. Behnke, A. R. "The Relation of Lean Body Weight to Metabolism and Some Consequent Systematizations." *Annals of the New York Academy of Sciences* 56 (1953), 1095–1142.

11. Behnke, A. R. "Military Aspects of Underweight and Overweight." Research and Development Technical Report USNRDL-TR-205, *Biology and Medicine* (1957), pp. 1–60.

12. Behnke, A. R. "The Estimation of Lean Body Weight from Skeletal Measurements." *Hum. Biol.* 31 (December 1959), 295–315.

13. Behnke, A. R. "Anthropometric Fractionation of Body Weight." *J. Appl. Physiol.* 16, no. 6 (1961), 949–54.

14. Behnke, A. R. "Comment on the Determination of Whole Body Density and a Resumé of Body Composition Data." In *Techniques for Measuring Body Composition*, edited by Josef Brožek and Austin Henschel. Washington, D.C.: National Academy Sciences National Research Council, 1961.

15. Behnke, A. R. "Quantitative Assessment of Body Build." *J. Appl. Physiol.* 16 (November 1961), 960–68.

16. Behnke, Albert R. "Anthropometric Estimates of Body Size, Shape, and Fat Content." *Postgraduate Medicine* 34 (1963), 190–98.

17. Behnke, A. R. "Anthropometric Evaluation of Body Composition Throughout Life." *Ann. N.Y. Acad. Sci.* 110, part II (September 1963), 450–64.

18. Behnke, A. R. "Morphologic and Metabolic Changes Associated with Aging." In *Clinical Metabolism of Body Water and Electrolytes*, edited by J. H. Bland. Philadelphia: W. B. Saunders Company, 1963.

19. Behnke, A. R. "Role of Fat in Gross Body Composition and Configuration." In *Fat As A Tissue*, edited by Kaarė Rodahl and Bela Issekutz, Jr. New York: McGraw-Hill Book Company, 1964.

20. Behnke, A. R. "Physique and Exercise." In *Exercise Physiology*, edited by Harold Falls. New York: Academic Press, Inc., 1968.

21. Behnke, A. R. "New Concepts in Height-Weight Relationships." In *Obesity*, edited by Nancy Wilson. Philadelphia: F. A. Davis Co., 1969.

22. Behnke, A. R., B. G. Feen, and W. C. Welham. "The Specific Gravity of Healthy Men." *J.A.M.A.* 118 (February 1942), 495–98.

23. Behnke, A. R., O. E. Guttentag, and C. Brodsky. "Quantification of Body Configuration in Geometrical Terms." Research and Development Technical Report USNRDL-TR-204, *Biology and Medicine* (1957), pp. 1–34.

24. Behnke, A. R., O. E. Guttentag, and C. Brodsky. "Quantification of Body Weight and Configuration from Anthropometric Measurements," *Hum. Biol.* 31 (September 1959), 213–34.

25. Behnke, A. R., E. F. Osserman, and W. C. Welham. "Lean Body Mass." *Arch. Int. Med.* 91 (May 1963), 585–601.

26. Behnke, A. R., and J. Royce. "Body Size, Shape, and Composition of Several Types of Athletes." *J. Sports Med. and Phys. Fitness* 6 (June 1966), 75–88.

27. Behnke, A. R., and W. E. Siri. "The Estimation of Lean Body Weight from Anthropometric and X-Ray Measurements." Research and Development Technical Report USNRDL-TR-203, *Biology and Medicine* (1957), pp. 1–38.

28. Behnke, A. R., and W. L. Taylor. "Some Aspects of Recent Findings Pertaining to the Body Composition of Athletes, Obese Individuals and Patients." Research and Development Technical Report USNRDL-TR-339, *Biology and Medicine* (1959), pp. 1–24.

29. Benedict, F. G. "A Study of Prolonged Fasting." Carnegie Institute of Washington, Publ. No. 280 (1915).

30. Berg, B. N., and H. S. Simms. "Nutrition and Longevity in the Rat." *Journal of Nutrition* 71 (1960), 255.

31. Boling, E. A., W. L. Taylor, C. Entenman, and A. R. Behnke. "Total Exchangeable Potassium and Chloride, and Total Body Water in Healthy Men of Varying Fat Content," *J. Clin. Invest.* 41, no. 10 (1962), 1840–49.

32. Borhani, N. O., H. H. Hechter, and L. Breslow. "Report of a Ten Year Follow-up Study of the San Francisco Longshoremen." *J. Chron. Dis.* 16 (1963), 1251–66.

33. Boyd, Edith. "The Specific Gravity of the Human Body." *Hum. Biol.* (December 1933), pp. 646–72.

34. Boyd, Edith. *The Growth of the Surface Area of the Body.* Minneapolis: University of Minnesota Press, 1935, p. 53.

35. Brown, C. H., and J. H. Wilmore. "Weight Training in Female Athletes." Paper presented to the American College of Sports Medicine. Annual meeting, Albuquerque, New Mexico, May 1970.

36. Brown, C. H., and J. H. Wilmore. "Physical and Physiological Profiles of Champion Women Long Distance Runners." Paper presented to the American College of Sports Medicine. Annual Meeting, Toronto, Ontario, May 1971.

37. Brožek, J., F. Grande, J. T. Anderson, and A. Keys. "Densitometric Analysis of Body Composition: Revision of Some Quantitative Assumptions." *N. Y. Acad. Sci.* 110, Part I (1963), 113–40.

38. Brožek, J., and A. Keys. "The Evaluation of Leanness-Fatness in Man: Norms and Interrelationships." *Brit. J. Nutr.* 5, no. 2 (1951), 194–206.

39. Buskirk, E. R. "Underwater Weighing and Body Density: A Review of Procedures." In *Techniques for Measuring Body Composition*, edited by J. Brožek and A. Henschel. Washington, D.C.: National Academy of Sciences National Research Council, 1961.

40. Clarke, H. Harrison. *Physical and Motor Tests in the Medford Boys' Growth Study.* Englewood Cliffs, N.J.: Prentice-Hall, Inc., 1971.

41. Clarke, H. H., L. R. Gesser, and S. B. Hunsdon, "Comparison of Upper Arm Measurements by Use of Roentgenogram and Anthropometric Techniques." *Res. Quart.* 27 (December 1956), 379–85.

42. Consolazio, C. F., R. E. Johnson, and L. J. Pecora. *Physiological Measurements of Metabolic Functions in Man.* New York: McGraw-Hill Book Company, 1963, p. 298.

43. Craig, A. B., and D. E. Ware. "Effect of Immersion in Water on Vital Capacity and Residual Volume of Lungs." *J. Appl. Physiol.* 23 (1967), 423–25.

44. Crews, E. L., K. W. Fuge, L. B. Oscai, J. O. Holloszy, and R. E. Shank. "Weight, Food Intake, and Body Composition: Effects of Exercise and Protein Deficiency." *Amer. J. Physiol.* 216 (1969), 359–63.

45. Daniels, G. S., H. C. Meyers, Jr., and Sheryl Worrall. "Anthropometry of WAF Basic Trainees." *WAMC Technical Report 53-12.* Wright Air Development Center, Wright-Patterson Air Force Base, Ohio, July, 1953.

46. Drillis, R., and R. Contini. "Body Segment Parameters." *Tech. Report 1166.03.* N.Y. Univ. School of Engineering, Univ. Heights, N.Y. 10453.

47. DuBois, E. F. *Basal Metabolism in Health and Disease.* 3rd ed. Philadelphia: Lea and Febiger, 1936.

48. DuBois, D., and E. F. DuBois. "A Formula to Estimate the Approximate Surface Area of the Body if Height and Weight Be Known." *Arch. Int. Med.* 17 (1916), 863–71.

49. Edelman I. S., and J. Leibman. "Anatomy of Body Water and Electrolytes." *Am. J. Med.* 27, no. 2 (1959), 256–77.

50. Entenman, C., W. H. Goldwater, N. S. Ayres, and A. R. Behnke. "Analysis of

Adipose Tissue as a Key to Understanding the Mechanism of Body Weight Loss in the Human." Research and Development Technical Report USNRDL-TR-169, *Health and Biology* (1957), pp. 1–21.

51. Entenman, C., W. H. Goldwater, N. S. Ayres, and A. R. Behnke. "Analysis of Adipose Tissue in Relation to Body Weight Loss in Man." *J. Appl. Physiol.* 13 (July 1958), 129–34.

52. Fidanza, F., A. Keys, and J. T. Anderson. "Density of Body Fat in Man and Other Mammals." *J. Appl. Physiol.* 6 (1953), 252–56.

53. Filer, L. J., Jr., L. S. Baur, and Helen Rezabek. "Influence of Protein and Fat Content of Diet on the Body Composition of Piglets." *Pediat.* 25 (February 1960), 242–47.

54. Fomon, S. J. "The Male Reference Infant." In *Human Development*, edited by Frank Faulkner. Philadelphia: W. B. Saunders Company, 1966.

55. Fomon, S. J., R. L. Jensen, and G. M. Owen. "Determination of Body Volume of Infants by a Method of Helium Displacement." *Annals N.Y. Acad. Sci.* 110 (1963), 80–90.

56. Forbes, G. L., J. Gallup, and J. B. Hursh. "Estimation of Total Body Fat from Potassium 40 Content." *Science* 113 (1961), 101.

57. Forbes, G. B., and A. M. Lewis. "Total Sodium, Potassium and Chloride in Adult Man." *J. Clin. Invest.* 35 (1956), 596–600.

58. Garn, S. M. "Roentgenogrammetric Determination of Body Composition." *Hum. Biol.* 29 (December 1957), 337–53.

59. Garn, S. "Radiographic Analysis of Body Composition." In *Techniques for Measuring Body Composition* edited by J. Brožek and A. Henschel. Washington, D.C.: National Academy of Sciences National Research Council, 1961.

60. Garn, S. M., and R. W. Young. "Concurrent Fat Loss and Fat Gain." *Am. J. Phys. Anthrop.* 14 (1956), 497–504.

61. Gofman, J. W., H. B. Jones, F. T. Lindgren, T. D. Lyon, H. A. Elliott, and Beverly Strisower. "Blood Lipids and Human Atherosclerosis." *Circulation* II (August 1950), 161–78.

62. Gofman, J. W., Beverly Strisower, O. DeLalla, A. Tamplin, H. B. Jones, and F. Lindgren. "Index of Coronary Artery Atherogenesis." *Modern Medicine* (June 15, 1953), 119–40.

63. Hampton, Mary C., Ruth L. Huenemann, Leona R. Shapiro, Barbara W. Mitchell, and A. R. Behnke. "A Longitudinal Study of Gross Body Composition and Conformation and Their Association with Food and Activity in a Teen-Age Population." *Amer. J. Clin. Nutri.* 19 (December 1966), 422–25.

64. Hansard, S. L. "Radiochemical Procedures for Estimating Body Composition in Animals." *Ann. N.Y. Acad. Sci.* 110 (1963), 229–45.

65. Hathaway, Millicent, and Elsie Foard. "Heights and Weights of Adults in the United States." *Home Economics Research Report No. 10.* U.S. Dept. Agric., Washington, D.C.: U.S. Government Printing Office, 1960.

66. Heath, T. H. *The Works of Archimedes.* New York, Dover Publications, Inc., 1953, p. 258.

67. Hechter, H. H. "The Relationship Between Weight and Some Anthropometric Measurements in Adult Males." Research and Development Technical Report USNRDL-TR-206, *Biology and Medicine* (1957), pp. 1–11.

68. Hertzberg, H. T. E., E. Churchill, C. W. Dupertius, R. M. White, and A. Damon. *Anthropometry of Turkey, Greece, and Italy*, AGARDograph 73. Elmsford, N.Y.: Pergamon Press, Inc., 1963.

69. Hirsch, J., and J. L. Knittle. "Cellularity of Obese and Nonobese Human Adipose Tissue." *Fed. Proc.* (July-August 1970), pp. 1516–21.

70. Hunter, W. M., and F. C. Greenwood, "Studies on the Secretion of Human-Pituitary-Growth-Hormone." *Brit. Med. J.* 1 (1964), 804–7.

71. Johnston, F. E., and R. M. Malina. "Age Changes in the Composition of the Upper Arm in Philadelphia Children." *Hum. Biol.* 38 (1966), 1–21.

72. Karpinos, B. D. "Weight-Height Standards Based on World War II Experience." *J. Am. Stat. Assoc.* 53 (June 1958), 408–19.

73. Katch, F. I. "Apparent Body Density and Variability During Underwater Weighing." *Res. Quart.* 39 (1968), 993–99.

74. Katch, F. I., and E. D. Michael. "Prediction of Body Density from Skinfold and Girth Measurements of College Females." *J. Appl. Physiol.* 25 (1968), 92–94.

75. Keys, A., and J. Brožek. "Body Fat in Adult Man." *Physiol. Rev.* 33 (1953), 245–325.

76. Kodama, A. M. "In Vivo and In Vitro Determinations of Body Fat and Body Water on the Hamster." *J. Appl. Physiol.* 31 (August 1971), 218–22.

77. Lee, M. M. C., and C. K. Ng. "Postmortem Studies of Skinfold Caliper Measurements and Actual Thickness of Skin and Subcutaneous Tissue." *Hum. Biol.* 37 (1965), 91–103.

78. Lesser, G. T., A. J. Blumberg, and J. M. Steele. "Measurements of Total Body Fat in Living Rats by Absorption of Cyclopropane." *Amer. J. Physiol.* 169 (1952), 545.

79. Lesser, G. T., W. Perl, and J. M. Steele. "Determination of Total Body Fat by Absorption of an Inert Gas: Measurements and Results in Normal Human Subjects." *J. Clin. Invest.* 39 (1960), 1791.

80. Lesser, G. T., and G. Zak. "Measurement of Total Body Fat in Man by the Simultaneous Absorption of Two Inert Gases." *Ann. N.Y. Acad. Sci.* 110 (1963), 40–54.

81. Malina, R. M. "Quantification of Fat, Muscle and Bone in Man." *Clin. Orthopaed. and Related Research*, 65 (July-August 1969), 9–38.

82. Malina, R. M., and F. E. Johnston, "Relations Between Bone, Muscle and Fat Widths in the Upper Arm and Calves of Boys and Girls Studied Cross-Sectionally at Age 6 to 16 Years." *Hum. Biol.* 59 (1967), 211–33.

83. Maresh, Marion, "Changes in Tissue Widths During Growth." *Am. J. Dis. Child.* 111 (February 1966), 142–45.

84. Matiegka, J. "The Testing of Physical Efficiency." *Am. J. Phys. Anthrop.* 4 (1921), 223–30.

85. Mayer, Jean. *Overweight: Causes, Cost, and Control.* Englewood Cliffs, N.J.: Prentice-Hall, Inc., 1968.

86. McCammon, R. W. *Human Growth and Development.* Springfield, Ill.: Charles C Thomas, Publisher, 1970.

87. McCay, C. M., and M. F. Crowell. "Prolonging Life Span." *Scientific Monthly* 39 (November 1934), 405.

88. McMurrey, J. D., E. A. Boling, J. M. Davis, H. V. Parker, I. Caryl Magnus,

Margaret R. Ball, and F. D. Moore. "Body Composition: Simultaneous Determination of Several Aspects by the Dilution Principle." *Metabolism* 7 (September 1958), 651–67.

89. Moore, F. D. *The Body Cell Mass and Its Supporting Environment.* Philadelphia: W. B. Saunders Company, 1963.

90. Morales, M. F., E. N. Rathbun, R. E. Smith, and N. Pace. "Studies on Body Composition." *J. Biol. Chem.* 158 (May 1945), 677–84.

91. Murphy, H. F., T. Lohman, L. Oscai, and M. L. Pollock. "Potassium Scintillator as a Measurer of Fat." Proceeding of Symposia on Exercise and Fitness, ed. B. D. Franks. Chicago: Athletic Institute, 1969.

92. Myhre, L. G., and W. V. Kessler. "Body Density and Potassium 40 Measurements of Body Composition as Related to Age." *J. Appl. Physiol.* 21 (July 1966), 1251–55.

93. Newman, R. W., and R. M. White. "Reference Anthropometry of Army Men." *Report No. 180.* Quartermaster Climatic Research Laboratory, Lawrence, Massachusetts, September 1951.

94. Nichols, A. V., V. Dobbin, and J. W. Gofman. "Influence of Dietary Factors upon Human Serum Lipid Concentrations." *Geriatrics* 12 (1957), 7–17.

95. O'Brien, Ruth, M. A. Gershick, and Eleanor P. Hunt. "Body Measurements of American Boys and Girls for Garment and Pattern Construction." U.S. Dept. Agric, misc. publ. no. 366, Washington, D.C.: U.S. Government Printing Office, 1941.

96. O'Brien, Ruth, and W. C. Shelton. "Women's Measurements for Garment and Pattern Construction." U.S. Dept. Agric. misc. publ. 454, Washington, D.C.: U.S. Government Printing Office, 1941.

97. Osserman, S. F., G. C. Pitts, W. C. Welham, and A. R. Behnke. "In Vivo Measurement of Body Fat and Body Water in a Group of Normal Men." *J. Appl. Physiol.* 2 (June 1950), 633–39.

98. Osserman, E. F., G. C. Pitts, W. C. Welham, and A. R. Behnke. "In Vivo Measurement of Body Fat and Body Water in a Group of Normal Men." Naval Medical Research Institute, Research Report, 12 (1954), 55–66.

99. Pace, N., and Edith Rathbun. "Studies on Body Composition." *J. Biol. Chem.* 158 (May 1945), 685–91.

100. Parizkova, Jana. "Impact of Age, Diet and Exercise on Man's Body Composition." *Annals. N.Y. Acad. Sci.* 110 (September 1963), 661–74.

101. Parizkova, J., and L. Stankova. "Influence of Physical Activity on a Treadmill on the Metabolism of Adipose Tissue in Rats." *Brit. J. Nutr.* 18 (1964), 325–31.

102. Pascale, L. R., M. I. Grossman, H. S. Sloane, and T. Frankel. "Correlations between Thickness of Skinfolds and Body Density in 88 Soldiers." *Human Biol.* 28 (1956), 165–76.

103. Pitts, G. C. "Body Fat Accumulation in the Guinea Pig." *Am. J. Physiol.* 185 (1956), 41–48.

104. Pitts, G. C. "Studies of Body Composition by Direct Dissection." *Annals N.Y. Acad. Sci.* 110 (1963), 11–22.

105. Pitts, G. C., L. S. Bull, and G. Hollifield. "Physiologic Changes in Composition and Mass of Total Body Adipose Tissue." *Am. J. Physiol.* 221 (October 1971), 961–66.

106. Pryor, Helen B. "Charts of Normal Body Measurements and Revised Width-Weight Tables in Graphic Form." *J. Pediat.* 68 (1966), 615.

107. Rathbun, E. N., and N. Pace. "Studies on Body Composition." *J. Biol. Chem.* 158 (May 1945), 667–76.

108. Reba, R. C., D. B. Cheek, and F. C. Leitnaker. "Body Potassium and Lean Body Mass." In *Human Growth*, edited by D. B. Cheek. Philadelphia: Lea and Febiger, 1968.

109. Roth, J., S. M. Glick, R. S. Yalow, and S. A. Berson. "Secretion of Human Growth Hormone: Physiologic and Experimental Modification." *Metabolism* 12 (1963), 577–79.

110. Salans, L. B., J. L. Knittle, and J. Hirsch. "The Role of Adipose Cell Enlargement in the Carbohydrate Intolerance of Human Obesity." *J. Clin. Invest.* 46 (1967), 1112.

111. Schemmel, Rachel, O. Mickelsen, and J. L. Gill. "Dietary Obesity in Rats: Body Weight and Body Fat Accretion in Seven Strains of Rats." *J. Nutr.* 100 (September 1970), 1041–48.

112. Seltzer, C. C., R. F. Goldman, and J. Mayer. "The Triceps Skinfold as a Predictive Measure of Body Density and Body Fat in Obese Adolescent Girls," *Pediatrics* 36 (1965), 212–18.

113. Sheldon, W. H., C. Wesley Dupertuis, and Eugene McDermott. *Atlas of Men.* New York: Harper Brothers, 1954. Sheldon's technique is described by Dupertuis, C. W. and J. M. Tanner, *Amer. J. Phys. Anthrop.* 8 (1950), 27.

114. Shephard, R. J., J. Jones, K. Ishii, M. Kanek, and A. J. Albecht. "Factors Affecting Body Density and Thickness of Subcutaneous Fat." *Am. J. Clin. Nutr.* 22 (1969), 1175–89.

115. Simmons, Katherine. "The Brush Foundation Study of Growth and Development." *Mon. Soc. Res. Child Develop.* 9, no. 1 (1944).

116. Siri, W. E. "Apparatus for Measuring Human Body Volume." *Rev. Sci. Instr.* 27 (1955), 729–38.

117. Siri, W. E. "Gross Composition of the Body." In *Advance in Biological and Medical Physics*, IV, edited by J. H. Lawrence and C. A. Tobias. New York: Academic Press, Inc., 1956.

118. Siri, W. E. "Body Composition from Fluid Spaces and Density." In *Techniques for Measuring Body Composition*, edited by Josef Brožek and Austin Henschel. Washington, D.C.: National Academy of Sciences National Research Council, 1961.

119. Siri, W. E. "Body Volume Measurement by Gas Dilution." In *Techniques for Measuring Body Composition*, edited by J. Brožek and A. Henschel. Washington, D.C.: National Academy of Sciences National Research Council, 1961.

120. Sloan, A. W. "Estimation of Body Fat in Young Men." *J. Appl. Physiol.* 23 (1967), 311–15.

121. Sloan, A. W., J. J. Burt, and C. S. Blyth. "Estimation of Body Fat in Young Women." *J. Appl. Physiol* 16 (1962), 967–70.

122. Soberman, R., B. B. Brodie, B. B. Levy, J. Axelrod, V. Hollander, and J. M. Steele. "The Use of Antipyrine in the Measurement of Total Body Water in Man." *J. Biol. Chem.* 179 (1949), 31.

123. Steinkamp, R. C., N. L. Cohen, W. R. Garrey, T. McKey, G. Bron, W. E. Siri,

T. W. Sargent, and E. Isaacs. "Measures of Body Fat and Related Factors in Normal Adults: A Simple Clinical Method to Estimate Body Fat and Lean Body Mass." *J. Chronic Diseases* 18 (1965), 1291–1307.

124. Stern, M. P. "Relationship Between Fat Cell Lipid Content and Body Composition in Normal and Obese Human Subjects." Veteran's Hospital, Palo Alto, submitted for publication, 1972.

125. Stouffer, J. R. "Relationship of Ultrasonic Measurements and X-Rays to Body Composition." *Ann. N.Y. Acad. Sci.* 110 (1963), 31–39.

126. Strom, A., and R. A. Jensen. "Mortality From Circulatory Diseases in Norway, 1940–1945." *Lancet.* 1 (January-June 1951), 126.

127. Sutton, J., J. D. Young, L. Lazarus, J. B. Hickie, and J. Maksvytis. "Hormonal Changes During Exercise." *Lancet.* 2 (1968), 1304.

128. Talso, P. J., C. E. Miller, A. J. Carballo, and I. Vasquez. "Exchangeable Potassium as a Parameter of Body Composition." *Metabolism* 9 (1960), 456.

129. Tanner, J. M. *The Physique of the Olympic Athlete.* London: George Allen and Unwin, Ltd., 1964.

130. Tanner, J. M. "Radiographic Studies of Body Composition in Children and Adults." In *Human Body Composition*, edited by Josef Brožek. Elmsford, N.Y.: Pergamon Press, Inc., 1965.

131. Taylor, H. L., and A. Keys. "Adaptation to Caloric Restriction." *Science* 112 (August 1950), 215–18.

132. Taylor, W. L., and A. R. Behnke. "Anthropometric Comparison of Muscular and Obese Men." *J. Appl. Physiol.* 16 (November 1961), 955–59.

133. Trotter, M. A. "A Preliminary Study of Estimation of Weight of the Skeleton." *Amer. J. Phys. Anthrop.* 12 (1954), 537–51.

134. Tuddenham, R. D., and M. M. Snyder. *Physical Growth of California Boys and Girls from Birth to Eighteen Years.* Berkeley: University of California Press, 1954.

135. Turner, C. D. *General Endocrinology.* 3rd ed. Philadelphia: W. B. Saunders Company, 1960.

136. Von Döbeln, W. "Human Standard and Maximal Metabolic Rate in Relation to Fat-Free Body Mass." *Acta Physiol. Scand.* 37, suppl. 126 (1956), 79 pp.

137. Walser, M., and S. N. Stein. "Determination of Specific Gravity of Intact Animals by Helium Comparison with Water Displacement." *Proc. Soc. Exptl. Biol. Med.* 82 (1953), 774–77.

138. Welch, J. E. *Edward Hitchcock, M. D. Founder of Physical Education in the College Curriculum.* Greenville, North Carolina (East Carolina College), private printing, 1966.

139. Welham, W. C., and A. R. Behnke. "The Specific Gravity of Healthy Men." *J.A.M.A.* 118 (1942), 498–501.

140. Wetzel, N. C. "Growth in Medical Physics." In *Medical Physics*, vol. I. Chicago: Year Book Medical Publishers, Inc., 1944, pp. 513–19.

141. White, R. M. "Body Build and Body Weight in 25-year-old Army Men." *Hum. Biol.* 28 (1956), 141.

142. Willmon, T. L., and A. R. Behnke. "Residual Lung Volume Determinations by the Methods of Helium Substitution and Volume Expansion." *Amer. J. Physiol.* (April 1948), pp. 138–42.

143. Willoughby, D. P. "Anthropometric Method for Arriving at the Optimal Proportions of the Body in Any Adult Individual." *Res. Quart.* 3 (1932), 48–77.

144. Wilmore, Jack H. "Use of Actual, Predicted and Constant Residual Volumes in the Assessment of Body Composition by Underwater Weighing." *Medicine and Science in Sports* 1 (1969), 87–90.

145. Wilmore, Jack H. "A Simplified Method for Determination of Residual Lung Volumes." *J. Appl. Physiol.* 27 (1969), 96–100.

146. Wilmore, Jack H. "Validation of the First and Second Components of the Heath-Carter Modified Somatotype Method." *Am. J. Phys. Anthrop.* 32 (1969), 369–72.

147. Wilmore, Jack H., and A. R. Behnke. "Predictability of Lean Body Weight Through Anthropometric Assessment in College Men." *J. Appl. Physiol.* 25, 4 (1968), 349–55.

148. Wilmore, J., and A. R. Behnke. "An Anthropometric Estimation of Body Density and Lean Body Weight in Young Men." *J. Appl. Physiol.* 27 (July 1969), 25–31.

149. Wilmore, J., and A. R. Behnke. "An Anthropometric Estimation of Body Density and Lean Body Weight in Young Women." *Amer. J. Clin. Nutri.* 23 (March 1970), 267–74.

150. Wilmore, Jack H., R. N. Girandola, and D. L. Moody. "Validity of Skinfold and Girth Assessment for Predicting Alterations in Body Composition." *J. Appl. Physiol.* 29, 3 (1970), 313–17.

151. Wilmore, J. H., and W. L. Haskell. "Use of the Heart Rate-Energy Expenditure Relationship in the Individualized Prescription of Exercise," *Amer. J. Clin. Nutr.* 24 (1971), 1186–92.

152. Wilmore, Jack H., J. Royce, R. N. Girandola, F. I. Katch, and V. L. Katch. "Body Composition Changes with a 10-week Program of Jogging." *Med. and Science in Sports* 2 (1970), 113–17.

153. Young, C. M., M. E. K. Martin, M. Chihan, M. McCarthy, J. J. Manniello, E. H. Harmuth, and J. H. Fryer. "Body Composition of Young Women." *J. Am. Dietetic Assn.* 38 (1961), 332.